DAVID TORRANCE ....oadcaster who spe-
cialises in the politics and history of the long-running debate about Scottish
independence. After being educated in Edinburgh, Aberdeen and Cardiff he
worked as a newspaper and television reporter before taking a brief career
break to dabble in politics at Westminster. For the past seven years he has
been a freelance commentator as well as the author or editor of more than
ten books about Scottish and UK politics, biography and history. Like all
good Scotsmen he has lived in London for long stretches, but is currently
based in Edinburgh.

By the same author:

The Scottish Secretaries (Birlinn, 2006)
George Younger: A Life Well Lived (Birlinn, 2008)
'We in Scotland': Thatcherism in a Cold Climate (Birlinn, 2009)
Noel Skelton and the Property-Owning Democracy (Biteback, 2010)
Inside Edinburgh: Discovering the Classic Interiors of Edinburgh (Birlinn, 2010)
Salmond: Against the Odds (Birlinn, 2011)
David Steel: Rising Hope to Elder Statesman (Biteback, 2012)
Whatever Happened to Tory Scotland? (ed.) (Edinburgh University Press, 2012)
The Battle for Britain: Scotland and the Independence Referendum (Biteback, 2013)
Great Scottish Speeches I (ed.) (Luath Press, 2013)
Great Scottish Speeches II (ed.) (Luath Press, 2013)
Britain Rebooted: Scotland in a Federal Union (Luath Press, 2014)
Scotland's Referendum: A Guide for Voters. With Jamie Maxwell. (Luath Press, 2014)

100 Days of Hope and Fear

How Scotland's Referendum was Lost and Won

DAVID TORRANCE

Luath Press Limited

EDINBURGH

www.luath.co.uk

First published 2014
Reprinted 2015

ISBN: 978-1-910021-31-6

The author's right to be identified as author of this book
under the Copyright, Designs and Patents Act 1988 has been asserted.

The paper used in this book is recyclable. It is made from low chlorine pulps produced
in a low energy, low emission manner from renewable forests.

Printed and bound by Bell & Bain Ltd., Glasgow

Typeset in 11 point Sabon

To the 100 per cent

Contents

The photographs in this book are all © the author unless otherwise stated.

Introduction

In a postscript to his 1999 diary of the first Scottish Parliament election campaign – *Scotland Reclaimed* – the former *Herald* journalist Murray Ritchie gazed into his crystal ball:

> Sometime in the future, it is reasonable to predict, the Holyrood and Westminster Parliaments will be run by opposing political parties, most probably with the SNP governing Scotland. When that day comes the Scottish Parliament will have a critical influence over Scotland's and Britain's destiny, and the people who voted for Home Rule will be asked to decide in a referendum whether they want their country to remain an integral part of the United Kingdom or to reclaim its independence.

Given others were busy predicting that devolution would kill Nationalism 'stone dead', it was a prescient conclusion. Less than eight years after Ritchie's diary was published the SNP formed its first – minority – administration, while just over five years following that election victory a referendum on independence was agreed between the Scottish and UK governments, due to be held on 18 September 2014.

This, then, is an account of the 100 days (roughly speaking) that separated the beginning of the formal campaigning period and the weekend following the referendum itself. Before embarking on this, I had only ever kept a diary while travelling, so keeping a detailed account of my homegrown activities proved an interesting departure. To give some useful context, throughout the referendum campaign I was based in Edinburgh, having moved back to the city of my birth, upbringing and schooling from London a few weeks before. Not only did this mean I was able to vote, but also Edinburgh was, of course, where all the 'action' was.

When I say Edinburgh I mean, of course, Scotland, for although based in the capital I travelled to other parts of the country as often as I could, usually (but not always) in connection with the campaign. Only occasionally did I return to London – although that provided a much under-rated perspective on what was happening in Scotland – and only a few times did I go abroad, including to the European Parliament in Strasbourg and to cover another independence referendum in Barcelona. Otherwise, for much of this diary

I was conscious of living in a Holyrood bubble – literally staying a minute or so from the Scottish Parliament and inhabiting, by and large, the area between there, Waverley Station and The Tun, home to BBC Scotland. Later I moved to Newington and, although further away, it felt much the same.

Inevitably, therefore, most of the people who feature in this diary are drawn from that bubble, for which I make no apology: in terms of providing insights and the 'inside track' throughout the long referendum campaign, those involved in either Yes Scotland or Better Together were obviously the best individuals for me to seek out. Given the nature of politics and journalism, many of them were also friends (or in some cases, such as my father, close relatives). And given the often-sensitive nature of what I was told, many individuals are not named.

Diaries are inevitably self-indulgent things, full of 'I' this and 'I' that, but while hopefully giving an insider's perspective of an historic constitutional event, it might also shed some light on the working life of a freelance journalist which, in my humble experience, is much misunderstood, if not actively disparaged. Indeed, being a journalist during the referendum – particularly a non-aligned one – was frequently an uncomfortable experience. The adage of 'I disapprove of what you say, but I will defend to the death your right to say it' (often misattributed to Voltaire) ceased to apply; any piece of analysis with which a campaigner (usually pro-independence) disagreed was dismissed as 'biased', while 'facts' often became little more than a matter of opinion.

How was it written? Initially, at least, it was bashed directly into my laptop at the end of each day but over time, and as I got busier, I developed a habit of keeping daily notes and finishing the entries every few days or so. There were, of course, exceptions: I only finished writing the last seven or eight entries more than a week after the big day itself. I was, among other things, exhausted. As were many others, not least those directly involved in either campaign, and especially following a political process that had occupied more than two years of our lives.

Too often 'historic' is a term abused by journalists and politicians, but on occasion it is entirely justified. If a democratic vote that might have ended the 307-year-old marriage between Scotland and England (not to mention the relatively younger United Kingdom), thereby turning conventional political wisdom on its head, could not be termed 'historic' then it was difficult to think what would.

Indeed, the independence referendum, a wide-ranging national conversation lasting more than two years, generated much hyperbole: things, gushed journalists, would never be the same again (usually they were precisely that), while the status quo was not an option. The debate also had a habit of raising big questions – about inequality, political engagement and the balance of power(s) within the UK – only to answer them in small, superficial ways; endless discussion about 'independence' (however defined) and that ambiguous term 'more powers' filled the vacuum left by any significant discussion of political *ideas*.

In terms of the two campaigns, Yes Scotland and Better Together, yet another journalistic cliché was invoked, chiefly Mario Cuomo's aphorism that one must 'campaign in poetry' but 'govern in prose'. On both sides of the constitutional divide genuine poetry rarely intruded into an often dry, cost-benefit analysis of the pros and cons of independence. Although it was not immediately obvious, meanwhile, the Yes campaign seized control of the narrative early on: having cast the debate in voters' minds as a battle between hope and fear, positivity and negativity, it became much easier to delegitimise criticism of independence – however compelling – as 'scaremongering' or, at the very least, 'bluff' and 'bluster'.

This was Yes's greatest strength, taking the campaigning prowess developed by the SNP at the 2007 and 2011 Holyrood elections to new heights, while harnessing the energy of existing and emergent groupings such as the Greens, National Collective and Radical Independence Campaign. And although in policy terms it was an uncomfortable blend of utopian 1980s left-wingery and orthodox free-market economics (very much reflecting that of the SNP under Alex Salmond), its messaging was sharp, disciplined and well-targeted, the ironic consequence of the focus-group politics it so derided among the 'Westminster elite'. Yes Scotland was above all a brand, an advertising campaign attempting to convince voters that its constitutional product was superior to that on offer from competing Unionist salesmen. Salesman, of course, are not renowned for either consistency or principle, and indeed a lot in the Yes prospectus was fantasy politics: independence was presented as bringing an end to the 'Westminster system', chiefly neoliberal economics (only to replace it with implicitly superior *Scottish* neoliberalism), austerity, control by 'elites', corporate interests, and so on. But by framing the choice as Yes or No to austerity, Yes or No to neoliberalism, or even Yes or No to 'Tory rule', it compelled many hitherto hostile to Nationalism to pick a side. Arguments that had once been the preserve of the Left became mainstream, and were taken remarkably seriously.

And while back in the real world it was difficult to imagine an independent Scotland, by a peculiar twist of faith, becoming the first developed country to somehow defeat free-market economics, or that the SNP had (uniquely) found a way to combine low taxes with high spending, many articulate individuals and campaigning groups were more than prepared to believe that voting Yes might at the very least provide that opportunity. Having been encouraged by Yes Scotland to envisage independence in any way they liked (so long as they also backed, paradoxically, the Scottish Government's White Paper), many did precisely that: projecting their earnest political desires – Left, Right or whatever – upon the independence canvas. As a result, Yes often ended up being imbued with semi-mystical (and incredibly wide-ranging) powers of political transformation.

Another central argument of the pro-independence campaign was the apparent divergence between the political cultures of Scotland and England (Wales and Northern Ireland were generally ignored) since the 1980s, something emphasised again and again while given intellectual succour by the likes of the historian Sir Tom Devine, one of many high-profile (and relatively late) converts to the Yes cause. In terms of social attitudes and the economy, however, there was much that pointed to convergence between Scotland and the rest of the UK during that period. What remained – most notably in attitudes to the European Union – amounted to what Freud dismissed as the 'narcissism of small differences'.

But a strong and clear electoral divergence, of course, made this claim of Scottish exceptionalism superficially easy to make, and it enjoyed wide support among Scotland's chattering classes and sections of the commentariat. There was much talk of distinct 'Scottish values', although rarely defined and accompanied by a strong denial (usually by Nationalists) that this was anything other than avowedly 'civic' Nationalism. Only it was rather difficult to reconcile the claim that anyone could become 'Scottish' by assimilation while also asserting the idea that Scotland was somehow 'different'. But then Orwellian Doublethink was a persistent feature of the campaign.

The 'othering' required by Nationalism, meanwhile, took subtler forms, with many in the pro-independence camp resurrecting decidedly old battles. Despite claiming to be positive and forward-looking, a lot of Yes arguments rested upon age-old Tory bashing. Only independence, it was posited, would enable Scots to get the governments they voted for, only that was only true if Scots a) were particularly savvy floating voters or b) living in a one-party state which, even with an overall SNP majority, Scotland certainly was not. So ridding Scotland of the Conservatives, however undemocratic that sounded, was a mantra of the pro-independence campaign. And by Tories, Yes increasingly meant *all* Unionists, be they blue, red or yellow.

This was essentially political tribalism, and necessarily blind to obvious ironies. While denigrating Tories and Toryism, Yes Scotland only departed very subtly from SNP economic orthodoxy, which was decidedly conservative in nature. Often, for example, it appeared to be running out of

STV political editor Bernard Ponsonby speaks to Professor James Mitchell on referendum night at Pacific Quay.

taxes it intended to cut following an affirmative vote: Corporation Tax (no matter how low the UK rate fell), VAT (in certain cases), Air Passenger Duty (if not abolish it altogether) and those levied on the North Sea oil industry. All of this was repackaged as 'competitive advantage', just as the wider all-things-to-all-men policy agenda was sold as 'social democracy', although its resemblance to that in any of the oft-cited Scandinavian countries was more rhetorical than real.

The Yes campaign's economic conservatism manifested itself most ostentatiously in its approach to the mooted currency of an independent Scotland. In fact the SNP's policy of retaining Sterling – at least as an interim measure – dated from 2005 but only came under prolonged scrutiny once the formal referendum campaign got under way in the autumn of 2012. Even for Alex Salmond this was massively inconsistent: having long depicted the pound as a 'millstone round Scotland's neck', the First Minister now lauded it as 'as much Scotland's Pound' as it was England's (an argument he did not, naturally, apply to other shared assets like Trident). And deploying his considerable gift of the economic gab, Salmond also argued that monetary and fiscal policy were somehow completely separate (the Eurozone crisis rather suggested the reverse) while justifying his proposed currency union on the basis that most of Scotland's 'trade' was with England.

That, of course, sounded like a Unionist argument rather than a Nationalist one, although Salmond played up his Unionist credentials (defence, regal, currency and social) whenever and wherever possible. He also rarely missed an opportunity to extol the virtues of Scotland's prosperous economy while simultaneously arguing that it was somehow being held within a Westminster straightjacket. The historian Tony Judt's assertion that Scottish identity rested upon a 'curious admix of superiority and ressentiment' had never appeared more pertinent.

But of course the Yes campaign, like Better Together, had diligently studied the Quebec playbook. Back in 1995 the province's Yes campaign had promised Quebeckers they could keep the dollar (as well as the Queen as head of state) in the event of secession from Canada, while a crucial part of its near win against the federalists had come through convincing voters that what had once sounded unreasonable (chiefly continuing good relations with roc, the Rest of Canada) were actually both reasonable and, more to the point, possible.

The Parti Québécois had also made much of awaiting 'winning conditions', and those certainly existed in the Scotland of 2012–14: austerity economics at the behest of an Old Etonian Conservative Prime Minister, ukip on the march and a weak and divided Labour Party. And, like their Canadian cousins, the snp indulged in the intellectual somersaults associated with any Nationalist party trying to win an election or referendum campaign. Rather than diminishing Britishness, it was argued, independence would *strengthen* what it presented as little more than a *geographic* identity akin to that in Scandinavia.

Just as the 1995 referendum had often concerned an independent Quebec's place in the North Atlantic Free Trade Agreement, in 2014 there was much speculation about an independent Scotland's future within the European Union. And while weak on the likely terms and conditions, the Yes campaign basically won the broader point that a newly autonomous Scotland would remain at the heart of Europe (where it had been, after all, as part of the uk for more than four decades), although it never made clear why sharing sovereignty with the ruk (rest of uk) was such a bad thing but doing so (increasingly) with Spain, Portugal and Italy was a compelling necessity. Indeed, many Yes critiques of the British Union – that it was economically 'broken', unequal and so on – applied equally, if not more so, to the European version.

Given that broader context of 'ever closer union' with the Continent, Yes never successfully squared the circle of promising continuity and the preservation of five out of six of Scotland's 'Unions' (in Alex Salmond's terminology) – regal, currency, social, European and defence – with the prospect of transformational, if not radical, change. As Fintan O'Toole put it in an eloquent piece for the *Sunday Herald*:

> Freedom does not arrive just because you declare it. And if it ever does arrive, it is complicated, constrained and contested. Too much has happened to too many dreams of national liberation for any sensible citizen to believe in a great moment of transformation after which everything will be simpler, purer, better.

One of those constraints, an independent Scotland's membership of NATO, had been neutralised by the SNP early on, but at the same time it seemed ill-prepared on other sovereign fronts, too long dependent upon a slogan ('independence in Europe') rather than reasoned policy when it came to the EU, and in the confusing position of actually arguing *against* 'independence' when it came to monetary policy. In retrospect, particularly given the high Yes vote, it might even have been a little bolder on both fronts: acknowledging a degree of uncertainty on EU membership, for example, while preparing the intellectual ground for an 'independent' Scottish currency pegged to Sterling. Neither might have produced a majority, but it would at least have left the Yes campaign a lot less exposed.

But then it is worth remembering that the long-coveted independence referendum actually caught the SNP by surprise, meaning that, in pretty short order, the party had to develop comprehensive policies relating to welfare, defence and economics that had hitherto been unnecessary under the devolutionary status quo. And despite having at its disposal the (usually) well-oiled machine of the Civil Service in Scotland, it often lacked adequate means to do so. Frequently prevailed upon to justify or explain positions and policies that either did not exist or did so in an embryonic state, the normally slick Scottish Government often looked less than confident in its arguments.

The referendum campaign, meanwhile, also found the formal No campaign – Better Together – on a steep learning curve. Arguing *for* independence (no matter how weak the arguments) came naturally to politicians and activists who had long dreamed of their Big Idea, but the same could not be said for Unionists who had, certainly for much of the 20th century, simply taken the status quo to be a self-evident truth, so obviously *a good thing* that it required little explanation or defence. If Nationalism could be, in Michael Billig's description, 'banal', then so could its constitutional corollary.

Simply being cast as the 'No campaign' presented obvious problems when it came to a battle between apparently 'positive' and 'negative' visions of Scotland's future, although presenting a negative in a positive light was not impossible, for the pro-Union campaign (as some tried in vain to call it) had started well: in early 2012, a few months before the formal launch of Better Together, Prime Minister David Cameron had set out a warm, ecumenical vision of Scotland's place in the Union, while the campaign's initial branding, 'Better Together' and the slogan 'the best of both worlds' (so good the Yes campaign later tried to purloin it), were far from the 'Project Fear' of Yes caricature. In reality both campaigns were a mix of hope and fear, only No struck a less effective balance than Yes.

More broadly, it proved difficult for the three parties that comprised the No campaign – Labour, Conservative and Liberal Democrat – to sell effectively a vision of Scotland in the Union when it was perfectly clear there was no agreement as to what that was. This was all the more problematic given the blurring between two of those involved, both minority concerns north of the border but nevertheless both in government at a UK level, and between two historic opponents, Labour and the Conservatives, with Labour undoubtedly suffering guilt by association. And that they, Labour, were in 'cahoots' or 'in bed' with the Auld Enemy, was something about which Nationalists never tired of reminding them.

'No complacency' was long a mantra for the three Unionist parties, but in truth that is precisely what they were. This was understandable, up to a point: faced with polls that consistently showed a strong No lead, and up against arguments which – to Unionists – were manifestly absurd, it was all too easy to rest their laurels on age-old 'Nat bashing' techniques and aim for the jugular. Again this was fine, but only up to a point: negative campaigning *could* work, as the 2011 campaign against the Alternative Vote demonstrated, but not if it was considered an end in itself, divorced from a broader and more positive meta-narrative.

Which was not to say Better Together's chosen targets – the European Union, currency and pensions – were not effective. Often they were, although good points were frequently overstated or, in the case of the Yes campaign's mooted currency union, poorly presented. So instead of ruling it out, more in sorrow than anger, the Chancellor George Osborne (a poor choice of messenger in any case) unwittingly cast his currency veto in terms of Westminster versus Scotland, which offended – if only in the short term – even Scots inclined to support the Union. Osborne also argued that an independent Scotland would not, under any circumstances, be able to *use* the pound when, given it was a fully tradable currency, that clearly was not the case. All of this served to make a perfectly reasonable economic critique, and one supported by an army of independent experts and economists, a lot less compelling than it might have been.

And the Unionist side often fell victim to framing they had allowed their opponents to establish early on, so while they were pointing out the risks of independence to pensions (an important point about cross-border schemes ought to have caused the Yes side significant problems), the economy, university research funding and so on, Yes Scotland, and particularly the SNP, were busily eroding their opponents' standing in the debate and therefore their effectiveness. As a consequence all sorts of spurious arguments gained a surprising degree of currency, not least the supposed 'threat' to the Barnett Formula from voting No (what, pray, would have happened to it under independence?) and, more damagingly, to the NHS in Scotland. Although short on supporting evidence, Yes successfully convinced many wavering voters that independence was the only way to 'save' the NHS from Tory cuts (which did not, in reality, exist) as if that carried no risks of its own to public spending.

But then a lot of the Yes side's anti-Union arguments, albeit exaggerated, resonated because they contained an element of truth. Taking the longer view, it was true that Scotland occasionally 'got' governments it did not vote for (although in certain cases the same was true of England), while the legislative records of the Scottish and UK Parliaments certainly pointed to different priorities in certain policy domains. And while Scottish public life certainly was not free of 'elitism' and products of a private education, they did not dominate the airwaves to quite the same extent as Messrs Cameron and Osborne.

In retrospect, Better Together – like Yes Scotland – was much too reticent in prosecuting its core case. Although it rightly pointed out that Scotland had long benefited from higher per capita public spending than other (although certainly not all) parts of the UK, it seemed wary of talking up the fact that in the space of three decades Scotland had gone from one of the poorest parts of the country to one of the wealthiest, a truism regularly betrayed by the Scottish Government's incessant use of healthy economic data from precisely that time frame. A more confident No campaign might have flagged up the fact that this transformation had taken place under Conservative and Labour governments, of which the SNP viscerally disapproved. But then articulate proponents of the Union often seemed in short supply: the popular former Liberal Democrat leader Charles Kennedy, for example, was notable by his absence, while the former Prime Minister Gordon Brown only belatedly sang a song of Union, and very effectively too.

Given the nature of the campaign, particularly the seemingly endless goodies promised by the pro-independence camp (with only the slightest of caveats), it was a bidding contest Better Together could never in reality win. For they were defending the often unpleasant status quo while Yes were gazing towards future the sunlit uplands of a more easily defended future. The biggest bidding contest of all, meanwhile, manifested itself in constitutional terms. While Yes pointed to the prospect of controlling *all* policy levers (it glossed over obvious exceptions, such as monetary policy) under independence, No promised 'more powers' to further improve the devolutionary status quo.

Yet doing so raised lots of awkward questions about the existential case for the UK: if the only 'positive' argument lay in loosening that Union yet further, then what did that say about the essential integrity of the 300+-year-old Anglo–Scottish Union? And when even the Scottish Labour Party toyed with devolving elements of the pan-UK Welfare State (they had been particularly vulnerable to SNP attacks about the 'bedroom tax'), it prompted obvious soul searching about what exactly it was that bound the nations and regions of the UK together, if not what Gordon Brown called the 'pooling and sharing' of both risk and resources. And why on earth were more powers being promised when those agreed by the cross-party Calman Commission were yet to come into force?

But then the constitutional approach of British governments since the late 1990s had essentially been reactive rather than holistic, *ad hoc* rather than uniform in application, something that propagated the very British habit of muddling through. Only the Liberal Democrats sold a comprehensive vision of the UK as a federal country, but of course they did so from a position of relative weakness. Many of the arguments Labour had made in the 1980s, meanwhile, came home to roost, not least the general charge that a Conservative government lacked the mandate – moral and electoral – to 'rule' Scotland. Such a small 'n' Nationalist pitch posed obvious problems when it came to defending the mandate of a minority Tory/Lib Dem Coalition several decades later.

It was into this febrile atmosphere that the three Unionist leaders, David Cameron, Ed Miliband and Nick Clegg, launched their belated mission to save the UK in the final dramatic weeks of the campaign. Having resolved early on not to make the same mistakes as the federalists in Quebec nearly two decades before, in certain respects Better Together failed to learn from very similar constitutional history: when the gap between No and Yes narrowed (as it had in 1995) Britain's Unionists responded with a renewed 'vow' (or rather timetable) for more powers and even a Montreal-style rally in London's Trafalgar Square. Sure, both had been longer-term strategies but the optics remained bad: panicky, hasty and just a tad desperate. At long last Tom Nairn's 37-year-old charge about Britain being 'broken' appeared to have some credence.

Some siren Unionist voices argued that the Prime Minister ought never have agreed to a referendum in the autumn of 2012 and that even having conceded one ought to have agreed to a second option on 'more powers'. Given the circumstances, it was easy to be an armchair critic, but in reality neither critique stood up under scrutiny. Considering the SNP's considerable 2011 mandate, the UK Government realised early on it had little choice but to agree to a plebiscite on independence, while the beguiling simplicity of a second (or was it third?) question was in fact anything but: not only had no one actually defined what 'devo-more' might look like (the term 'devo-max' had always been a red herring) but such a formulation would have caused both sides significant problems, the Unionists in terms of agreeing a deal and the Nationalists when it came to securing party agreement to something that would have certainly beaten its preferred independence option.

In retrospect it was timing that proved Cameron's big mistake. Carelessly conceded by the Prime Minister in the course of unguarded remarks at Dover House in London, a two-year timescale enabled Yes Scotland to plan a slow-burn, under-the-radar insurgency; a swifter referendum, even one held by the end of 2013 rather than 2014, would have forced Nationalists' hands before they were ready. But then the whole referendum affair exposed Cameron's strategic weaknesses. Very much a reactive, day-to-day politician, he was evidently better at planning a long-term General Election campaign than the preservation of the country he led.

So the referendum debate brought out both the best in Scots, such as passionate idealism, but also the worst, not least nostalgic tribalism, much of it noisily manifesting itself on Twitter, Facebook and other online forums, more akin to echo chambers than virtual platforms for measured debate. Furthermore, the long debate gave rise to the view that there somehow existed swift, cost-free solutions to long-standing and deeply complex problems. Too often it was little more than political escapism.

It was also necessary to separate the quantity of referendum debate from its quality. Certainly it was true that more Scots ended up engaged with politics in general and the Scottish Question in particular, but more often than not this engagement was at the level of student politics. Bankers are evil! No more Tory governments! Nationalists are racist! A lot of people might have agreed with such sentiments, but to depict it as a deep reflection on big, important issues would have been to admit to a tenuous grip on contemporary reality.

The first casualty of the referendum war, inevitably, was nuance. Recent history was manipulated (by both sides) to justify contemporary arguments while corrections on points of fact or analysis were often dismissed as pedantry or a distraction from the 'real' issues, whatever those happened to be. In economic terms much of the discourse was illiterate and reductive with, at one point, both Yes Scotland and Better Together attempting to quantify in monetary terms the relative benefits of 'independence' and 'the Union'. Danny Alexander, the Chief Secretary to the Treasury, and Alex Salmond, the First Minister, even issued largely meaningless predictions of future rates of economic growth, productivity and employment. Crystal ball gazing was no longer confined to travelling circuses.

While benefiting – to some extent – from a general anti-politics mood, Yes Scotland also managed to insulate itself from that all-pervasive cynicism. Alex Salmond somehow succeeded in convincing a large number of Scots that he, unlike other here-today-gone-tomorrow politicians, would actually deliver on his promises. And what promises they were; amid widespread (and justifiable) skepticism about jam tomorrow pledges, Yes simply promised even more jam: no austerity, earlier retirement, more generous pensions, potentially higher public sector wages and permanently free university tuition, all paid for via stable, or in many cases reduced, taxation.

Many otherwise jaded commentators completely failed to separate what was being promised from what was actually deliverable, even though recent history was littered examples of 'positive' centre-left campaigns fuelled by high expectations (step forward Messrs Obama and Hollande). At the same time, and despite strikingly low approval and trust ratings, most polls still suggested a majority of Scots were prepared to go with the more sober and less flashy status quo. Did that mean Project Fear had prevailed? Or that voters had seen through what one critic dubbed 'Project Pollyanna'?

On 18 September 2014, the United Kingdom of Great Britain and Northern Ireland came within 383,937 votes of having to grapple with the issue of its continued existence. More than four million 'Scots', generously defined, participated in the referendum on Scottish independence held that day, and when the votes were counted only 10.6 per cent separated the winners from the losers, a much closer margin than either side had anticipated for much of the two-year campaign.

Finally given the right to self-determination, a majority of voters in Scotland had self-determined in *favour* of the Union, which at the very least removed one rhetorical line of attack from the Nationalist armoury. But at the same time it seemed clear a large number of those voting No had done so in the expectation of Scotland being granted even more autonomy within that continuing Union. As the former Liberal leader Michael Ignatieff observed of two similar referendums in Quebec: 'Canadians were able to joke that what Quebeckers really wanted was an independent Quebec inside a united Canada.' Perhaps a majority of Scots had reached that same seemingly paradoxical position.

Whatever the case, the margin of victory for No only looked decisive because polls had narrowed so dramatically in the closing weeks of the campaign; a year or so earlier and Unionists had spoken confidently of securing a 2/1 No vote or, at the very least, 60/40. So in that context a 55.3 per cent No vote was best viewed as a reprieve rather than a victory for the status quo. (As one correspondent in the *Herald* letters pages quipped, it was a shame the ballot paper hadn't taken a leaf out of Scots Law by including a 'not proven' option.) It was also difficult for Better Together to claim any great credit, given the often-uninspiring nature of its two-year campaign. Initial analysis revealed that the vast majority of those voting No had decided to do so early on and had not budged, while other analysis showed that perhaps as much of a quarter of the electorate was motived to vote No out of opposition to independence, and most for the first time in several years; it was even tempting to conclude that No had won in spite of the official pro-UK campaign, not because of it.

Paradoxically, the pattern of Yes and No voting across Scotland gave the major parties on each side cause for concern: many SNP strongholds (at Holyrood or Westminster) decisively voted No while Yes secured a majority in two urban Labour heartlands, Glasgow and Dundee. On the night, Labour faces had the most furrowed brows, and indeed in several respects they only had themselves to blame: not only electoral defeat in 2007 and again in 2011, but its lack of strategy, lack of ideas, lack of life and lack of maturity when presented with the opportunity to develop its once-coherent record on devolution. The fact that a clear majority of Scots aged less than 55 voted Yes also pointed to a demographic problem for Unionists: like Republicans in the US, it seemed support for their cause would diminish over time.

On the other hand, however, those among the '45 per cent' who argued that the outcome was down to media bias, scaremongering, a last-minute 'vow' of more powers or even a British-led conspiracy were wide of the mark. Equally important had been that the pro-independence arguments (though not all of them) had not made sense to a majority of electors, who had also found the promised riches too unrealistic, the intellectual contortions too obvious and (an often underrated factor) the remaining pan-UK bonds too strong. With that uncomfortable reality in mind, there was little to be gained from arguing (as many did online) that 'we wuz robbed', or lapsing (as certain Yes-supporting columnists did within days of the result) into 'we told you so' preaching. After all, lots of people had said lots of silly things before polling day: the Scottish Parliament would be abolished, Westminster would take 'revenge'; even that Scotland might fade away as a distinct political entity.

Yet the experience of similar constitutional debates in other countries demonstrated that much of this was far-fetched. Quebec in particular carried two main lessons: first that the question was bound to come round again, and second that the predominant pro-independence party need not suffer as a result of one, or even two defeats. In Canada the Parti Québécois won provincial elections following both its referendum losses in 1980 and 1995, and in Scotland polling suggested the SNP was on course to do the same in 2016.

But it would do so, of course, under new leadership. The big surprise of the day after the referendum vote had been the resignation of Alex Salmond, although in retrospect it should not have been such a shock. After all, he had served the second of two decade-long terms at the helm of his party and, approaching 60 years of age, he must have been exhausted. More to the point, Salmond's acute political antennae told him that although he had done more than anyone else to bring about that decisive moment, it would be better left to someone else, almost certainly his deputy Nicola Sturgeon, to exploit political terrain he judged 'redolent with possibility'.

Indeed, speaking at the launch of her leadership campaign, Sturgeon hinted that the Conservatives' desire to hold an in/out referendum on the UK's membership of the EU by the end of 2017 might present an opportunity to reopen the issue, although at the same time she had to take care not to encourage talk of a Quebec-style 'neverendum'. And if the Scottish Question was asked again, sooner or later, then even some Unionists realised that with 'independence' normalised in the minds of voters and the prospect of more austerity, UKIP success and Middle Eastern conflict likely to justify certain warnings about a No vote, the status quo might not be so readily defended the second time around.

With that in mind, it was also a mistake for the Unionist parties to convince themselves that the solution lay solely in delivering more devolution for Scotland. Rather, if the referendum had revealed anything, it had been that the problem went much deeper than that. Most analysis showed that the main driver of Yes votes had been discontent with the 'Westminster system'; it was about trust and legitimacy, and that was not easily fixed with yet another cross-party devolution commission. The BBC journalist Allan Little put it best in a pre-referendum edition of *Panorama*. Future generations of Scots, he concluded, 'will need reasons to love and trust the Union as our parents and grandparents did, rather than simply to fear the alternative'.

In the summer of 2013 the US polling guru Nate Silver had stated the then orthodox view that the Yes campaign had 'virtually no chance' of victory, positing that only a 'major crisis', most likely originating in England, could conceivably alter that dynamic before 18 September 2014. That it ended up having precisely that – a chance of victory – simply served to demonstrate that the nature of political prediction, as Silver wrote elsewhere, was as unreliable as it was extensive. Reading this diary back during the editing process it was clear that, like Silver, I got a lot of things wrong (including the likely margin of victory) but also many things broadly correct. At least I can plead, as journalists often do, that I was probably right at the time.

David Torrance

100 Days of Hope and Fear

Friday, 30 May 2014 (Edinburgh)

Today marked the beginning of the 'official' regulated period, or the ironically named 'short' campaign (actually 16 weeks). Bit of a damp squib in media terms, little more than Blair McDougall and Better Together types 'knocking doors and speaking to undecided voters' in Govanhill. I suspect Yes Scotland and the SNP had something planned, but the European election result put a kybosh on its 'two countries moving in opposite directions' stuff. Obviously winning a third MEP would have given them a pre-referendum electoral boost, but then they didn't, thus they kept quiet.

Meanwhile I was still nursing my ego having watched Iain Macwhirter talk about the referendum at Summerhall in Edinburgh the evening before. Apropos of nothing he mentioned me in response to a question from the audience, claiming I'd said on Twitter that there'd be a civil war between England and Scotland if the latter became independent. Obviously I'd said nothing of the sort (I'd simply mentioned the Anglo-Irish trade war of the late 1920s) and intervened to say so. Iain looked a little taken aback (obviously he had no idea I was in the audience) and later mumbled a half apology. The chap next to me also used the exchange as an opportunity to accuse me of writing 'negative' articles.

The thing is, Iain is very good at such events: funny, engaging, frequently insightful, but also has a tendency to adopt unfortunate terminology (at one point he and his questioner happily discussed Danny Alexander being 'sent north' to lecture Scots on economics, when in fact he'd travelled 'south' from his Inverness constituency); the Chancellor had come to Edinburgh on a 'day trip'; £300bn in oil revenue 'went south' and Scotland saw none of it, which is just nonsense. He was critical, however, of the SNP on Corporation Tax.

The event was very chattering class Edinburgh (there were amused coos when I intervened). One lady told me on the way in that, like Iain, she'd moved from supporting Labour to embracing independence. 'No one told me when I joined Labour that it was a Unionist party,' she said, which struck me as an odd thing to say. To Iain's credit, he later texted me to apologise and offer lunch, which of course I accepted. I read the extra chapter in the paperback edition of his *Road to Referendum* book (Cargo), which was very good. The only bit I think he overstates (as at the event) is the impact of George Osborne's 'sermon on the pound', which he seems to think fatally undermines the 'moral' basis of the Union.

Saturday, 31 May 2014 (Glasgow)

Up early to get the 7.15am train to Glasgow to take part in the *Shereen* programme (BBC Scotland), which is always good fun. It was a nice day so I brought my bike and cycled from Queen Street to Pacific Quay (the cycle path along the Clyde had more or less reopened). Also on the show was Ian Blackford, a former SNP treasurer and a fully paid-up member of the human race. We jousted, as ever, but good-naturedly, agreeing that both Danny Alexander and Alex Salmond's economic forecasts a few days before had been based more on wishful thinking than hard facts (though Ian's instinctive loyalty eventually kicked in).

Before the recording Ian conceded that the Unionist parties hardening up their 'more powers' offers made it harder for them (Yes Scotland) to push a Yes vote, not something that's publicly conceded, for obvious reasons. After the show I cycled through Kelvingrove Park to meet Duncan Sim, one of my tutors at UWS (University of the West of Scotland), to discuss a seminar we're both doing next Saturday. He was sporting a colourful Yes badge on his jacket.

Monday, 2 June 2014 (Glasgow)

Back through to Glasgow to watch the Scottish Tories unveil their long-awaited Strathclyde Commission report on more powers following a No vote. The setting was the Clydeport building on Robertson Street, which I've loved since I used to attend Airtricity meetings there a few years ago,[1] an architectural manifestation of Glasgow's former status as a global centre of shipping and trade. After a rather lacklustre opening pitch from Lord Strathclyde himself (clearly a useful figurehead more than anything else), Ruth Davidson did a turn.

It was pretty impressive. Importantly, she looked as if she meant it, fielded questions effectively and was at her engaging best: quite a contrast with a few years ago, when I and others were rather hastily writing her

---

1 I briefly worked in PR in mid-2007 and Airtricity was one of my accounts at Edelman.

Lord Strathclyde unveils his Scottish Conservative Party report on further powers for the Scottish Parliament.

off politically. The press pack seemed quite impressed too (I met Chris Deerin from the *Scottish Daily Mail* for the first time), which made an interesting change, but then the report itself was short and to the point, recommending – as expected – the full devolution of income tax (though not, oddly, thresholds), some additional welfare powers, and so on. Some parts, particularly a UK-wide committee of the devolved parliaments and assemblies, hinted at a federal approach but obviously didn't use that word.

Everyone was very chipper. Afterwards, Tory MSP Jackson Carlaw told me he found the whole exercise 'liberating', finally laying the 'ghost' of Margaret Thatcher to rest. Chatting to Adam Tomkins, a constitutional lawyer at Glasgow University, who of course had heavily influenced the whole thing, I suddenly remembered that Ruth had referred to the Barnett Formula being in its 'death throes' when she launched the Commission more than a year ago, yet when Tom Strathclyde was asked about Barnett he moved swiftly to declare it alive and kicking. 'The trouble with you,' Adam said to me, 'is you remember lines in old speeches.'

That aside, the shift in Scottish Tory thinking (apart from being long overdue, the Welsh party got to this point 15 years ago) is striking. Later Alex Fergusson (another Commissioner) told me he'd been astonished at how quickly the mood changed among his colleagues – initially he'd assumed he'd have to resign as a result of not agreeing with the recommendations. He and Jackson Carlaw also said Margaret Mitchell (formerly a hardliner on more powers) had surprised everyone by enthusing about the report in the group meeting. There was some method in this madness: while she considered the 2012 Scotland Act incoherent and dangerous, the Strathclyde Commission, she believed, had sorted it all out.

Tuesday, 3 June 2014 (Dundee & Edinburgh)

Today was dominated (at least in my head) by a Q&A with Alex Salmond I was chairing in Dundee as part of the Five Million Questions (5MQ) project. I don't mind admitting to being quite nervous about the whole thing, but in the event I held it together. It was quite clear he didn't really want to be there at all (which was understandable, we had rather bounced him into doing it) and, having arrived, only met the Principal (with whom he was rather curt) and Michael Marra (whom he clearly remembered from his Labour days, but now director of 5MQ), only greeting me as we headed into the packed lecture theatre. Dawn Campbell took a picture of the four of us at the entrance, in which Salmond grinned and I looked pained.

He is a rock star politician: before he'd even sat down the punters were whistling and clapping (some had turned up two hours early just to get a seat), while on the way out he was delayed by requests for selfies and autographs. Not many politicians in this cynical age have that star quality. Still, in the space of an hour all his strengths and weaknesses were on show, the low blows ('I'll never be as conservative as you' he quipped at one point), chuckling at his own jokes, weird (and lengthy) digressions and obvious irritation at even the politest interruption from me.

I tried to put myself in his shoes. Obviously reading my stuff (and he clearly does) must be annoying, but then all politicians have to put up with criticism and not all politicians behave like he does (Nicola Sturgeon, for example, is usually charming, but then she mostly gets praise). Despite the onslaught, I think I managed to get some interesting stuff out of him when it came to his shifting views on income tax, immigration and so on. Charm was in short supply, even his reference to my 'meticulous' chronicling of his

With (left to right) Michael Marra, Alex Salmond and Pete Downes at Dundee University.
(Photo: Five Million Questions)

life ('he knows more about me than me') sounded like damning me with faint praise. Because of this I missed the Labour rally in Glasgow, although I had made it along to that morning's press conference in Edinburgh. Gordon Brown was very, well, Gordonish, clumsily referring to the 'Scottish Assembly' and speaking a bit out of turn when it came to more powers (he was scathing when someone asked how it felt to be 'outbid' by the Scottish Tories). There was a flash of humour when Cameron Brooks from the *Press & Journal* asked how the referendum compared with his time as PM. 'I'm enjoying this,' he said, clearly not intending it as a joke but breaking into his slightly awkward grin when he realised that most of us had taken it that way.

The more positive framing of the No message was interesting: we were handed printed material which said 'I'm voting No', 'No thanks', etc, and also a 1997-style pledge card. Brown was a little better on evening telly, although Dennis Canavan did his usual eye-popping red-in-the-face routine when asked to comment: he didn't trust the 'Tories', nor should Gordon, etc. More interesting was Douglas Alexander versus Nicola Sturgeon on BBC2's *Scotland 2014*, a programme which, after a shaky start, is beginning to find its feet. Sarah Smith asked decent questions and Douglas, generally a class act, did his thoughtful ecumenical bit while Nicola, also a class act, talked down the Unionist parties' offers of more powers as a 'lowest common denominator' offer, but then I guess she had to do that. The reality is that fixed-term Parliaments at Westminster have significantly altered the political dynamic and if the three Better Together parties don't make good on that pledge between 2015 and 2016 then they'll be in serious trouble.

Wednesday, 4 June 2014 (Edinburgh)

A fairly quiet day beyond the launch, or rather re-launch, of the Edinburgh University Press book Scotland's Choices by Guy Lodge (of the IPPR), Jim Gallagher and Iain McLean. It was upstairs in Hemma, which was handy, but rather thinly attended, most probably because the skies had opened up outside. Birlinn publisher Hugh Andrew was there, as were two former permanent secretaries at the old Scottish Office (Sir Russell Hillhouse and Sir Muir Russell). Iain McLean told me he'd tried to make Gordon Brown's forthcoming book (My Scotland, Our Britain) less 'Gordonish' while a nice Catalan woman whose name I forget told me she'd seen the Catalan documentary featuring me, Tom Devine, et al. She was impressed by its 'balance', which she added forlornly was much rarer in the context of Catalonia's own referendum debate.

After that I went to see End of Tomorrow at the Omni, an enjoyable enough piece of sci-fi fluff starring Tom Cruise and trading on the 70th anniversary of D-Day, although with aliens instead of Nazis. Talking of Nazis, a Twitter storm was already erupting as I took my seat, the ever-reliable Pat Kane having taken umbrage at Alistair Darling referring to 'blood-and-soil' Nationalism in an interview with the New Statesman. For dramatic effect he conflated this with Nazi ideology rather than a fairly innocuous reference to ethnic nationalism (he kept tweeting it in the original German, 'blut-und-boden', for even more dramatic effect). I took issue with that and got flak for 'defending' Darling's comments (which I hadn't), revealing my true colours, and so on.

It later emerged that Darling hadn't used those words but had agreed ('at heart') with Jason Cowley when he used the term in a question. This didn't stop the usual suspects drowning in phoney outrage and at one point even Mike Russell (the Education Secretary) waded in, saying one of my tweets was 'unworthy' (a rather pompous word), Darling should apologise, etc. I responded by pointing out to him and others that a) Darling hadn't used those words and b) Salmond had called the BBC's Ric Bailey a 'Gauleiter' back in 2012, a clear reference to a regional Nazi administrator. At this point most of my attackers went rather quiet. Funny that.

That aside, some of Darling's comments had been ill advised, particularly as he'd been leading calls for a civilised, respectful debate. Most controversially he said Salmond's response to UKIP's election win (that television coverage of Farage et al had been 'beamed' into Scotland) was 'something that Kim Jong-il would say'. Tellingly, Salmond called on Darling to apologise for that but not the blood-and-soil bit, perhaps aware his own Nazi allusion would be thrown back at him.

Thursday, 5 June 2014 (Edinburgh)

First Minister's Questions was predictably pointless, although Ruth Davidson quoted the economist Andrew Hughes-Hallett back at Salmond on overestimated oil revenues and he ducked the point. Afterwards Ruth ambled up to me in the Garden Lobby and thanked me for calling out *The Times'* columnist Alice Thomson on giving her age (in a column that morning) as 37 rather than 35. Also chatted to Tom Gordon from the *Sunday Herald*. He thinks Salmond will resign swiftly no matter how high the Yes vote is (assuming a No), as he hates being cast in the role of loser *à la* 1999–2000 when he was briefly opposition leader in the Scottish Parliament. He referred to a recent blog by Paul Hutcheon (also of the *Sunday Herald*), which quoted a source saying the FM was 'unlikely to lead the SNP into the 2016 Holyrood election – a role earmarked for Nicola Sturgeon'. Although I've always thought Salmond would stay on as First Minister (after all he has a separate, and rather large, mandate), I found Tom's reasoning quite convincing.

The Leader of the Western World's indyref intervention livened up the afternoon. I tweeted about the parallel with Clinton and Quebec in 1995 and it earned me the top interview slot on Radio 4's *PM* with Eddie Mair (useful thing, Twitter). Spoke to Ramsay Jones from Downing Street (who came up with the genius 'Nobama' hashtag) beforehand and he mischievously feigned ignorance, saying he had no idea 'precisely' what Obama would say, which more or less gave the game away. Mair picked me up (rightly) on my assertion the whole thing had been co-ordinated, but I simply pointed out that Obama's response to a journalist's question clearly hadn't been ad-libbed (indeed the phrasing was similar to Clinton's in 1995). The fact David Cameron was standing alongside looking studiously surprised also underpinned my point.

Making the best of a bad situation, Salmond cleverly threw the phrase 'yes we can' back at Obama, knowing he couldn't denigrate or delegitimise him as he routinely does other critics of independence. Still, it's not good for them; years spent cultivating DC opinion and that's what happens, not even a neutral line, which had been the indication until now. Someone from Yes Scotland texted to say he found it difficult to gauge the reaction, which might even be neutral. Got me thinking that a lot of this to most people, even an intervention from the President, is just noise. Outside the bubble, hardly any of this registers – Danny Finkelstein once estimated five per cent – but it's chewed over endlessly by the likes of me.

Bruce Crawford, always the least tribal of Nationalists, told me at Holyrood the other day he thought Adam Tomkins was good value, and indeed he is on fine form at a Better Together meeting at Leith Academy that evening. The whole thing was entirely contrary to the impression of BT meetings I'd formed from Twitter: that they barely take place, if they do they're thinly attended, have bad speakers, and so on. This one was well attended (about 100 people), the three speakers were all very good and the questions informed and intelligent. Of course it wasn't at all representative, but those present clearly wanted validation for voting No.

At one point, having outlined the UK's record on international aid, Adam declared: 'Am I proud to be British? Damn right I'm proud!' an exclamation that could easily have gone wrong but was greeted with an enthusiastic round of applause. It was weird being back in Leith Academy, my old school. The seats in the theatre were the same uncomfortable plastic ones I remember from 20 years ago and when the bell rang it induced a Pavlovian churn of the stomach.

One lady came up beforehand to say she'd watched the Dundee Salmond Q&A on YouTube and was impressed I'd held my tongue given he was so 'condescending' (it heartened me that someone had noticed). The academic Tom Gallagher was in the audience and referred to the 'brass neck' of the pro-independence case (provoking another round of applause), as was Jill Stephenson, the prolific historian-cum-tweeter. Earlier Douglas Pattullo, who works for the Tory MSP (Sir) Jamie McGrigor, told me the most common thing he hears while telephone canvassing is 'my heart wants me to vote Yes but my head says No', even from Tories. That might be true, but those at Leith Academy certainly weren't feint-hearts. Had a quick drink on Leith Walk with Adam and a bright Labour activist called Cat Headley.

Friday, 6 June 2014 (Edinburgh)

Spent most of a very summery day at the Raeburn Room in Old College at a Scottish Constitutional Futures Forum event called '100 Days to Go: Four Nations and a Union'. Aileen McHarg from Strathclyde University kicked off with what was essentially an articulate Yes case: the UK state is unreformable, the pro-independence vision isn't about Nationalism but building a better future, Unionism is indefensible, etc. Oddly, it wasn't terribly academic, i.e. lots of assertions and vague assumptions interspersed with cautious bits of balance ('Westminster is an all-purpose bogey man for everything bad'). Some observations were interesting though: that the debate would for many Yes voters reinforce their discontent with the status quo, while equally it might reinvigorate the Union for No voters, shifting the perception away from Colin Kidd's 'wallpaper', or 'banal', Unionism.

Neil Walker from Edinburgh University made the point that the third question or option 'hadn't gone away', despite (successful) efforts to kill it off during the Edinburgh Agreement negotiations. Being an academic, he couldn't resist a pop at the media, saying that to the London media Scotland was 'just an alternative to Crimea' (a bit of an exaggeration), although he was right to say its attention was 'sporadic'. But of course it cuts both ways – how many Scottish journalists and commentators write about English politics in a sympathetic or knowledgeable way?

Nick Barber from Oxford University spoke very entertainingly about England but made lots of basic errors (he said tuition fees had been introduced in England because of Scottish votes). He balanced out Aileen by being unequivocally anti-independence ('I like living in a multi-national state... they're more tolerant, more attractive... that's why I'd be sorry to see it go'). I sat next to a chap from Yes Scotland, who seemed to enjoy it all; Better Together doesn't seem to bother attending events like this.

A chap called Dan Wincott from Cardiff University was also interesting, talking about the UK's 'accidental constitution' (or rather its territorial extent was accidental), its 'pantomime' quality (in that it's usually behind you) and how Wales and Northern Ireland were the 'forgotten' bits of the UK, which of course is true. Talking of the Province, John Morison from Queen's compared what's happening in Scotland with the run-up to the 1998 referendum on the Good Friday Agreement, i.e. endless analysis from constitutional lawyers but more limited interest from the general population, and once it was all over interest tailed off significantly. That's the sort of talk that keeps me awake at night.

Although I understand the need for academics to have seminars, this one just confirmed my suspicion that constitutional lawyers are better on theory than they are on politics, which is a bit of a weakness, given the referendum and independence are both intensely political. Many of them seemed unaware of significant developments: citizenship, for example, was discussed without reference to the Scotland Analysis paper that conceded an independent Scotland would lead to 'dual citizenship', but then they probably don't read newspapers.

After soaking up the sun I got diverted via the STV studios to speak to *Channel 4 News* about Better Together hiring M&C Saatchi to handle its communications in the last four months of the campaign. There was a rather feeble attempt by Yes Scotland to rubbish this on the grounds that Saatchi had handled the Tories' 1979 election campaign, but as Better Together pointed out (untypically swiftly), both the SNP and Scottish Government had used the same ad agency as the Conservatives and UKIP.

In haste (and because it was still sunny) I appeared unshaven, wearing a Frank Sinatra T-shirt (folk on Twitter thought it was Ian Brady!) and looking, as someone later put it, as if I'd come straight from the students' union. After that I had food with Dominic Hinde of the Scottish Greens then cycled down to Leith for a drink with a cultural sector type who's planning to vote No. Wonders shall never cease.

Sunday, 8 June 2014 (Edinburgh)

Writing my *Herald* column took most of the afternoon but I was quite pleased with it, using Obama and 'yes we can' as a hook for exploring the quixotic nature of positive campaigning. Alex Massie had an interesting (and diligently balanced) feature in *Scotland on Sunday*, including a quote from a Yes Scotland 'source' which predicted that in the end the referendum question would simply be framed as a: 'vote for Scotland or a vote against Scotland? A vote even against the concept of Scotland.' For some reason I found that quite chilling.

Sunday Politics Scotland on BBC1 had an interview with John Reid, further proof that Labour is finally wheeling out (or perhaps dusting off) its 'big beasts' as polling day approaches. Reid, who gave a speech in Stirling yesterday, was good if a little pompous, arguing that those intending to vote No are every bit as Scottish as those planning to vote Yes. He also effectively outlined Better Together's strategy for the next 100 days: emphasising the economic advantages of being part of the UK, the risks associated with independence and thirdly, the emotional argument (which he conceded applied to both sides). Over the next few weeks, predicted Reid, 'arguments of the head and the heart' would 'come together'. Blair McDougall, interviewed on Radio 4's *Westminster Hour* later that evening, did much the same routine, so it's obviously the agreed 'line'.

Monday, 9 June 2014 (Edinburgh)

Up early to speak to *Good Morning Wales* about there being '100 days to go' in the referendum campaign. It's actually (as I told the producer) 101 days, but no one seemed to mind. Later, at a Yes Scotland photo call to mark the same pre-versary, Peter Murrell (the SNP's chief executive) blamed the BBC for the timing, and specifically Glenn Campbell, which I thought was quite funny. Meanwhile Blair Jenkins (who admired my Brompton at a café near Dynamic Earth) unveiled a new total for the Independence

Declaration (nearly 800,000 signatures), although I find it difficult to take that seriously (is anyone actually going to check?).

Later that morning I went along to the 'female Cabinet', which came over as a bit tokenistic and woolly (independence will be 'good' for women, etc), although Nicola Sturgeon was typically cogent. Entertainingly, she kept referring to the gathering (again at Dynamic Earth) as 'all-women' despite there being almost an entire row of male journalists (including me) at the back. Beforehand a lawyer called Carol Fox, who said she knew Michael (my brother), politely accused me of being too 'relaxed' about Thatcherism, whatever that was supposed to mean.

I regretted not heading through to Glasgow for a Better Together rally in Maryhill (the calling notice hadn't sold it particularly well), which judging from Twitter and television footage was quite an event: 'real' people spoke about their commitment to the Union and Alistair Darling made a speech which, at least judging by the text, was better than usual. After lunch with the ever-engaging Peter Geoghegan and a nice chap from the *Washington Post* (he interviewed me for a piece he was writing on the 'youth' vote), we went to a rather pointless photo call with Darling at the West End, only saved by some amiable chat with Jim Naughtie, Daniel Johnson, Severin Carrell *et al*.

I got completely soaked cycling back to Holyrood in the rain but had dried out (almost) by the time I needed to ride down to Powderhall Rigg for dinner with Roddy Martine, Sheena McDonald and her partner Allan Little, the BBC network correspondent whom I met briefly at the Strathclyde Commission event last week. It was a fun evening and there was, inevitably, a lot of referendum chat as well as reminiscing about the Edinburgh arts scene of old. 'How many books have you written?' asked Allan at one point. 'About ten,' I replied, trying and failing not to appear a prick. Sheena and Allan dropped me off in a taxi and I caught up with evening telly. Salmond was on STV (looking tired and fed up) saying Yes was within 'touching distance' of victory, although of course that's an exaggeration. There was one interesting bit, when the FM said 'we asked in 2012 to include the devo-max option in the... referendum and David Cameron said no to that,' which to my knowledge was the first time he'd been that unequivocal.

Tuesday, 10 June 2014 (Edinburgh & Dundee)

Gordon Brown appears to have gone a bit mad, or that's how it appeared at first, telling a Westminster Lobby lunch that it would be a 'good idea' for David Cameron to debate with Alex Salmond, criticising the UK Government for framing the debate as Britain 'against' Scotland and issuing 'patronising' material (last week's Lego stuff, for example). 'Countries,' he added for good measure, 'can be lost by mistake.'

It didn't exactly look, um, better together, but in retrospect it made more sense. He clearly does his own thing, but it seems likely Brown's remarks were targeted at wavering Labour voters and thus intended to reassure them that the wicked Tories weren't beyond reproach. I texted Neil Mackinnon later on (former Scottish Lib Dem spin doctor) and he said he 'would not be surprised to find out that he believes that he personally can turn the whole thing around'. 'And you know what?' he added. 'He might very well be able to!'

I've always thought Brown an asset to the campaign, for all his quirks and faults. I still remember canvassing during the Glenrothes by-election in 2008 and finding even SNP supporters were rooting for him: Fifers considered him one of their own, and there was also an underdog aspect to it. He had a piece in today's *Guardian* that also demonstrated obvious talents (this line in relation to welfare):

> Yet this system of pooling and sharing resources would be the first casualty of Scotland's departure from Britain. So what is the basis of the SNP claim that, having smashed the UK's system of redistributive transfers, an independent Scotland would be a more equal place? There is none. The SNP has refused to match Labour's commitment to raise the top rate of tax to 50p; refused to agree – even with Boris Johnson – to reform stamp duty with a millionaires' mansion tax; refused to contemplate a new top band for council tax for the most expensive properties. Nor do they have plans to redistribute income or wealth through a bankers' tax or any other means.

Of course for most of his time as Chancellor Brown didn't do any of that either, although his credentials when it comes to redistribution of wealth are certainly better than the First Minister's, who's told the *Daily Record* that no matter what happens in September he plans to contest the 2016 elections. 'I intend to stand again in 2016,' he told David Clegg. 'Whatever the political circumstances, there will be an election in 2016 and the people will choose the First Minister.'

Kezia Dugdale (a Labour MSP), who I saw later on, reckoned he had to say that to prevent speculation, but – as I pointed out – there hasn't been any. I suppose it could be power play with Nicola Sturgeon, who after all wants to be leader/FM and 2016 is arguably her best shot at that. I'm amazed Salmond has been so definitive, not his style at all. I only saw the story following a highly enjoyable lunch with David Greig (the playwright) at a nice restaurant called Kyloe in the West End. He was thoughtful and interesting, with chat ranging across the referendum, culture and also theatre. I told him I'd enjoyed *Dunsinane* but hadn't understood *San Diego* ('I don't think anyone did,' he remarked self-deprecatingly). He was refreshingly conscious that art ought to engage as widely as possible, thus Hugh MacDiarmid – however interesting – didn't really qualify. I showed him my copy of Alasdair Gray's book (which I'm reading) and of course we covered the settlers and colonists stuff, on which we were (mercifully) in agreement.

At one point in Gray's book (full of baffling digressions and bad history, ancient and contemporary) there's an astonishing sentence where, in the process of revisiting – and defending – his earlier essay, he lists several 'good settlers of whom I approved because, although English, they had funded a play or exhibited pictures of mine'. So there we have it; not only can English immigrants be classified as 'good' or 'bad', but also the criteria is how much public money they've sent Gray's way!

In a similar vein, Janet Street-Porter interviewed Robin McAlpine of Common Weal fame for a BBC programme I watched later, based on her (rather tenuously) walking around different bits of Scotland. 'It's not that we don't like you [the English],' he said at one point, 'it's that you're not part of our lives. We put on the television and your news and our news are about different things. The 6 o'clock news we see up here from London may as well be coming from France for as much relevance as it's got to us.' Robin is of course trapped in a bubble where everyone agrees with him and the Common Weal thus his Salmond-like tendency to speak on behalf of the nation, but it was still a pretty weird thing to say: what about the millions of Scots who have English partners, relatives, friends or colleagues? So much for the social union.

I mentioned this and Gray's book to Chris Whatley at Dundee University later, and he looked amused at my summary (this involved gesticulating). I was there to chair a debate on independence and children's policy as part of the Five Million Questions project (in fact, its penultimate event) and felt a little out of my depth, as it wasn't my field at all. Only when the discussion moved on to taxation did I become more comfortable, and pushed Aileen Campbell (the Children's Minister) on that because I knew she'd be uncomfortable (and she was), falling back on the usual lines about growing the economy, social justice and so on. Overall, however, she was very impressive: personable and obviously on top of her brief.

On the train back to Edinburgh (beautiful evening), Professor Kay Tisdall (a Canadian, we inevitably touched on Quebec) and I chatted with a couple of passengers, a lady who got off at Kirkcaldy (No) and a chap from Aberdeen who worked for a charity (didn't say but also probably No). They spoke about the uncertainty of independence; I said there was uncertainty on both sides but they looked unconvinced. Later someone tweeted at me saying they'd been in the same carriage 'trying not to join in the Indy debate'.

The journalist Tom Rowley, whom I met a few weeks ago, had a great piece in the *Daily Telegraph* examining what made seven pro-indy folk tick: he asked the actress Elaine C. Smith how the Nesbitts (as in Rab C. and Mary Doll) would have voted in the referendum, and she laughingly told him to ask Ian Pattison, their creator.

> So I do. His reply is typically acerbic: For thousands of impoverished voters like Rab and Mary Nesbitt, the referendum will offer a unique opportunity to choose who screws them over, Holyrood or Westminster,' he writes. 'Either way, life will go on as normal. In the event of a Yes vote, Rab will not be blind to the irony of queuing at a food bank with a Saltire painted on his face, shouting "Free-dom".'

I thought of this later on when I popped down to Tesco on Holyrood Road to buy some ice cream. At one counter was a copper taking a statement from a member of staff because there'd clearly been an 'incident', while at another was Education Secretary Mike Russell in a pin-stripe suit. 'Hi Mike,' I said, slightly conscious we'd sparred on Twitter just last week. 'Ah,' he boomed, 'everyone's here. Now at least I don't have to tweet at you.'

Wednesday, 11 June 2014 (Edinburgh)

Lunch with Iain Macwhirter, 'penance' (his word) for misrepresenting something I'd said on Twitter about Ireland to an audience at Summerhall a couple of weeks ago. We sat outside at Urban Angel on Hanover Street and chatted, inevitably, about the referendum. Perhaps surprisingly, we found ourselves in agreement on most points, although he has a tendency (as I told him) to overstate certain points (i.e. the impact of Osborne's currency intervention) and he is, like Lesley Riddoch, obsessed with Norway *et al*.

We touched on the day's stories: Campbell Gunn's email to the *Telegraph* questioning Clare Lally's credentials as a 'real' mother (he later apologised but the whole thing was a bit grubby) and, of course, J.K. Rowling's £1 million donation to Better Together and 1,600-word blog on her website about why she was voting No. Iain said it captured perfectly why he reckoned fewer women would be voting Yes, i.e. not necessarily hostile to independence but just worried about the consequences.

Speaking at a Napier University event that evening (I cycled to Craiglockhart along the canal; lovely evening), Nicola Sturgeon was pitch perfect when someone in the audience asked about Rowling. While obviously indicating that she didn't agree with its conclusion, nevertheless 'what she wrote was very thoughtful' (which it was). On independence generally Sturgeon was, as ever, authoritative and engaging. A Yes vote, she told a mostly open-minded audience, would not be a 'magic wand' (an unintentional Rowling reference), while saying interesting things about the European Union ('not a huge enthusiast for ever more integration') and an intelligent question about whether or not rUK would be the sole successor state in the event of a Yes vote ('a matter of negotiation', so she didn't actually answer).

Having spotted Paul Hutcheon and me sitting near the back (it was a big lecture theatre, so she has good eyesight), Sturgeon also avoided media bashing when invited by another member of the audience ('I don't think the media are biased', a quote I considered putting on a T-shirt). The questions were good and she dealt with them very well, although the only applause followed a question about Trident, which betrayed the relatively well-heeled Edinburgh South audience.

Chatted to Peter Murrell afterwards, who appeared at the back, presumably to drive Nicola home: he mentioned that the FM had been enthusing about last week's Five Million Questions event in Dundee, which came as a surprise, given his mood on the night. Also saw Rab McNeil (former *Scotsman* sketch writer, now also a *Herald* columnist) and the local MSP Jim Eadie, who'd chaired the event. I described Sturgeon as 'Scotland's Hillary Clinton' and he agreed that she had a similar appeal among women and gay men.

Thursday, 12 June 2014 (Liverpool)

Up early to get the train to Liverpool (via Wigan), mainly to see Charles Kennedy speak in the evening but also – because the forecast was good – to cycle around and finally see Birkenhead. Thankfully, the weather was glorious, so I caught the ferry ('cross the Mersey), got off at Kingsway then cycled up to New Brighton then doubled back on myself to Birkenhead itself. Some glorious architecture including the Georgian Hamilton Square designed by an Edinburgh architect and thus, unsurprisingly, looked a bit like Edinburgh. Caught the ferry back to Liverpool – the Liver Building looked incredible in the sunlight – then cycled along to the docks and up to the Adelphi Hotel (which has seen better days), where Kennedy was due to speak at 5pm.

Lord Alton (who I interviewed about David Steel a while back) introduced Kennedy, saying he was a 'key figure' in Better Together (!), and he went on to very amiably deliver a rather short speech which I'm pretty sure was ad-libbed, though he's so good that it still came across well. He didn't so much set out a case against independence; indeed he said Alex Salmond *et al* had advocated a lot that he found 'compelling'. He also repeated criticisms of his own 'side' for giving the impression 'economic Armageddon' would follow a Yes vote. Kennedy was much better under questioning – funny, engaging and reasonably frank – and he said the three Unionist parties would issue a 'joint statement' on more powers 'next week', which he probably wasn't supposed to say, rightly criticised the Yes campaign for conflating policy with the constitution (on Trident, for example) and said that just as he wouldn't stop pushing for AV despite its defeat in a referendum, nor should Nationalists stop agitating for independence even following a No vote. 'It won't go away,' he said, although he worried about 'Scotland becoming more divided almost irrespective of the outcome.'

The audience were mainly Roscoe regulars (and lots of them, the ballroom in the Adelphi was almost full) and expat Scots, the latter reminding me that Liverpool is a microcosm of the UK, full of English (obviously), Scots (a legacy of shipbuilding and other old heavy industry), the Irish (the city's 'Scotland' Division used to elect an Irish Nationalist MP) and Welsh, North Walians having always looked to Merseyside rather than Cardiff. On the way south I read a good *Guardian* column by Martin Kettle praising Gordon Brown for using the 'f' word (he'd written on Monday that the upshot of a No vote could be 'a system of government as close to federalism as you can have in a nation where one part forms 85 per cent of the population'), arguing that federalism 'is one of the great awakening issues in the debate about what happens after 18 September'. I texted Martin plugging my recent book (*Britain Rebooted: Scotland in a Federal Union*), although obviously it's a bit late...

Kennedy was also asked about federalism, which he said should 'eventually' be the way forward for the UK, although he described England, rightly, as the elephant in the room. The aim, he added, would be to keep the UK 'together' while also recognising its various 'escape valves', although he acknowledged that he or his party wasn't currently 'winning that argument in England'. Heading back north on the train (it was a beautiful evening) I could feel my federalist instincts deepening: Merseyside – centred upon the great metropolis of Liverpool – is screaming out to be a federal unit but, of course, Brown *et al* are only really interested because of the impending referendum and will probably stop mentioning the 'f' word once it's all over. Meanwhile a few others and I will plug away, not least at this year's Edinburgh International Book Festival, when I'll be sharing a platform with Henry McLeish who – like Brown – uses the 'f' word rather tentatively.

Something called the World Cup has begun; I'll need all my powers of avoidance to pretend it isn't happening. Bernard Ponsonby from STV told me the other day he reckoned a combination of that, Wimbledon and the Commonwealth Games would push the referendum down the news agenda and thus things would only get going properly in early August. Peter Murrell said something similar the other night. In fact, he pinpointed the kick off (pardon the pun) as 4 August, the day *after* the Commonwealth Games closing ceremony.

Friday, 13 June 2014 (Edinburgh)

Coffee with Helen Ross and Per Johansson, an engaging Swede who heads up the European Parliament's office in Edinburgh. He made the point that the election of a UKIP MEP in Scotland actually gave them an opportunity to re-engage with the arguments for and against EU membership, which I thought was interesting. Helen also said they could fund a trip to Strasbourg or Brussels if I wanted, which of course I fully intend to pursue.

Meanwhile Hillary (Clinton) has spoken and Salmond responded, not as deferentially as he did with Obama, taking issue with her reference to hoping the UK wouldn't 'lose' Scotland as if, as the FM put it, it was a piece of property. Later that day the Bishop of Rome also waded in, saying 'all division' of states worried him and that it had to be examined 'case by case' (in other words, Yugoslavia fine; UK not). Kevin Pringle also tweeted an interesting snippet from *Private Eye* that claimed (probably correctly) Number 10 had repeatedly leaned on Her Majesty to make a helpful statement *a la* 1977. Sensibly, they'd been repeatedly rebuffed.

There's still pressure on Campbell Gunn to resign but the FM is holding firm so he'll probably be fine. That ongoing row and the online reaction to Rowling's donation (summarised by BuzzFeed) has of course been very damaging for the Yes campaign's attempt to win over female voters. Campbell had clearly taken his cue from Wings over Scotland (Stuart Nicolson, the FM's official spokesman, has in the past praised it to me) in sending the email to the *Telegraph*, and visiting Dad (an SNP foot soldier since the mid-1960s) this afternoon I teased him about the incident exposing the SNP as the 'nasty party'. He retorted that Labour was nasty too (which is true), but then they have nothing on the Scottish Government's campaigns of denigration and character assassination. The bullying tone, of course, comes from the top.

Claire Stewart from STV later told me the post-FMQs briefing yesterday afternoon had been rather tense, with Stuart Nicolson admitting that Campbell had 'clearly not' abided by the special advisers' code of conduct.

Of course Stuart is friendly with Simon Johnson at the *Telegraph*, who's now written stories critical of both Campbell and Stuart so, as Claire said, 'friendships are being tested' and there's a generally 'bad vibe' in Holyrood. It can only get worse over the next 95 days or so.

Saturday, 14 June 2014 (Melrose)

Hugh Andrew drove us both down to Melrose for the Borders Book Festival, telling me *en route* that he'd heard Alexander McCall Smith would soon be making public his support for the Union, which would be almost as big as Rowling, given his reach and following. The Book Festival itself was predictably tweedy, like being at a posh country wedding, and indeed I met Allan Massie (Alex's father) for the first time, who was standing on the steps of the main house wearing a cravat, tweed jacket and smoking a cigar. I had to clamber over Sally Magnusson and Kirsty Wark sunning themselves in order to introduce myself.

He was very charming, telling me that Alex and I were two of the only journalists writing about Nationalism from a position of respect (truer of Alex than me, but it was nice of him to say). We ruminated on the likely result in September and found ourselves in broad agreement. Was odd talking to him; a vision of Alex in 30 years' time – the same charm, mannerisms and appearance only, of course, older.

Also saw Lord Steel (still complaining about the lack of publicity for the biography I wrote of him nearly two years ago), Michael Moore and his wife, Jim Naughtie, Angus Macleod from *The Times*, and Judy Steel wandering around wearing a NASA T-shirt. Apparently there's a poll out tomorrow showing a 52/48 split against independence, which just confirms my suspicion that polls are no longer worth paying attention to. Spoke to Rob Shorthouse, communications director of Better Together, who said they weren't concerned because their private polling was 'solid' (although there is a tendency to tell different journalists different proportions). I mused that in a week where the leader of the western world, a possible future leader of the western world, the Bishop of Rome and a best-selling international author had all (sort of) supported the No campaign then they had reason to be smug. All Yes Scotland has managed in response was someone from River City and a former president of STUC.

After cycling from Melrose to Dryburgh Abbey Hotel (about half an hour with lots of hills), had an early dinner in Gattonside with Paul McNamee (who edits *The Big Issue*) and his wife Jane Graham, a columnist with the *Belfast Telegraph*. We then caught a cab back to Melrose for the Gordon Brown gig. He was doing his 'no notes' routine, pacing around the stage in an amiable fashion, but I'd heard most of the lines and gags before so found it hard to engage. Afterwards I got him to sign my copy of his book (*My Scotland, Our Britain*) and he was charming, perched on the edge of the desk rather than sitting behind it. 'You're the writer aren't you?' he asked, '*Herald* columnist? I think some of your stuff is very good, and I see you've been writing about federalism.' I admit to being a little star-struck, but useful fuel for the ego.

One lady (wearing a Yes badge) at the festival later told me that Brown, like 'all Scots at Westminster', had been treated badly, mentioning the Earl of Bute. I cited Ramsay MacDonald before realising I was in danger of agreeing with her point. Perhaps he was, but it had relatively little to do with him being Scottish. In the *Scotsman* that day he protested (in response to reports he'd criticised the No campaign), rather defensively, that not only had he 'praised Better Together, its leader Alistair Darling, called for the main debates to be Salmond vs Darling but also stated that he'd benefited "from conversations with friends in, and leaders of, Better Together"'. He's always, of course, done his own thing, but it's still remarkable to witness his new, referendum-inspired lease of life. After the event I got pissed with Paul, Jane and Allan Price from BBC Scotland (very bright and now producing Jim Naughtie); the taxi driver who took Paul, Jane and me back to our hotels said the Borders were solidly against independence (not exactly a surprise) but didn't actually say what he thought.[2]

Sunday, 15 June 2014 (Melrose)

Dryburgh Abbey Hotel, like the Book Festival, is very tweedy: breakfast all clattering tea cups, eccentric waitresses and bored elderly couples trying to make conversation after 50 years in each other's company. I managed to get up reasonably early and read a very moving piece in *Scotland on Sunday* by Gordon Aikman, Better Together's head of research, who as I learned a week or so ago has been diagnosed with Motor Neurone Disease and has only a few years to live. He's only 29, bright, attractive and could have done anything he wanted after the referendum. Puts everything in context. I broke my usual rule and donated £20 to a charity researching the disease.

Speed-read Gordon Brown's book, which is actually much more substantial than the referendum potboiler I'd been expecting. It basically reaches the same conclusions as *Britain Rebooted*, i.e. regional English devolution, a written constitution (eventually), a federally reconstituted

---

2 A ComRes poll subsequently found that (with Don't Knows excluded) 70 per cent of those living in the south of Scotland planned to vote No compared to just 30 per cent intending to vote Yes.

House of Lords, stressing 'interdependence' and reconciling Nationalism and Unionism, while puncturing pro-independence arguments about reducing inequality. After that I visited Dryburgh Abbey just across the road, saw Sir Walter Scott's grave, then exhausted myself climbing a steep path to see a rather tacky statue of William Wallace, and cycled back to Melrose to check out the Abbey – all terribly Scottish.

After writing my *Herald* column (on Brown's book) I went in to see Jim Sillars versus Lord (Michael) Forsyth, which was a bit of a damp squib. In his opening pitch Sillars referred to the 'audacity tae think the way the establishment tells you not tae think', at which point Judy Steel, still wearing her NASA T-shirt, burst into solitary applause. Otherwise he deployed some old lines ('Scotland is the only nation that ever discovered oil and people got poorer') and ended by quoting from the opening section of *In Place of Fear II*:

> On 18 September, 2014, between the hours of 7am and 10pm, absolute sovereign power will lie in the hands of the Scottish people. They have to decide whether to keep it, or give it away to where their minority status makes them permanently powerless and vulnerable.

He sounded genuinely angry (and a little raspy), adding with a flourish that if a majority of Scots voted Yes then, 'I say to working-class people at long, long, long last our time will have come'. The tweedy audience applauded politely, although there were clearly some Yessers in the house, for they heckled Forsyth's opening pitch (shouting 'rubbish!' when he mentioned Darien and RBS) and one guy even walked out, heels clicking melodramatically. Forsyth invoked Sir Walter Scott ('a good Tory') and made some nice asides (to Jim), i.e. 'leaving Europe is just about the only argument I can think of for Scottish independence'.

Indeed, as the debate wore on it became clear the pair agreed about more than they disagreed on: Europe, the unworkability of a currency union, that moves towards devo-max would require the consent of the whole UK, etc. Summing up, Sillars said independence was the only chance of achieving socialism while Forsyth said it amounted to inviting Scots to 'make a leap in the dark' (at which point Judy approvingly yelped 'Yes!').

Predictably, the debate – although engaging at points – didn't lead anywhere terribly useful. Both Forsyth and Sillars are undoubtedly big beasts, albeit from a bygone age, but banging on about socialism and 'Great' Britain belongs in the 1980s. Forsyth I think sensed this, for when I spoke to him afterwards (he was touchy about a 'pop' I'd had at him in a recent column) he wondered out loud whether anyone's mind had been changed as a result. A tweedy old guy then shook Forsyth's hand and exclaimed: 'I think we've got it in the bag' (the referendum); Michael just looked at him quizzically and said, 'Oh, do you?'

I also bumped into Zoe MacDonald in the signing tent, patiently waiting to take Jim back to Edinburgh. Forsyth had paid tribute to Margo at the start of the debate, which was decent of him, and I told Zoe how moving I'd found her mother's memorial service. She said Jim was doing okay but tired due to his speaking schedule (I got the impression he was working through the grief by keeping as busy as possible). I'd seen Donald (Dad's cousin) and Sandy as I left the event, both looking well, while I got a lift to Cameron Toll from a Book Festival driver who turned out to be Roddy Martine's cousin (Iain). Scotland really is a village.

Monday, 16 June 2014 (Edinburgh)

Walked and cycled up to Calton Hill in glorious sunshine for a 'joint declaration' from the three Unionist party leaders on 'more powers'. I'd already flagged up the unfortunate historical symbolism in an article for newsnetscotland, i.e. a bunch of activists standing on the National Monument (Edinburgh's Folly), which of course was left unfinished after three years. I suggested to Craig Davidson (a Labour spin doctor) that they spin it so that they want to complete the unfinished business of devolution, but he didn't look convinced (later on *Scotland 2014* Alistair Carmichael referred to the 'devolution journey' being 'completed', so there you go).

It was little more than a photo call, but of course the purpose was obvious: to demonstrate they're serious about devolving more power in the event of a No vote. The declaration itself (trailed in yesterday's *Scotland on Sunday*) was inevitably vague, asserting the sovereignty of the Scottish people (as did Nicola Sturgeon in a speech at the Playfair Library about an interim written constitution, although as Adam Tomkins later pointed out, there was a conflict between both HM and the 'Scottish people' being sovereign) before fudging what powers would actually be devolved. Alex Salmond was also in Orkney promising the islands more powers if they vote Yes, which is an amusing microcosm of the Unionist parties' pitch to Scotland (i.e. we'll give you more powers if you vote No).

The *Herald* had a weird story about 'Quebec independence experts' Bernard Drainville and Alain Gagnon warning Scots they'd 'pay the price' in reduced power and influence at Westminster if they rejected independence, something I raised with a well-placed Canadian source ('bullshit' was his curt response), who I met after cycling back down from Calton Hill. He felt it made the mistake of reading across from Canadian to UK politics, where

Johann Lamont (Labour), Willie Rennie (Lib Dem) and Ruth Davidson (Conservative) preparing to make a 'joint declaration' on Edinburgh's Calton Hill.

of course a different dynamic applied.

He (of Scottish extraction) was very interesting on Quebec, saying that the language issue was no longer as salient and praised the UK's unwritten constitution as a strength rather than a weakness (he cited the Canadian Provinces' failure post-1995 to agree a new constitution in support). Re the referendum, said his Government was 'worried' about the result, reckoned Whitehall had been 'tone deaf' (particularly in wielding the Post Office/ Royal Mail as a virtue of the Union immediately prior to privatising it) and complacent, and said the general view of Canada – as with most other western countries – was that the UK was an important ally and ought to remain intact. He said the BRIC countries might want the UK cut down a peg or two for geopolitical reasons but otherwise he couldn't gauge any support for Scottish independence internationally.

Also said he was amazed the SNP and Yes Scotland got away with so many obviously bullshit arguments (i.e. John Swinney saying today he'd borrow his way out of austerity) and I said it was down to poor political opposition and a poor media. He then pointed out that the Irish media was still of higher quality, which was an (irritatingly) good point, got me to sign a copy of *The Battle for Britain* and then I headed into the Scottish Parliament where I bumped into James Mackenzie (formerly of the Scottish Greens) who told me the only thing he could think of that 'Westminster' (a 'failed' system in his eyes) had achieved since 1951 was the Open University.

Sir Malcolm Rifkind (who's announced he'll be campaigning in Scotland during August and September) had a piece in the *Evening Standard* with a couple of interesting points, chiefly (of the SNP's 'independence in Europe' stance): 'Why is sharing a parliament and sovereignty with the Portuguese, Greeks and Hungarians desirable and acceptable but sharing the House of Commons with the English and Welsh anathema?'

Later I risked peak Gordon by going with Susan Dalgety (an old *Evening News* colleague and former Scottish Labour adviser) to see Brown and (Sir) Tom Devine in conversation at the McEwan Hall. It was very establishment: Tim O'Shea kicked things off followed by Gordon Brown reading out (without flinching) congratulations on Devine's knighthood from the PM and First Minister. Gordon cross-examining Sir Tom was more interesting than the other way round, Devine is a better historian than he is a commentator: talked up the 'profound' differences between Scotland and England (in truth they've become *more* alike rather than less), predicted the 2015 General Election would be a 'flash point' (I've heard that before) and kept using foreign phrases and words like 'accidentalia' and referring to 'Scotia' (rather than just 'Scotland').

He was more sensible when pushed by Jim Naughtie to consider what might happen following a Yes or No vote: the former would give rise to 'exciting' but also 'very considerable administrative challenges' while the latter would result in a 'core' of voters (30 per cent) being 'terribly, terribly disappointed', much worse than in 1979, so that pledges on more powers would have to be met. I'd concluded exactly the same thing in my newsnetscotland piece the night before.

Had a quick bite to eat with Susan afterwards, always a pleasure. She was quite gloomy about the result, assuming it would be a No or 'very close', but I told her I reckoned it would be 60/40 against, as apparently does Darling. I'm told Brown believes it will be closer to 55/45, but then he's naturally pessimistic.

(Susan, who's keeping an online indyref diary, later blogged that it had been 'a perfectly pleasant event – and thanks to my old mate David Torrance for the invite. David has written 12 (yes 12) books at some ridiculously young age. I remember showing him how to work the phones at the *Evening News*. What happened?)

Tuesday, 17 June 2014 (Edinburgh)

Had breakfast with my contact from Yes Scotland at quite a good Italian café on Waterloo Place. Said after the weekend polls he felt more confident about the result (though I still got the impression he thought they'd lose), said there'd be lots of prominent business backers coming up (mmm) and that Wealthy Nation (Michael Fry and Peter de Vink's outfit) would be touring quite soon (I'm not sure he regarded this as a good thing). Said he'd watched me interviewing the FM in Dundee online and thought he'd been quite condescending at points and that he'd been quite worried about it in advance but raved about it afterwards (not, I fear, a tribute to my interrogative skills). Was scornful about Paul Hutcheon's blog scenario on what Salmond might do following a No vote; said he'd certainly run in 2016 no matter what, his name on the ballot paper was worth 10 per cent of the vote, and so on. Rather cryptically, he also added that Hillary Clinton would 'regret' her comments later on but couldn't tell me why...

After a swim I got changed and met Douglas (Pattullo) to walk up to the Carlton Hotel for the Scottish Parliamentary Journalists' Association lunch with Sir John Major (there were great views of St Andrew's House from the Highland suite). His speech was only okay, basically an explanation of where he once stood on devolution and how he viewed the current debate ('like any Englishman I have a stake'). He continually used the words 'separation' and 'separatist' which became a bit irritating, but there were some nice lines ('facts are often far less enticing than emotion, but they last longer') good arguments (why on earth would Scotland want to leave the UK 'and join another much less successful Union'), nice historical allusions (he quoted from the 1521 John Mair, a distinguished Scottish Catholic philosopher, whose surname tended to be Latinised as Major), wider political points (he said it would be 'absolute folly' for either Scotland to leave the UK or the UK to leave the EU) and reasonable frankness (he admitted Lord Strathclyde's recent commission was a 'lesser position' than his as articulated in 2011, i.e. devo-max).

Strikingly, Major looked pretty much the same as he did as Prime Minister, even though he's now 71. He had a little dig at 'expensively schooled' colleagues who hadn't realised he'd been quoting Orwell in referring to 'Old maids bicycling to holy communion through the morning mist' (he also had a nice lyrical passage describing the four parts of the UK which I regretted not noting down) and repeatedly emphasised that 'this is not just about Scotland', arguing that the 1998 Scotland Act had been a bad piece of legislation because it had ignored England, although it was a disingenuous point since a) that wasn't his (or others') argument at the

Ruth Davidson attentive as Sir John Major explains that : 'like any Englishman I have a stake'.

time and b) if Labour had tried to legislate for regional English devolution at that time he (and his party) would probably have opposed it. All in all his comments would get written up more for who he is (or was) rather than because he said anything that interesting, while the main 'line' – that the SNP had chosen the 700th anniversary of the Battle of Bannockburn in a deliberate attempt to stir up 'anti-English feeling' – is just wrong (and even if true hasn't worked, ticket sales for the event have been a disaster). I chatted briefly to him on the way out, reminding him he'd attended the book launch for my biography of George Younger back in 2008, but it was obvious he didn't really remember. I added that Margaret Thatcher had been there too and he said, smirking, 'Oh, did we talk?'

After that I headed home to change again and bash out a short presentation for an Edinburgh University summer school seminar I'd agreed to take part in on the social aspects of the independence debate. Despite being written in great haste this seemed to go down quite well with a couple of dozen PhD students and a smattering of academics. The Q&A was particularly good and when I mentioned that some EU citizens I'd met were reticent about voting in the referendum a couple of (I assume) Scandinavian girls intervened and said they wouldn't be on 'ethical' grounds, although one other said she would be. A heavily unscientific straw poll at the end found four intending to vote Yes, about twice as many No and a few Undecideds. Afterwards one of the staff told me I'd presented it all 'much better than most academics would have,' which I guess was a compliment.

After a quick bite to eat with Neil Freshwater and his girlfriend Kristen I cycled to a bar called the Hanging Bat on Lothian Road to have a drink with Lewis, then saw Colin Firth and Reese Witherspoon in a pretty good movie called *Devil's Knot*. Marco Biagi was on *Scotland 2014* being sanctimonious about nuclear weapons ('it's a matter of principle'), another survey having shown that a majority of Scots are not, as the SNP likes to believe, ardent CNDers. Nats have always overstated this point, but they don't much care when rigorous research contradicts views they ascribe to the 'Scottish people'. Faslane, said Biagi (who's actually among the best of the SNP backbenchers) had a 'tremendous' future ahead of it as HQ of the Scottish Defence Force, but I doubt anyone working there at the moment believes that.

Wednesday, 18 June 2014 (Edinburgh)

Had lunch with Chris Deerin (*Scottish Daily Mail* columnist) at a place on George Street, first time I'd met him properly. He was enjoyably undiplomatic and feels no need to be balanced about the SNP or Yes campaign. Said he reckoned the campaign had busted the 'myth' that Scots were fundamentally different from the English. Predicted the result would be 60/40 against.

Afterwards I popped into his office (Charlotte Street Partners), which was like a bachelor crash pad: Xbox and trendy fridge (full of Irn-Bru, a client) in the corner and large flat-screen televisions. I had a can of Irn-Bru as I chatted to Andrew Wilson, who was as engaging as always. Said he still believed the campaign was going well (though not with much conviction) and that for Yes to still be polling in the mid-40s despite all that No had thrown at it told its own story (he had a point there); he also reckoned John Major's comments yesterday would have played badly. He was a bit put out that the press were still all over the BBC Radio Scotland show he was supposed to be doing with the Labour MSP Kezia Dugdale. There'd been (predictable) outrage that she was getting paid despite being an elected politician, so the BBC capitulated and crowbarred in a presenter (John Beattie, not yet public), but Andrew was worried Kezia would pull out rather than endure it all.

Had a beer in the sun with Alex Massie and got a call from someone at Downing Street, flagging up the 'greatest hits' Scotland Analysis paper coming out tomorrow. 'Are we vulnerable on any points?' he asked, rather sweetly. I then cycled up to St Mary's Street to catch the beginning of a National Collective 'session', at which I was eyed suspiciously (or perhaps sheepishly, I wasn't sure) by a few people. Gerry Hassan was there, ostensibly to 'come out' (as he put it), i.e. describe his 'journey' to Yes. I had to rush off to get the train to Glasgow, so only saw a Northern Irish lady describe her 'journey'.

On the train I bumped into Paul Sinclair and Craig Davidson from the Scottish Labour Party and the journalists Paul Kilbride (*Daily Express*) and Magnus Gardham (*Herald*), who were all on good form. I asked what Paul (Sinclair) made of the YouGov poll (60/40 against) and he indicated that he thought that was about right. Humza Yousaf was in the same carriage, chatting amiably with other passengers (including one wearing a 'No Thanks' badge) about foreign policy, Iraq, Pakistan and his ministerial schedule. As we got off he complimented my hair, which has now become a running joke.

It was still light so I cycled along the Clyde to Pacific Quay and ended up getting made up next to Jackie Bird (she was being quite starry). Patrick Harvie was there, sharp as ever, talking about Spain potentially vetoing Scottish entry to the EU, then Kevin McKenna and I did no more than five minutes at the end talking about Ed Balls on the currency union and Morrison's banning English World Cup songs in its Scottish branches. It was our bad luck to be on *Scotland 2014* on a slow-news day, and we didn't even get to talk about the only interesting story, which was the writer Jeanette Winterson murdering a bunny rabbit and eating it (and posting pictures on Twitter).

On the drunks' train home I got an email via my website complaining about my comment that a currency union would probably happen, no matter what Better Together said:

> You are described as a Unionist, therefore I assume, like me, you are greatly concerned at the prospect of Scotland being torn out of the UK. I found your comments on this evening's *Scotland 2014* less than helpful to the cause. Asserting that post independence, whoever is Chancellor will let Mr Salmond have his way on a currency union must put you right up there on his Christmas list! So in effect you take the Nationalist view that anything anyone says in opposition to them is a lie & constitutes bullying. We cannot afford the luxury at this critical point in time of saying anything that gives credence to the outrageous claims of the nationalists.

I didn't bother replying.

Thursday, 19 June 2014 (Edinburgh)

A contact of mine at Downing Street also texted me about what he accurately called my 'brief' appearance on Scotland 2014: 'Do you really think Labour or the Conservatives would be able to sell a currency union on the doorsteps of English marginal seats only months after they had lost a referendum?' This was a reasonable point, but I just replied saying it had worked out okay with the Irish Free State in the early 1920s. He responded: 'I don't think you can really compare the 1920s when electorates were less well informed and clearly had no experience of eurozone-style currency union crises. Besides it wasn't exactly the same kind of CU the SNP are proposing.'

Got my hair cut at a hipster barber called Ruffians on Queensferry Street. Stewart Kwan ('probably voting No'), who did my hair, said his customers did mention the referendum but at the moment the World Cup took precedence. Had lunch after and read the newspapers, as well as tweets about Kezia Dugdale pulling out of the BBC Radio programme, as Andrew Wilson had predicted.

It was another sunny day so I toyed with skipping a European Parliament briefing I'd agreed to attend about the recent elections (handily, I had a *Westminster Hour* interview to do just before). It was actually quite good, with a chap called Simon Hix from the LSE who, admittedly, knew more about the English scene than Scotland. Beforehand Christina McKelvie ('What are you doing lurking at the back?') sat next to me and chatted for a while, although she wasn't exactly over friendly. 'It's just the thought of a Conservative/UKIP Coalition that terrifies me,' she chipped in at one point, although Hix made it clear that seemed unlikely. There was a man in the audience wearing a kilt, though it wasn't clear why, and also someone from the European Movement who asked plaintively: 'Why did 140,000 Scots vote for UKIP?' Hix didn't really answer, pointing to disaffected Tory and Labour voters; but when I said that couldn't really be the case because both their shares of the votes increased, he looked a bit annoyed. McKelvie looked pleased when he said BBC coverage of the Euro elections had been 'shockingly bad', implying that Downing Street had leaned on executives in London.

After that I cycled to North Castle Street for a Charlotte Street Partners 'at home'. No sooner had I entered than Andrew Wilson insisted on taking a picture of me with the First Minister, who was chatting amiably with some suits at the other end of the office. Salmond was quite game, taking the Peroni out of my hand and then striking an amusing pose. He then introduced me to a businessman as 'my biographer', having also asked

First Minister Alex Salmond asks why he's not featured on David Torrance's T-shirt.
(Photo: Andrew Wilson)

why he wasn't on my T-shirt (as opposed to Frank Sinatra); 'Mrs Salmond', he said, had been making noises about going to a Rod Stewart concert. I found myself liking him again.

Spent a long time chatting to Eddie Barnes from the Scottish Tories and my contact from Yes Scotland. The latter said he thought Ruth *et al* were *sincere* about more powers and when Eddie asked him if he'd wanted a 'devo-max' option on the ballot paper he said 'too fucking right'. I mentioned that Salmond had let slip on television exactly that, but he just smirked and said, 'What the First Minister meant to say was...' More seriously, he repeated something others had told me, chiefly that a third option wouldn't have got through the party conference. They then started thrashing out a fantasy 2015 coalition deal (my Yes contact reckons a Cameron victory is virtually certain) involving Capital Gains Tax and Corporation Tax. All they could agree on was Air Passenger Duty.

It was a very corporate do, full of Edinburgh's managerial class, but also a smattering of arts types, including Nick Barley from the Edinburgh International Book Festival. I spoke to one Yes supporter who was utterly scornful of the Radical Independence Convention *et al*, adding he'd be quite happy to see the frontiers of the state rolled back under independence. There he overlapped with the Tories in the room. Eddie told me that Michael Crow had been unfairly lumbered with the 12-seat target back in 2010 (the former party chairman had blurted it out to some hacks when slightly drunk) and this time round it was a more modest four: DCT (Dumfriesshire, Clydesdale and Tweedale, Moore's seat; Perthshire; and WAK (West Aberdeenshire and Kincardine). We agreed that Ruth was now a convincing front(wo) man for the Tories and that Murdo Fraser, who narrowly lost the Scottish Tory leadership contest in 2011, might actually have struggled to pull it off. Also complained about Ben Thomson of Reform Scotland dissing the Strathclyde Commission in the *Herald*. 'It gets to the point,' said Eddie, 'where he's got to decide which side he's on.'

Friday, 20 June 2014 (Edinburgh)

Hungover, so not a productive day beyond lunch with some Tory contacts in Parliament and then an afternoon of coffee and reading in the sun. In the evening I cycled over to the 'other' Edinburgh, to see Stewart's Melville production of Sondheim's *Sweeney Todd*. It was very good, though anything Jason (Orringe, also my flatmate) does as musical director is generally of a high standard, and the school's theatre is better equipped than many professional venues I've been to.

In the interval he introduced me to a sixth former who's about to study politics at Sheffield University and who wanted advice about becoming a political journalist (he'd read my biography of Salmond, which was impressive for an 18-year-old). I gave him all the usual tips, but he seemed bright enough to realise what was involved; I also said it was impossible to predict what state the 'media' would be in in three or four years' time. He told me both Alistair Darling and MSP Alex Neil had been to the school to speak about the referendum, but when I asked how fifth and sixth year divided in terms of opinion he laughed and said it was 'solidly against' independence with only one or two Yes voters. As Jamie Maxwell has always said, there is a class dimension to this referendum.

At home Jason's mother (visiting for the show) seemed surprised he had a vote in the referendum – I said we (the Scots) had generously granted him one. She said she'd probably vote No if she was resident in Scotland but otherwise protested that she didn't feel very strongly about it. When I asked how she'd feel about Jason living in another country she said she 'hadn't thought about it like that' before adding that even if Scotland became independent she wouldn't think of it as a 'different' country.

Saturday, 21 June 2014 (Edinburgh)

Wandered over to Holyrood for 'Pride Scotia' prior to the march up the Royal Mile to the City Chambers. Saw Colin Macfarlane from Stonewall Scotland who was typically amusing and quite interesting on the same-sex marriage stuff; said the Scottish Government had been dragging its feet again, something he nudged Whitehall into dealing with. After marching (or, more accurately, wheeling my Brompton up the road) to the Mercat Cross saw Ruth Davidson (who ostentatiously mentioned her 'girlfriend'), Sarah Boyack et al.

The speeches were generally dire but mercifully brief. One lady shouted about 'Nazis' in Scotland, by which she meant anyone to the right of her (almost everyone), and 'North West infidels who come up from England'. Of course she meant UKIP, but seemed blissfully unaware that hyperbolic rhetoric simply fuels Euroscepticism rather than defeats it. By amusing contrast, I then caught a bus to Balerno to speak to a (very) Tory garden party as a favour for Cllr Dominic Heslop. Everyone looked very bored as I meandered through 15 minutes on the referendum and how the Scottish Conservatives should view it as an opportunity rather than a threat, but I got a bottle of Single Malt and some chocolates out of it, so all was well.

My hosts' son (who worked for Skyscanner) seemed convinced the Tories' determination to devolve Income Tax meant he was going to get 'hammered', which was a curious interpretation of Scottish Tory strategy. Afterwards I cycled back to the city via the Water of Leith, although a wrong turning meant this took nearly an hour and three quarters rather than half that.

Sunday, 22 June 2014 (Edinburgh)

Listened to BBC Radio Scotland's first Crossfire programme, the cause of a typically Beeb PR disaster over the past few days. Lesley Riddoch tweeted that it was 'unlistenable', which wasn't quite fair (like lots of long-serving ex-Beeb employees, she rarely misses a chance to slag them off), but it was pretty pedestrian stuff. The presenter simply got in the way while Andrew Wilson and Pam Duncan (an articulate enough Labour activist) meandered through the usual fare. Getting an interview with Claire Howell (the architect of SNP 'positivity') was a nice touch, although even that couldn't save it.

Spoke to Better Together Campaign Director Blair McDougall about TV debates, the *Sunday Herald* having revealed that, assuming David Cameron maintains his refusal to go head to head with Salmond, the FM will joust with Alistair Darling. Apparently STV are insisting on 16 July ('Scotland 500' format) while the Beeb is planning an extravaganza at Glasgow Hydro with 12,000 schoolchildren a few days before 18 September (given how they generally poll, Yes can't be happy about that).

Blair said the BBC had been 'ridiculous' about negotiations so was happy STV had 'stolen a march'. Also very frank about Cameron vs Salmond ('something we desperately wanted to avoid'), while he said focus groups found AD 'reassuringly dull' but AS 'not working well', thus why the latter had been reigning in what Blair (accurately) called his 'breathless chuckle'. More widely, and discounting Panelbase and Survation, he reckoned 60/40 against was about right. Said the twin image of a single mother coping with a disabled child (Claire Lally) and the FM saying 'she shouldn't be upset but if she is I'll get someone else to apologise' played very badly for Yes. 'If you had to embody things women voters don't like about him [Salmond],' he said, 'then that was it.'

Blair also agreed with Murrell *et al* that a combination of the World Cup/Commonwealth Games/Wimbledon would probably drown out the referendum until early August but said Better Together would still be 'upping the tempo' because they were now at the stage where folk were making up their minds and it'd be madness to waste that. Flagged up the Rosyth carrier launch on 4 July (I pointed out it was Independence Day in the US), saying a 'more obvious statement of security and stability of the UK' you couldn't ask for.

Watched the 'Duggy Dug' newsnetscotland video online and it was pretty desperate stuff: vote No and the NHS will be privatised, Barnett scrapped, tuition fees reimposed, and so on – almost all just wrong or at the very least highly questionable. Why Brian Cox agrees to voice this stuff is beyond me. My Yes Scotland contact texted me: 'As you say AS not the best debater. Darling clear favourite at this point :-)' I asked him to expand and he said a TV debate wasn't Salmond's 'natural territory' and therefore on 'first inspection Darling is favourite' although he'd 'love AS to surprise on the upside'. This suggests they have something up their sleeves.

Wrote my *Herald* column on the forthcoming Bannockburn events and later watched Fergus Ewing on *Sunday Politics Scotland* trying (but failing) to put a positive spin on poor ticket sales, cost, etc. At points he quoted website addresses and PR puff to such an extent that Gordon Brewer (who seems to have found a new lease of life now *Newsnicht* is no more) accused him of being a 'used-car salesman'. All a bit embarrassing, but then he's a minister largely because of his surname.

Richard Keen QC, the Scottish Tory chairman, has struck again, dismissing Labour's devo proposals as 'incoherent, unworkable and confused', among other things: of course he has a point, but to say so to anyone who'll listen (i.e. a journalist) is astonishingly naïve. His was an incredibly bad appointment, the usual view that having a big hitter from another profession (i.e. the law) is a good move. It usually isn't. Tom Gordon later told me that he hadn't even needed to wheedle it out of Keen; it was his opening gambit!

Monday, 23 June 2014 (Coatbridge)

Made my *Today Programme* debut, discussing the Bannockburn anniversary with Professor Murray Pittock, although we ended up agreeing with each other, probably not what the producer intended.

In the evening I got a train to Motherwell and then changed to get off at the intriguingly named Whifflet near Coatbridge. Bumped into Professor Tom Gallagher, wearing a 'UK OK' badge and in a reasonably charming frame of mind. Said he was planning to write a biography of the Portugese dictator Salazar. He walked and I cycled to the very new looking Saint Andrew's High School, also emblazoned with images of the Pontiff. Outside two locals admired my bike and asked what I was doing in Coatbridge:

> Me: Seeing George Galloway.
> Lady 1: What's he doing?
> Lady 2: Telling us to say naw.
> Lady 1: Oh that, I've nae idea how ahm gonnae vote.
> Lady 2: You look a bit like Will Young.

I hadn't quite appreciated that it was under the 'NO Thanks' banner, so Elaine Smith (the local MSP) kicked things off and Tom Clarke (the local MP), ponderous and red-faced, rambled his way through a lengthy introduction, although he got a big round of applause when he said his constituents had 'more in common' with steel workers in Corby than with the 'dukes and lairds' who run Scotland. Finally, he basically begged Labour voters 'not to fall for that trick', the 'trick' being the idea that only independence could deliver socialism.

Then it was Gorgeous George's turn to speak, sporting a black fedora and a black suit, white shirt with no tie. There were some nice lines ('If Britain's so bad how come they want to keep so much of it?'), allusions to his greatest hits ('If the US Senate couldn't shut me up, you'll [cybernats] will never shut me up!') and clever ways of framing complex issues ('I've been divorced – more than once – and believe me it's never amicable'). There was a crowd of several hundred people, two of whom walked out when he got stuck into independence (this is becoming a fixture, the same thing happened with Lord Forsyth in Melrose). He also picked at old wounds, getting a round of applause for a reference to 'scab' drivers during the miners' strike.

It was, like Sillars vs Forsyth, good political theatre, and interesting to hear a Left critique of independence (fleshed out in an 'Official Booklet') and, like the Better Together meeting I'd attended at Leith Academy, intended to make folk already inclined to vote No feel good about it. Surprisingly, Galloway has buried the hatchet with his old party, saying at one point that 'everything that's good in this country came from Labour'. He also got really worked up when explaining (or 'adumbrating') why opposing Scottish independence didn't contradict his stance on Palestine or Irish reunification ('Scotland is not an occupied country.').

I left just as the Q&A got under way, making a bit of a mad dash to get to Coatbridge Sunnyside (on my bike) to get the direct train back to Waverley. It was a nice evening and the area was actually quite scenic (my snobbish brain had expected otherwise); trundled back to Edinburgh through stations with lots of exotic names I'd never heard before. Cycled to the Village Pub in Leith expecting to catch the *Great Yes, No, Don't Know, Five Minute Theatre Show*, only to find it had finished. Watched some of it online later on.

Tuesday, 24 June 2014 (Edinburgh)

To The Tun to do another interview about Bannockburn, about which I have little to say of any use (in the event it wasn't even used on *Reporting Scotland*). Popped into Holyrood after and had a long chat with Simon Johnson from the *Telegraph*, now 'persona non grata' (his term) with the Scottish Government following his coverage of the Gunn/Lally affair (in which spin doctor Campbell Gunn had been accused of 'smearing' Labour activist Clare Lally). He's now busy causing them trouble over the Local Income Tax story (not, of course, local at all) that, for some bizarre reason, the First Minister said on a radio phone-in he'd pursue after independence. Simon says he's spoken to people at Yes Scotland who think the result will divide 62/38 against.

Ben Jackson at Oxford emailed me an advance copy of the next edition of *Renewal*, including an editorial that had already gone online. In a similar vein to Ben's *Political Quarterly* piece it amounted to a pretty compelling deconstruction of Nationalist ideology. For example:

> Nothing could be more indicative of the intellectual crisis of Scottish nationalism than the fact that this political movement, which set out criticising the British state for its attachment to feudal totems and international finance, has ended up relying on the monarchy and the Bank of England as the guarantors of a Scottish 'independence' that approaches parody (Scottish Government, 2013).

And also, later on:

> In comparison to the Scottish nationalism of 1999 or even 2007, that of 2014 lacks a coherent account of either the state or the economy. In its place, a politics of assertion, rejection and blind hope has emerged. The style and mode of the SNP's argumentation has become correspondingly vague, simplifying, and wilfully obfuscatory. Both its fabled 'positivity' and its quickness to blame arise from a comfortingly voluntaristic conception of politics, in which Scotland's problems can be attributed to malign foreign institutions that are wilfully frustrating the natural genius of its people.

Ouch. Of course it won't provoke a response, for there's now no one in the SNP with the intellectual gravitas to attempt a rebuttal (Ben's *PQ* piece was similarly ignored).

Had lunch with Andrew Kerr from BBC Scotland at Hadrian's Brasserie (expensive, but good grub). He filled me in on internal politics while I (reluctantly) conceded that all those arguing that the Beeb is having a bad referendum have a point. Later, David Ross from Better Together called to effectively brief against STV, it having apparently bowed to pressure from the FM not to hold the first televised debate on its preferred date of 16 July (having also told Better Together this was non-negotiable). He then sent me an 'insider' line to the effect that STV had 'simply rolled over', but the upshot was that while Salmond had agreed – in principle – to the STV debate, Darling had withdrawn due to the date change. This allowed Yessers to depict Darling as 'feart' (like the Prime Minister). Of course it was more complicated than that, but then all is fair in love and referendums.

The day had brightened up so I cycled to the National Museum of Scotland for the *Spectator*/Brewin Dolphin debate on independence, or rather the proposition that 'independence is the greatest threat to Edinburgh'. Speaking for the motion were the Labour MP Ian Murray (cogent enough, and the only one to deal with the motion), Annabel Goldie (uninspiring but made a good point about basing a Scottish Defence Force in Faslane when it'd spend most of its time defending the North Sea) and George Galloway (on firebrand form even if a lot of lines were recycled from Coatbridge). Speaking against were Andrew Wilson (looking defensive and not really on form), Jeane Freeman (the best) and Blair Jenkins (dry as dust, practice clearly doesn't make perfect).

More to the point, the audience was overwhelmingly against independence from the start. Amusingly, once all the plebs had taken their seats those there as guests of Brewin Dolphin filed in from the back all besuited and affluent, and whenever Andrew made one of his usual points (i.e. 'you can be British and vote Yes') they tittered in a slightly snide way. Freeman's social justice pitch (woolly, as usual) obviously fell on deaf ears although, oddly, Galloway, who when not speaking sat chewing gum and staring impassively ahead, went down extremely well. As Alex Massie later tweeted: 'The end times are upon us: Galloway cheered to the echo by an audience of Edinburgh lawyers, bankers, fund managers etc.'

Galloway was also typically melodramatic, declaring at one point there would be 'havoc if you vote Yes in September'. He also duffed up Andrew Wilson, referring to him as 'Fred the Shred's spin doctor', a point Andrew didn't deal with at all well. During the Q&A, however, he hit the nail on the head when – following a slightly garbled attempt to reassure from the Yessers – he looked at the audience and said, 'it doesn't sound certain does it? Are you up for it?' And then, more darkly, 'What kind of nutter would vote for that?' Although expressed in pungent terms, Gorgeous George had tapped into what a big chunk of voters actually think about the whole thing. His main peroration was also – in places – quite eloquent, for example this in the context of the Second World War:

> And not one person asked in that summer and autumn of 1940 and into 1941 if the pilots who were spinning above us defending us from invasion from the barbaric horde were from Suffolk or Sutherland. We were people together on a small piece of rock with 300 years of common history. That's what they want to break up and all the rest is balderdash.

Wilson and Freeman were, at points, surprisingly frank, the former admitting that RBS operations had effectively decamped to London well before the crash, while the latter conceded 'there is no guarantee that an independent Scotland would take all the right decisions' (just that it would get the parties it voted for running the government), while Blair Jenkins also agreed with the chairman, the typically even-handed Andrew Neil, that 'Scotland is over-centralised' ('Who's responsible for that?' asked Neil rhetorically). The debate also got a bit bad-tempered, Jeane telling Galloway at one point to 'stop telling lies' and, when asked about the 'more powers' pledges from the Unionist parties: 'I wouldn't trust it as far as I could spit.'

Most of the questions directed at the panel were hostile to independence, so much so that an old guy next to me said he felt sorry for those on the left as they'd chosen a 'sticky wicket'. As we filed out he also told me he doubted it was a 'representative audience', which was an understatement. I watched Andrew Wilson make his way along the row of speakers to shake hands with them all but – seeing him approach – Galloway diligently avoided him (very childish). Afterwards I had a couple of pints with Alex Massie, James Corbett (from ThinkScotland) and Chris Sibbald (from Charlotte Street Partners).

Wednesday, 25 June 2014 (Edinburgh)

Nipped up to Starbucks on the Royal Mile for coffee and overheard the barista responding to a query about Scottish banknotes from an American lady in front of me. 'It's still the same country,' he said without missing a beat, 'at least until September.'

A very silly row about the TV debates rumbles on, the FM now saying he'll debate Darling on 5 August (STV) but Better Together still in a huff about the change of date. Spoke to my Better Together contact and he said Blair McDougall et al were keen to have the debates sooner rather than later, while Yes Scotland would prefer to have them all in August for obvious reasons.

Had a drink with Rory Scothorne of the fringe communist group 'Mair nor a roch wind'. Engaging as always, said he was preparing a review of my federalism book (to which he's sympathetic) and is still intending to vote Yes ('just') in the hope that it'll mobilise the Scottish Left, nudging newly politicised Yessers into a more class-based critique of the SNP. I suppose that might happen, but I'm too cynical to go along with fantasy politics – although if I did make that leap I'd probably end up in leftist territory (if not communism). Rory also confirmed that the Radical Independence Campaign's intention was to form a political party post-referendum to take the place of the SSP & Greens, although its expectation that they'd swallow their pride and make way for the new force (whatever it's called) seems quixotic. Apparently Ben Wray is the 'intellectual' driver of this strategy, while Messrs Foley and Ramand are providing the substance. Just before we finished up I saw through the window Mike Russell and several other SNP MSPs looking very jolly, making their way down Holyrood Road.

Thursday, 26 June 2014 (Edinburgh & Glasgow)

Murdo Fraser got a lot of attention all day because of remarks he'd made advocating a federal UK the day before at a Queen's University conference in Belfast (at which, he told me via Twitter, I was much cited). Murdo, of course, has been heading in that direction for years, only now it's more topical folk are interested. I did a clip for ITV Border backing him up and then watched FMQs from the Holyrood gallery. Salmond was actually on good form, referring to the 'Scottish Conservatives in any of their manifestations' and, later, to 'federal Fraser', which was a good line. The *Herald* and *Scotsman* had reasonably constructive editorials on his proposals (the former more so), while Yes Scotland spun that Murdo was shoring up their argument for independence. I forwarded this press release to him with the exclamation 'Nationalist!' 'I've been called,' he replied, 'much worse.'

After FMQs and quickly swinging by the launch of 'English Scots for Yes' (what next, 'No voters for Yes?') – a bearded guy from County Durham said he recognised my *Herald* picture byline – I cycled up to Ramsay Garden for an International Futures Forum seminar with a couple of journalists I can't name, as it was conducted under Chatham House rules. The first was very good, arguing that Better Together had bounced back from its 1987-style 'wobble', that Darling was 'a saintly man for having put up with it all' and that HQ, once full of 'scared-looking kids' was now full of 'proper politicians'. The other said his English-born wife had decided to vote Yes because it was the only thing that would 'make Scots stop whingeing' (except it wouldn't), and otherwise was rather gloomy: there'd be a 'lot of poison' in the months ahead, Yes Scotland would try to frame the referendum as a 'vote for or against Scotland' while Murdo's federalist pitch was a 'piece of nonsense', not least the prospect of forcing 'Balkanisation' (that word again) on England (not actually what Fraser was arguing).

I asked what they reckoned Salmond would do post-referendum and they both took the conventional Media Tower line that he'd resign quite quickly and make way for Nicola, although I still think that's a misreading of Salmond: he wants ten years as FM and an election hat-trick, a bit like the much-maligned Blair.

After speaking to a Dutch journalist who was working on a 10,000-word piece about the 'disunited UK' I caught a train to Glasgow and then cycled to Glasgow University (quite a decent evening) for a Reform Scotland event at which Michael Moore and Murdo Fraser were speaking. I mischievously asked Moore who was going to be the most federalist ('I defer to my new federalist friend,' he replied, gesticulating at Murdo), then he asked: 'What are you going to do in September?' It's a good question. I said I'd probably have an existential crisis.

Moore's speech, or 'vision' as Reform Scotland had it, was solid enough but not exactly inspiring. He spoke about 'Devolution 3.0', cautiously suggested some more powers, and finished by warning that Unionists had to 'move fast and lead or we'll find the people of Scotland have left us behind'. Murdo's was much more engaging (he rebutted 'federal Fraser' with 'separatist Salmond'); he's now basically a born-again federalist and his speech even lacked most of the usual qualifications. He quoted from my recent book, as well as David Melding's work (though not Gordon Brown's, which he later told me he hadn't read). Turning Ron Davies' maxim on its head, he said 'federalism is very much an event and not a process'.

Afterwards I went for a curry with a couple of well-placed Conservatives on Ashton Lane just off Byres Road. One was interesting on the Calton Hill Declaration, saying he was surprised that the party had agreed to two lines in the statement, the opener about the Scottish people being sovereign (he said David McLetchie, as a lawyer, used to 'go ballistic' about that), and also the sentence committing to Scottish representation at Westminster remaining as it is (in contravention of party policy).

The other was also fascinating on the Strathclyde Commission. I asked to what extent Lord Strathclyde had actually engaged with the whole thing and he smiled knowingly before saying that he'd objected to the devolution of Capital Gains and Inheritance Tax so they were taken out (as they had to 'give' him something), largely because Tory voters would worry about it. He also highlighted the fact that the report said they weren't devolved for 'good reasons' but didn't actually give any. They both agreed that the PM and Chancellor were completely 'on board' about more powers after the referendum.

Friday, 27 June 2014 (Edinburgh)

Cycled to The Hub at the top of the Royal Mile to watch Ed Miliband (who was 30 minutes late) speak to the usual circle of party activists (Margaret Curran claimed there were Undecideds there but I couldn't see any). His speech was standard 'I'm in Scotland' fare, name-checking John Smith, Keir Hardie and – with a bit more originality – Jennie Lee (on the basis she sat for an English constituency). 'You're in the midst,' Ed said at one point, 'of an all-consuming referendum.' He got that bit right.

At an SPJA lunch a couple of hours later he wandered in wearing a 'No Thanks' badge looking awkward (as he does generally, but particularly so in Scotland). His speech was better than the morning's effort, quite relaxed and self-deprecating, recalling being forced into hiding when it emerged he'd been drafted in to help with the 1999 Holyrood election campaign. Otherwise it was very touchy-feeling, expressing his belief that 'the battle of ideas matters... much more important than photo opportunities'. He also went after the SNP on inequality, arguing that No was the truly 'progressive' choice (as trailed in today's *Herald* splash), and so on. More interestingly, he reckoned the independence referendum would come to be viewed as a 'defining moment' for the UK, like 1945 and 1979. 'Ideas are what win referenda,' he said, again slightly clumsily, 'what win elections.' There wasn't long for questions but he largely played it safe, saying 'Barnett has served us well and I've got no plans to change it' and that Better Together should 'steer very clear of alliances' with UKIP.

Outside the Scottish Labour referendum battle bus ('VOTE NO' emblazoned on the side) Torcuil Crichton from the *Daily Record* introduced me to Ed M:

> Ed M: We've met before haven't we? [He probably says this to everyone.]
> Me: Yes, I worked in the Commons' Press Gallery for a year...
> Torcuil: David is Alex Salmond's biographer.
> Ed M: Oh, when's your book coming out?
> Me: It came out three years ago [I added that a third edition would only be published once Salmond resigned.]
> Ed M: It should be published now!

And with that he was off to Airdrie, Port Glasgow and other places that must appear like alien territory to a gawky, but I guess basically decent, guy from a leafy suburb of north London. Will he win next year's election? I still think it's possible, although his biggest handicap is his basic weirdness; the electorate don't like someone who they can't see on the steps of Number 10.

Listened to Derek Bateman's very chummy interview with Alex Salmond online. 'The things I can't say about the BBC,' said the FM at one point, 'he [Bateman] says about the BBC,' more or less an admission that he can't stand BBC Scotland. Salmond claimed lots of folk were registering to vote having not done so since the Poll Tax (although he didn't offer any evidence); repeated his prediction of an 80 per cent turnout (still think that's way too high) and burbled on at (great) length when Bateman asked him about interrupting Lawson's 1988 Budget speech. This was, in itself, quite revealing, for Salmond genuinely thinks of it as a great achievement rather than just an inspired PR stunt. 'Could we revert to my question?' said Derek after several minutes' worth.

This had been about his (Salmond's) 'motivation'. The FM responded about his grandfather and early lessons in Scottish history to which, to his credit, Derek responded that surely Better Together would accuse him of 'romantic nationalism' rather than hard-headed stuff about economics. Salmond said his Nationalism was 'completely civic' and added – taking his script from Wings and Pat Kane – that Alistair Darling had agreed what motivated the SNP was akin to a 'Nazi slogan' in his interview with the *New Statesman*. 'Scotland,' he said, 'is like a great tartan' (yuk), then undermined his own argument by simply asserting that an independent Scotland 'will do better because it's a nation', which is pure existentialism.

Got some welcome escape from the indyref in the evening, first with an Edinburgh International Film Festival screening of *Tony Benn: Will and Testament*, a beautifully made but hagiographic documentary about the late Wedgwood Benn, then Wynton Marsalis and Jazz at the Lincoln Centre across the road at the Usher Hall; some amazing stuff, including a guest appearance from Nicola Benedetti.

Saturday, 28 June 2014 (Stirling)

Got the train through to Stirling early-ish (an Orange march was kicking off as I left) for Armed Forces Day and Bannockburn Live. Both very badly organised: website for the former provided lots of information except for the important stuff, i.e. route, timings, best vantage points etc. I watched the main procession kick off from the Castle Esplanade, although it was small and strangely unimpressive. After bumping into a bunch of Tories draped in Union flags I cycled to Bannockburn but had to queue to collect my already purchased ticket, the queue being the same as that for those buying on the day, thus it was very long.

This took about 45 minutes and I got recognised:

Old guy: Hey, you on the telly?
Me: Sometimes.
Old guy: You're one o' the No guys.
Me (smiling weakly): I'm professionally neutral.
Old guy (in a friendly way): Aye, right!

There were lots of Yes badges and it was quite busy, contrary to general press speculation that the punters were staying away. Once into the site it was raining (though not heavily) and there was another long queue for the 2pm re-enactment. Just as I got to the entrance it was declared full up, and given there were lengthy queues for just about every other event (except a lacklustre music stage) there wasn't really much for me to do but leave.

Bumped into Andy Wightman, who shared my general impression of the (bad) organisation. I then cycled back to the main Armed Forces Day site, but it too was very busy and I'd lost the will to live by then. Sat in a café reading *The Economist* before getting the train back to Edinburgh.

Sunday, 29 June 2014 (Edinburgh)

Brunch with an engaging duo, Simon Akam (a posh Englishman) and Fin Young (a slightly less posh Scotsman), who were working on a feature and longer e-book for *Newsweek*. They asked a series of intelligent questions, so I had fun riding all my usual hobby horses – i.e. the SNP's rhetorical social democracy, the convergence of Scottish and English social attitudes, federalism, etc – and they admitted that their UK tour had challenged both their assumptions. Fin, for example, said he'd always bought into long-established arguments about Scotland's 'distinct' political culture (and indeed he still doggedly clung to them in a few of his questions to me). Simon said his grandfather was Dr Jeremy Bray, the former Labour MP for Motherwell, which was slightly unexpected.

Mum texted to say, simply, 'The fish has expired', by which she meant a goldfish she and Dad had kept in an absurdly small plastic tank for the last few years. Otherwise, day was spent writing my *Herald* column (a response to federalist cynics), finishing a surprisingly good book on the referendum by a French academic called Didier Revest ('Senior Lecturer in British Civilisation Studies' at the University of Nice-Sophia Antipolis) and finishing a short chapter on Scotland for a guide to the 2015 General Election being edited by Iain Dale.

Monday, 30 June 2014 (Basel & Strasbourg)

Caught the tram to the airport for the first time, and although it took longer and cost more than the usual bus it was still enjoyable enough for that not to matter. Mixed response to my *Herald* column on the weakness of the arguments deployed against federalism. 'Great article in *Herald* debunking McWhirter [*sic*] nonsense,' texted Murdo Fraser. 'The Natterati panic over federalism shows what a good idea it is!' While Jackson Carlaw messaged me on Facebook, rather snidely, to say: 'Murdo says, David does is my unfortunate and disappointed conclusion' (it should be the other way round!).

EasyJet flight to Basel slightly delayed, but very easy to get into the city once I arrived: a fast bus straight from the terminal to the main railway station. Spent a few hours happily mooching around – a fine cathedral

(Munster) and good weather – also finished reading *Gottland*, a great little book on 'mostly true' tales from 'one half' of Czechoslovakia. The train to Strasbourg departed from a special French section of the railway station. I dozed and typed up some notes.

Former First Minister Jack McConnell called in the evening (a first), flagging up a speech he's making tomorrow to mark the 15th anniversary of the Scottish Parliament getting its powers on 1 July 1999. He explained that his intention was to reclaim devolution or 'Home Rule' within the UK, saying he hadn't been 'comfortable' with the tone of the campaign thus far and felt those leading it weren't inclined to talk up Holyrood or all its deeds over the past 15 years (interesting). Also said it would be 'relentlessly positive'. Just the other week I was asking Susan Dalgety (who used to work for him) why he wasn't more involved.

At around 9.30pm I made my way through Strasbourgians loudly celebrating a World Cup win over Nigeria and met Ian Duncan (the newly-elected Scottish Tory MEP) and his assistant Andrew Johnston (formerly of the Holyrood broadcasting unit) for dinner *al fresco* in Petite France. Good chat and good grub. Ian knows the European scene well so he was having no trouble getting into the swing of things. We made a (slightly drunken) bet about how many seats the Scottish Conservatives would win in 2015; I said one and Ian said four. We shook on 10 Euros or a bottle of wine, I can't quite remember which. If it's two, three or less (and indeed more), the bet's null and void.

Tuesday, 1 July 2014 (Strasbourg)

The *Herald* had a typically elegant letter from Neal Ascherson (now living back in Scotland it seems) politely dismissing my column on federalism, although he referred to two failed attempts to devolve power to the north-east of England (there's only been one, in 2004). Walked to the European Parliament since it was a nice day and spent the morning navigating the 'reimbursement' office, which culminated in me being handed several large Euro notes to refund travel and accommodation costs – it almost made me a Europhile. *En route* I passed the outgoing Commission President (José Manuel Barroso) looking tanned and relaxed. He must be glad it's all over.

Slept in so missed Farage *et al* turning their backs on 'Ode to Joy' at the opening session, but caught a bit of plenary session later on when the vice presidents were elected. Entertainingly, MEPs started casting their paper ballots before being instructed to and when a Member objected the chairman simply remarked 'sometimes democracy takes on a life of its own'. David Coburn, the new Scottish UKIP MEP, was there, ostentatiously

A kilted UKIP MEP David Coburn at the European Parliament in Strasbourg.

wearing a kilt (with a very long sporran). This obviously attracted a lot of media interest and he told me he didn't want the SNP to be the only ones flying the 'banner' for Scotland. 'They don't wear kilts any more,' he added, 'do they?' Later Pat Kane tweeted a picture of someone from ITV interviewing Coburn with the comment: 'Ok. Tartanry just ENDED.'

After a quick chat with a Catalan MEP I caught up with Messrs (Ian) Hudghton and (Alyn) Smith in the press bar, although we then relocated to another, quieter, spot on the other side of the building. They were a little cagey: not unfriendly but clearly meeting me out of obligation rather than camaraderie. I asked how they thought the referendum was going and there was a revealingly nervous grin from Ian and the standard (half-hearted) line that it's 'going well'. Alyn expanded a little, saying the biggest factor were the Undecideds and polling not matching his experience on the ground, but I can't help feeling that exaggerates the number of the former and underplays the significance of the latter. This was later reinforced when Peter Kellner posted a blog on YouGov basically demolishing the methodology used by pollsters (Panelbase, Survation, etc) that have been showing a much smaller gap between Yes and No. The key paragraph was:

> A number of recent polls have produced widely-reported stories that the contest is close. They are wrong. It isn't. The No campaign is well ahead. Its lead has held up for some months. Unless things change markedly in the next 11 weeks, Scotland will vote to remain in the United Kingdom, and by a decisive enough margin to settle the matter for many years to come.

Ouch, not least because that's aimed at the outfit we've been using at Five Million Questions/*Daily Record* (and indeed it was Michael Marra who flagged it up).

Also caught up properly later in the afternoon with the new UKIP MEP David Coburn who told me, apropos of nothing, that he thought there was a 'stench of fascism' about the SNP. 'They're a nasty bunch,' he added, and wondered out loud if there might be 'violence' in the event of a Yes vote (I said I doubted it, although some people might say silly things). 'Scotland's not fundamentally different, we've got the same bigotries as England,' he said when I asked about his election. 'We produce lots of clever people but it doesn't mean we're morally superior to the rest of the human race.'

I asked how he explained the UKIP vote rise and he reckoned it mainly came from people who hadn't voted before (there's probably something in that), as well as 'sheer fear of the SNP; people are reverting to type' (there's probably something in that too). David Martin, my last coffee of the day, said Coburn clearly wasn't the idiot some thought he was, pointing out that he was already a deft exploiter of the media. Said he'd detected a shift away from Yes during the European election campaign, much stronger Nos, and so on. Seems to read my column, which is good, and mentioned that Gordon (Brown) believes the Scottish Conservatives could win five seats based on his 'analysis' of the Euro election results.

Another dinner *al fresco* and some nice Alsatian beer; amused myself by thinking of turning this journal into a pale imitation of Roy Jenkins' much-mocked *European Diary*, which was more a catalogue of good lunches and fine wines than political life in Brussels and Strasbourg.

Wednesday, 2 July 2014 (Strasbourg & Frankfurt)

Up early after not very much sleep to meet Catherine Stihler at the European Parliament. Effusive and very friendly. Mentioned to a fellow Labour MEP from Yorkshire that I'd interned at Anne Begg's office while a student and when she worked there too. We talked – inevitably – more about

Scotland than Europe, although the two subjects meshed at various points. Like David Martin, she'd detected a hardening No vote during recent campaigning, but on the potential for the UK leaving the EU she was much gloomier. Repeated what others have been saying to the effect that Lord (Michael) Howard rather than Andrew Lansley was being lined up for the Commissioner's job, while she predicted that the European Parliament vote on Juncker in a few weeks could throw up a surprise or two.

More interesting polling from YouGov, including the finding that 56 per cent of Scots believe there'd probably be further devolution in the event of a No vote, vis-à-vis 31 per cent who are cynics (predictably, 65 per cent of Yessers think there won't, as compared with 80 per cent of No voters, who think there will be); so basically the cynics are highly concentrated among those already determined to vote Yes. Ian Bell, meanwhile, responded to my column in the *Herald*, skilfully focusing on my weakness, i.e. the lack of English desire for federalism. He made a reasonable case, although it still skirted over several of my points.

Had the afternoon to mooch around sun-drenched Strasbourg, and memories of my last visit there nearly 17 years ago came flooding back: I'm pretty sure I first met David Martin back then, while I ended up doing the same boat trip – basically a loop around the city – I'd done as a 20-year-old. I remember how terrified I was of travelling solo then compared with the relative ease with which I do it now. I had to muster courage just to go into a shop. At Strasbourg railway station portly German girls kept smiling pleasantly at me. I'd forgotten what a joy French and German trains were: punctual, clean, amazing toilets and announcements in English which, unlike their British counterparts, tell you useful things such as what platform your connecting train will be on. Today's papers have pictures of former French president Sarkozy looking crumpled in the back of a car – he's been questioned in connection with corruption. How very French.

Rory Scothorne sent me his draft review of my federalism book by email, which I scanned while waiting for my connection to Frankfurt at a station called 'Karlsruhe'. Inevitably, I fell far short of his communist utopianism (curious that he's so cynical – rightly – about utopian Nationalists) but nevertheless it was thoughtful and typically well-written: 'Torrance still struggles to escape his past entanglements with the Scottish right' (I thought I'd escaped them years ago) and 'Torrance has secured himself a prominent position in the referendum debate, partly through the strategic use of nice jumpers and expertly crafted hair, but largely on merit' (I ought to put that on a National Collective T-shirt), but, more seriously, he concluded that my proposals deserved 'far better than the lazy impossibilist critiques to which [my] proposals have been subjected'. I can live with that.

Will Self has a nice line in this week's *New Statesman*: 'I never feel I have the measure of a city until I've walked across it and felt its heft with my feet.' I know what he means – even though it was a 40-minute walk from the sprawling Frankfurt am Main railway station to my rather seedy hotel, I still walked it and felt I had some measure of it by that evening. Also saw the familiar Eurozone symbol outside the European Central Bank *en route* – now surrounded in the detritus of protest, against bankers, globalisation, etc.

Thursday, 3 July 2014 (Frankfurt)

Trust the Prime Minister to deliver a speech in Edinburgh while I'm in Germany, although it doesn't sound particularly inspiring: imploring the 'silent majority' of Scots to say No to a Nationalist 'minority' – except it's a pretty big minority.

Spent the morning and early afternoon mooching around sun-drenched Frankfurt. Not a huge amount to see or do, but it's an attractive enough German city. Saw Goethe's birthplace and then dropped in on Mario Draghi's monthly press conference at the European Central Bank. Achingly corporate: bankers wearing black suits uttering impenetrable jargon about the Eurozone economy and financial journalists (also wearing black suits) asking slightly less impenetrable questions. After half an hour of that I had to get a coach to Frankfurt-Hahn Airport that, like Glasgow Prestwick, is nowhere near the city in its name; in fact it's an hour and three-quarters away. Still, the countryside looked beautiful and it gave me a chance to catch up with various things.

Germany just looks so prosperous and orderly, remarkable for a country that barely functioned in my father's lifetime. Although Common Weal has touched on the German model, I couldn't help feeling an independent Scotland would have far more to learn from the EU's dominant Member rather than the Scandinavian nations we hear about *ad nauseam*. Agreed to do a down-the-line interview with *Scotland 2014* about the monarchy and independence, while STV also sent a cab to pick me up at the airport (making me feel very important) for a pre-record about the little indyref guide I've written with Jamie Maxwell.

Saturday, 5 July 2014 (Glasgow & Edinburgh)

Early train to Glasgow to take part in BBC Radio Scotland's *Shereen* programme, although there wasn't much politics so I wasn't at my best. Robert Dawson Scott was also on, an intelligent and decent guy who (being a former theatre critic) basically buys the 'cultural' argument for

Jim Murphy, Labour MP for East Renfrewshire, brandishes a bottle thrown by a heckler during a speaking engagement in Leith.

independence (whatever that is) but was at least willing to listen to my deconstruction of several Nationalist arguments he'd rather accepted at face value.

Once back in Edinburgh I cycled down Leith Walk to hear Jim Murphy, Labour MP for East Renfrewshire, do one of his '100 Towns' tour meetings, complete with an old Barr's Irn-Bru crate (or two) rather than a soapbox. It was good old-fashioned political campaigning with most of the entertainment coming from various attempts at heckling. Jim, it has to be said, took most of this in his stride. 'This isn't a *Braveheart* movie!' he quipped in response to one cry of 'freedom'; 'We can't base this on a mid-ranking Australian actor' (i.e. Mel Gibson). Also, 'I'm in favour of change! I want rid of both Governments' (good line).

There was some half-hearted heckling from a gaggle of Yes campaigners, including the Deputy Provost of Edinburgh, Deidre Brock. Being the Kirkgate, a lot of locals were also present, mainly women in the middle of their shopping who looked pleased at the free political theatre, although others were clearly (for lack of a better term) junkies who just wanted something to do. Murphy wasn't so hot when someone challenged him about Iraq, which was odd as it can't have been the first time he'd heard it. At one point an elderly chap showed off a massive scar on his stomach to make a point (I think) about the NHS, while there was consistent and incoherent heckling from one chap who appeared to have something against Fabians. 'The English can fuck off!' yelled someone as it drew to a close, to which Jim responded: 'I love beating England at tiddlywinks!'

Murphy caught sight of me at one point ('Hey, I heard you on the wireless this morning!') but otherwise he was an impressive bundle of campaigning energy. Rory Scothorne messaged me on Facebook suggesting it was all about preparing the ground for a future (Scottish) leadership bid, but I doubt Jim wants to abandon Westminster anytime soon. Someone tweeted a fuzzy picture of me chatting to Labour activists and said I'd been caught 'actively campaigning' for a No vote. Pathetic. The French Consul General was also there (he certainly gets around, also on a bike) and he told me his father had been an Algerian *pied-noir*, which must give him an interesting perspective on lots of things.

Sunday, 6 July 2014 (Glasgow)

Got the train to Glasgow to attend a curiously-titled event – 'Scotland on the Brink' – at Òran Mór at the top of Byers Road, organised by an American called Chris Agee, writer-in-residence at Strathclyde University. It was a typically luvvy affair, a well-heeled West End audience watching well-heeled writers and poets explaining (often not very well) their 'journey' to Yes (everyone's on a bloody journey, usually to pseuds' corner). Chatted briefly to Neal Ascherson beforehand, telling him that I always enjoy his elegant criticism of my *Herald* columns ('I respond to them because they engage me'); he then kicked things off by reading an essay reproduced in that day's *Sunday Herald*. Although this had some typically good lines ('For the last 15 years, we have been living in an informal, low-rise, lower-case union...'), a lot of it was highly generalised and full of caricature. Liz Lochhead, meanwhile, was good when reading from the opening of *Mary Queen of Scots Got Her*

Taking part in a Common Weal panel discussion at The Arches, Glasgow. (Photo: Stewart Wright)

Head Chopped Off but less so when reciting a short piece she'd written about Robert Burns for a recent Scottish National Portrait Gallery event. Susan Stewart, formerly of Yes Scotland, told me Ascherson's *Stone Voices* had been one of the 'key' texts in her transition from devolutionist to Nationalist, which demonstrates the power of good writing.

Mercifully, I had to leave before Alasdair Gray did a turn (his decorations inside Òran Mór were striking), no doubt to the usual unqualified adulation. Got a bit lost cycling to The Arches (Glasgow's cycle paths need some work) for a gathering of the Common Weal, so I turned up just in time for my panel discussion on the 'challenges' faced by the movement. It was surprisingly constructive, with one chap in the audience even saying he 'agreed' with my analysis (although he added the caveat of 'unusually'); and I warned them not to make the mistake of assuming all Scots shared their 'radical' thinking. The veteran SNP activist Isobel Lindsay also spoke and clearly couldn't quite understand why I'd been invited. Of course it's her son who's driving the whole thing (Robin McAlpine), so naturally she feels protective of it and him. Afterwards an acquaintance (who'd been in the audience) messaged me on Facebook saying he 'mostly' agreed with my comments. 'I was trying to be constructive!' I replied. 'I think you were,' he said. 'They need telt.'

Afterwards I mooched around for a bit, and when I passed the National Collective stall a young guy asked if I'd pose with their 'I Am National Collective' sign. Rather arrogantly I assumed he knew who I was so I agreed for a laugh, but it quickly became obvious neither he nor the photographer had a scooby that I was a journalist who wasn't exactly an uncritical admirer of their movement.

NC chap: Why are you supporting the movement?
Me: Er...
Him: Okay, then why are you voting Yes?
Me: Um...
Him: How are you voting?
Me: I'm a journalist.
Him: Okay, are you a Yes-voting journalist?
Me: I'm trying to stay professionally neutral.

The picture later did the rounds on Twitter to much – mostly good-natured – hilarity.

The author engages with the 'cultural case' for independence. (Photo: National Collective)

Monday, 7 July 2014 (Edinburgh)

Interviewed by two engaging chaps (one of whom used to work at STV) doing yet another indyref documentary project, but their questions were good. I can't keep track of all these things now, so goodness knows what I'll crop up saying on various films after the referendum. Today's papers had an interesting quote from Alistair Darling: 'We're making progress, which is why, with increasing confidence, I can say we will win, provided we continue to get our arguments across.' Whatever happened to 'no complacency'?

In the evening I watched two indyref documentaries with Peter, a Yes activist who lives in Dumbiedykes. The first, a Channel 4 *Despatches* programme was, as James Millar of the *Sunday Post* later tweeted, 'moronic', and also much too short at only half an hour. Although more or less balanced, its big 'story' was allegations of bullying by the Scottish Government from businesses including the Scotch whisky industry, although the evidence for this was pretty thin (I don't, however, doubt there's been intimidation). The second, a longer show by Robert Peston on BBC2, was much better, although necessarily simplistic when it came to the economic aspects of independence. It was fascinating watching both programmes with a confirmed Yesser: he saw bias everywhere, including tonal nuances in each script. To be fair, he made some good points amid general paranoia.

Tuesday, 8 July 2014 (Edinburgh)

Lots of faffing about in the morning while a photographer from the *Sunday Mail* took pictures of Jamie Maxwell and me for a feature relating to our independence voters' guide. It was raining so we did some indoors at the National Museum of Scotland on Chambers Street then drove to Calton Hill to do standard shots with the Edinburgh skyline in the background. It made me slightly late for my haircut at 11am. Jamie was scathing about last night's Peston programme on BBC2: didn't feature a 'single woman', was all pro-Union voices (simply not true), etc. But when I asked him to list three women he'd have interviewed he responded, rather weakly, 'I'm not Robert Peston,' which wasn't really the point.

Wednesday, 9 July 2014 (Edinburgh & Skye)

Superb weather for the (long) drive to Skye, having collected a rental car at Edinburgh Airport. We made good time to Pitlochry, after which it got a bit

Glendale, Skye.

gruelling, more so for Stefan (Knapik, a musician friend from London) who of course was doing all the driving. We crossed the Skye Bridge at around 5pm but it then took an inexplicably long time to get up to Glendale where Ian Blackford (the former SNP treasurer) had kindly agreed to put us up for the night. *En route* there was a Yes sign on the side of a building near the turn off for Dunvegan (Ian later said this had caused 'trouble'), while further up the road there was an ostentatiously large Union flag.

The views from Ian's home were stunning and he was, as ever, good company. His son and his girlfriend were also staying. I met his wife Ann for the first time, a bit of a Nationalist firebrand (but sensible with it) and, as she told me, a former leader of the opposition on South Lanarkshire Council, which must have been an experience. Lots of good chat and although I'd warned Stefan to be on his best behaviour by 1am (having driven to the coast for sunset views) he'd drunk so much that the word 'fascism' tumbled from his lips in relation to Nationalism (in general, not just the Scottish variety). Ian took it all in his stride.

Thursday, 10 July 2014 (Skye & Harris)

Good news! St Kilda Cruises are planning to sail tomorrow, which was a relief. Started reading Tom Steel's highly readable (but also highly unreliable) book *The Life and Death of St Kilda*. Once the islanders decided to evacuate they petitioned the then Secretary of State for Scotland (William Adamson) – another world in so many ways.

Before setting off (it was another sun-drenched day) Ian Blackford showed us his local Free Kirk where, interestingly for a geek like me, the Napier Commission took evidence for a couple of days in the mid-1880s. After bidding farewell we toured the Talisker distillery, although I could only muster so much interest in the process as opposed to drinking the stuff. The chap giving the tour recognised me, initially thinking I was an undercover inspector (I liked that idea), but then realised I was 'off the telly'. Later, at the hostel in Leverburgh, another guest also clocked me. He was polite enough but his tone darkened when he mentioned the Bella Caledonia website (for some reason he thought I wrote for them, which I don't). The perils of being a Z-list indyref celebrity.

Friday, 11 July 2014 (Harris & St Kilda)

Up reasonably early to catch the boat to St Kilda, accompanied by a mix of Europeans, Americans and some UKers. Weather worsened considerably as we cruised west, but the main thing was that we'd actually departed at all (I later learned that Saturday's trip was to be cancelled, and possibly Sunday's too). Arrived at around 11am to find a vast threatening sky hanging over the island. We were urged to do any walking first because the afternoon weather would probably make it much more difficult, so we headed up and then over, our reward (through heavy mist) being some stunning views at the other side.

After that we explored the old, mostly ruined village with its Main Street and 'Parliament', or rather the old Post Office outside which all the adult males would meet in the morning to discuss island affairs. It was very atmospheric. The boat headed back – via a tour of the nearby gannet-infested 'stacs' – at 3.30pm and we were furnished with cake, coffee and even whisky. St Kilda was as far removed as it's possible to be from the independence referendum, though I suppose its military and National Trust will be able to vote in September.

Saturday, 12 July 2014 (Harris & Lewis)

Weather abysmal but we set off more in hope than expectation to see the Callanish stones on Lewis, which I'd visited about a decade ago but couldn't really remember. Belatedly recalled that John MacLeod of the *Scottish Daily Mail* lived on the outskirts of Stornoway so I arranged to drop by. Said he was still 'probably' voting Yes and believed the result would be close, but when I pointed out that the SNP only got around 950,000 votes (due to the low turnout) in 2011 and that perhaps a third of those were No voters, he didn't demur when I concluded that going from that to, say, the 1.5 million votes necessary (assuming a 75 per cent turnout) to secure a bare majority, would be difficult if not impossible. Afterwards we drove all the way north to the Butt of Lewis, although the weather made this barely worthwhile. Lots of large wooden Yes signs and Saltires in these parts, prominently displayed by the roadside.

In the evening I worked on a first draft of my *Herald* column while Stefan entertained our fellow hostellers with an impromptu concert. One of the guests was a girl from Bournemouth doing her elective on Harris as part of her medical studies at Glasgow University.

Her: What sort of journalism do you do?

Me: Politics. Will you be able to vote in September?

Her: I don't know much about it but I think we're better together.

Surprising how often I hear people repeating that line – a measure, perhaps, of its effectiveness.

Sunday, 13 July 2014 (Harris, North Uist, Benbecula, South Uist & Eriskay

Ferry from Leverburgh to Berneray at 10.35am and it only took an hour. Weather (mercifully) better so spent the day driving south through North Uist (perfect beaches), Benbecula, South Uist and finally Eriskay, where we had a pretty decent meal at a restaurant called 'Am Politician' (after the boat in *Whisky Galore*). Yes support very much in evidence: a lady where we had lunch in Benbecula was wearing a Yes-branded blue fleece while a postman on Eriskay had attached a small wooden Yes sign to his mailbox. Somebody had even stuck Yes stickers on all the 'passing place' signs near the causeway connecting South Uist to Eriskay. It certainly feels like a place apart – English is usually in parenthesis here (if it appears at all).

Monday, 14 July 2014 (South Uist & Edinburgh)

Up early to catch the 7.30am Lochboisdale–Oban ferry. Dozed for most of the morning in the observation lounge, which had been rendered pointless by foul weather. Awoke to find there were even Yes stickers in the CalMac toilets. Madeleine Bunting had a good piece in the *Guardian* which, by coincidence, drew on her recent journey through the Hebrides (and in particular Lewis) to research a book on the history of the relationship between England and Scotland. She focused on 'Andrew', a Unionist who felt a little under siege in his community:

> The Yes campaign is an act of faith in the promised land; it resonates with a utopian language of Scotland's presbyterian history. 'It's milk and honey,' he says. But everything that doesn't fit that paradigm is photoshopped out of the picture. It's dishonest, Andrew argues, and can only lead to disappointment... [and] at this moment of passionate political engagement, Andrew doesn't talk about the subject, not even with friends. It's like being an atheist at a revivalist meeting. For Yes supporters the issue has become something to assert, celebrate and proclaim to the world as their identity.

I thought that was spot-on.

Eventually got back to Edinburgh at around 7pm and caught up with myself before taxiing to Edinburgh Quay to do STV's *Scotland Tonight* on social media and the indyref; made my usual points about it augmenting traditional campaigning rather than constituting a campaign *in itself*, and also the impossibility of conducting a nuanced political discussion in bursts of 140 characters. *En route* to the studio I saw on Twitter that William Hague was standing aside as Foreign Secretary, which was kinda unexpected.

Tuesday, 15 July 2014 (Edinburgh & London)

Busy morning of interviews with a chap from the *Toronto Globe & Mail* (doing a piece comparing Scotland's referendum with Quebec's) and a very Dutch correspondent from the Netherlands' equivalent of *The Times* (or so he said). Questions from both were inevitably general but perfectly reasonable. Photographer for the latter was particularly keen to get a photograph of me with my Brompton, which was good self-indulgent fun. Mark Mackinnon (of the *Globe & Mail*) was about to set off on a tartan tour of the Outer Hebrides, which, alas, is how a lot of international media still views Scotland. A producer from BBC1's *The One Show* emailed asking if Jamie (Maxwell) and I would do a turn next week, but mercifully both of us will be away.

Bumped into Kiran Stacey from the *FT* on the 2.30pm train to London (he's covering Scotland while Mure Dickie's on holiday) and otherwise caught up on indyref television I'd missed while I was in the Hebrides. An edition of *This Week* from Edinburgh last Thursday camped it up but was reasonably good, unlike the tired and generally hopeless *Question Time*, which came from Inverness the same night. Using a non-politician panel was a reasonable stab at doing something new, but the end result was Joan Burnie simply regurgitating standard Yes Scotland lines in an indignant tone and Ricky Ross (good hair!) being sanctimonious and peddling an absurd Yes bit of scaremongering about the Scottish NHS being privatised in the event of a No vote. Scott Hastings on the other hand was actually quite good, sensible and articulate, while the 'passionate Highlander' in the audience (who I'd already seen on YouTube) remained entertaining: 'We will keep our Union together in the name of Jesus!'

There was a bit of stooshie about Jean-Claude Juncker, the new European Commission President, ruling out further EU expansion in the next five years. Jumping the gun ever so slightly, various Unionists (though not the Scottish Tory MEP Ian Duncan) wielded this as incontrovertible proof that an independent Scotland wouldn't be admitted to the club quickly or easily. But not only had he been talking in the context of Eastern expansion, but his spokesman later confirmed he hadn't been referring to Scotland (which is clearly a different case by virtue of its 41-year-old membership as part of the UK). Sturgeon *et al* later accused Better Together of 'misrepresenting' Juncker's comments, and they had a point. Alistair Darling does tend to get carried away. For example the other day he said the consequences of independence would be worse than the economic crisis, which verges on hyperbole.

Wednesday, 16 July 2014 (London)

Took the scenic route from Clapton to Westminster, down the canal at Hackney Fields, through Limehouse Cut and then the cycle superhighway to Parliament Square. Nice, sunny day and the cycle paths and roads are a joy compared to the Third World conditions in Edinburgh. Usefully, my Lobby pass still worked so I was able to glide through the main gates as I used to last year (I still get a kick out of that).

Bumped into Quentin Letts from the *Daily Mail* as I tried to figure out where the All Party Parliamentary Group on Reform, Decentralisation and Devolution in the UK (a polite way of saying the 'f' word) was actually meeting. Told him I was seeing *Wolf Hall* at the Aldwych and *Great Britain* at the National later in the day and he expressed approval of the former but not the latter (apart from Billie Piper's performance). As it happens, he was correct, of which more anon. Also bumped into Ian Murray and we chatted about the recent *Spectator* debate in Edinburgh (he got flak for actually debating the motion). 'Only 64 days to go!' he said chirpily as he headed towards Portcullis House.

Finally figured out that the All Party Parliamentary Group meeting had been shifted at the last minute to Church House near Westminster Abbey so got there about half an hour late, entering just behind Sir Menzies Campbell, who was carrying a Panama hat. When he did his little spiel about federalism Lord (Nicol) Stephen nodded in my direction, obviously well aware I'm a born-again federalist with all the zeal of a convert (indeed more so than most Lib Dems). Talking of which, Alasdair McKillop did a reasonably constructive review of my federalism book for the *Scottish Review of Books* website, concluding that I'd argued 'with clarity and conviction, ably dismantling some of the theoretical objections to federalism', but on the other hand 'serious questions' remained as to how political and popular momentum would be 'generated to carry the UK to the federal future' I envision, which is fair comment. Some of the contributions at the APPG were reasonably interesting and Lord (Peter) Hennessy did a typically good job of chairing it. The noble Lords (George) Foulkes and (Jeremy) Purvis seemed quite pleased when I spoke to them afterwards, although Jeremy said administrative support was an issue and he'd like to produce something 'concrete' like a report.

Had a quick lunch with Lord (Bob) Maclennan on the Lords terrace and as ever he was fretting about the outcome of the referendum, saying plaintively at one point: 'I just can't understand why anyone would vote Yes.' An elderly Scottish peer sat next to Bob ('Haven't I seen you on television?') and it turned out to be Lord Kirkhill (John Farquharson Smith), who was Minister of State at the Scottish Office under Wilson and Callaghan in the late 1970s, indeed I remembered writing to him when I was researching my first book. He spoke knowledgably enough about the referendum as he digested a copy of *The Times*, but when he asked Bob about his 'leader' (i.e. Lord Hill) heading to Brussels, he didn't seem very interested.

After that I cycled up Whitehall to have coffee with a contact from Downing Street. He said the Prime Minister would be up in Scotland again before polling day ('but not loads') and that they were 'confident but not complacent' (the standard line). As usual he asked me 'what more we could be doing', but I couldn't really think of anything. Later I had a couple of Diet Cokes on the Commons terrace with Gregg McClymont, who was preparing for the weekend's (Labour) National Policy Forum in Milton Keynes, at which the party's manifesto will be sorted out, although as he wryly remarked that would be done prior to the public bit. Engaging as ever, he repeated his view that the Scottish Tories were making a strategic mistake in assuming that advocating more devolution would lead to electoral recovery, but when I pointed out the Welsh Tories had done precisely that he ducked the point by saying he didn't know enough about it. Like David Martin, Gordon Brown had told Gregg that he thinks the Conservatives could recover in Scotland at next year's General Election, perhaps winning four or five seats, but I just don't see it happening. (Later, Douglas Pattullo, whose judgement I trust, told me he was 'increasingly optimistic' that they'd retain DCT and take WAK and BRS (Berwick, Roxburgh and Selkirk.)

Beyond taking the Westminster temperature, most of the day was taken up seeing two plays, both dealing with 'England' at different points in its history. The first, Hilary Mantel's own adaptation of her book *Wolf Hall*, was engaging, funny and extremely well acted (apart from several fluffed lines, typical for matinees), although it petered out a little towards the end: the basic problem with historical drama is that the plot doesn't have any surprises... The audience was full of well-heeled and elderly Americans, one of whom exclaimed 'British history is really appalling' as she read the plot synopsis. Scotland was mentioned once or twice as a distant threat, whereas in Richard Bean's state-of-the-nation play *Great Britain* it was reduced to a hackneyed line about there being more pandas than Tory MPs in Scotland (when asked by the Tory leader what to do about it, 'Paige Britain' – geddit? – replies 'Kill the pandas'). Although it had its moments, and as Quentin said Piper was good in the lead role, it was much too cartoonish and lacking any real depth. I left at the interval, unusual for me, but the typically middle-class audience chortling at lots of cheap lines was just too much.

Thursday, 17 July 2014 (London & Edinburgh)

Left my brother's place in Clapton at 7am and got to King's Cross in only 25 minutes on my Brompton, far more quickly than I'd have managed on public transport. Got a bit of work done on the 8am train to Waverley, including a comment piece on federalism for Peter Geoghegan's *Political Insight* magazine. I'm even getting paid; freelance wonders will never cease. In the afternoon I did a Skype interview for an NPR-affiliated TV station in Missouri (it appeared to be attached to a journalism school). I was on with a chap from *Forbes* who just talked nonsense and a political scientist from Yale (entertainingly called David Cameron) who wasn't much better, although he did 'wholeheartedly' agree with my point about the UK becoming a properly federal state. In fact all three guests were called David, which made life for the presenter (Casey!) rather difficult. Apparently it's airing next week, though God knows who watches this stuff.

In the evening Waterstones on George Street was hosting a launch for the indyref idiots' guide (though I don't call it that publicly) I've written with Jamie Maxwell. Unfortunately he couldn't be there so the historian Owen Dudley Edwards spoke on his behalf, which I can't pretend I was looking forward to. Instead it and he turned out to be fine, although the turnout wasn't very good, no more than a dozen punters. Owen was even effusive in his praise of me as a writer and journalist, which came as a surprise given the blistering nature of his book reviews in *Drouth*. Even after the formal proceedings he kept up the charm offensive, saying he could tell how hard I tried to be 'fair' (harder, he conceded, than him) and that we must go for a coffee, etc; all very gratifying, if a little odd.

During the Q&A a lively exchange began about the degree of anti-Englishness in Scotland, to which I added that it was as generally benign and as harmless as anti-Scottish sentiment in England. Owen got visibly angry when talking about 'weapons of mass destruction' (Trident, in other words), which made me a little uncomfortable, but then maybe that's my trouble: I lack passion about politics (although educational stuff does get me a bit worked up). Otherwise a lady in the audience said England was keener on neoliberalism than Scotland (sigh) while a chap in a kilt rambled on about egalitarianism and folk songs.

A chap called Angus Reid also used part of the Q&A to talk about 'sovereignty' and the need for a written constitution (his book on this, *A Modest Proposal*, was also published by Luath). When I said that the sovereignty of the Scottish people was already a reality via several referendums he didn't look very happy, nor when I pointed out that it wasn't really clear what 'sovereignty' meant in practice as opposed to in theory. He had told me before the launch that he had been involved in the anti-Poll Tax protests of the late 1980s.

Dad, looking slim and tanned, nowhere near 67 (which he'll be in December) managed to get into an argument with Angus about something inconsequential, though it at least livened things up. As we left Angus insisted on giving me a copy of his book, which he had at his home on Heriot Row, confirming my instinctive impression of him as a champagne socialist (to be fair, he had already acknowledged living in 'a middle-class bubble'). He's also a leftie who's decided to vote No, partly out of general suspicion of all politicians but also because (refreshingly) he believes it's possible to make Scotland 'the best part of the UK', with which I agreed, preferably as part of a federal Union (obviously I was warming to him).

So he gave me a copy of his book and also decided to put my silhouette on one of the many walls in his unusually tall stairway, something he's done with various other people including his near neighbour John Macfie (indeed I recognised the outline of his beard). This was an unexpected way to end the evening. I also met his neighbour, an obviously affluent lady lawyer who looked appalled at the very mention of independence. I told her I reckoned the result would be 60/40 against, while Angus thought, at best, 57/43 against. I wonder if we'll all be proven wrong?

Friday, 18 July 2014 (Edinburgh)

Some fluff in today's newspapers about the LGBT 'case' for independence ahead of Glasgow Pride tomorrow. As ever, beyond vague stuff about an independent Scotland becoming a 'progressive beacon', it isn't entirely clear what the case rests on: if Yes was serious about attracting the pink vote then they'd offer free condoms or subsidised Kylie CDs. In truth, the record of successive Westminster governments (supposedly entirely reactionary) – New Labour and Con/Lib Dem – is so good as to make a contrary case almost impossible. But of course every campaigning box has to be ticked.

I mentioned this to Douglas Pattullo when we met for lunch at Holyrood. Alert as ever to council by-elections, he said the SNP had lost a councillor in Argyll and Bute the previous evening, further evidence (in his opinion, and he's usually right) that the Nationalist vote is declining when, particularly in advance of the referendum, you'd expect it to be going up, assuming momentum. Although I'm still wary of reading too much into local by-elections, Doug says he's increasingly convinced there's a trend against the SNP (though he thinks they'll still be the biggest party in 2016) and that the Scottish Tory vote will recover by enough to give them three seats (including DCT) next year. Again, I'm not so sure.

Back at the flat a girl buzzed to ask if she could distribute 'referendum information' in the stair, and of course I said yes. This turned out to be slightly misleading in that she was a branded Yes campaigner. On me answering the door she visibly recoiled and said, baffled, 'Oh, I wasn't expecting you, I'm looking for Jason Orringe.' I told her I'd make sure he got her propaganda (I mean information) when he got back from the US, but it was just one of those daft sliding scales they use to gauge how strongly voters are for or against independence. I can't believe they're still pushing this so close to polling day.

Later, as arranged, Jim Naughtie and a Radio 4 producer came round to interview Dad and I for a documentary on 'divided families'. I was a little wary of doing this as it more or less implied an allegiance, but Jim (professional as ever) was alert to this and pitched his questions accordingly. Caitlin (the producer) had asked me in advance to have some old SNP material to hand so I showed them a 1975 LP of 'SNP songs' I'd got on eBay a while back, endorsed – entertainingly – by Winnie Ewing. Jim read this out for the benefit of the microphone, as he did with an anti-English rant (about a 'cabal' intent on destroying Scottish nationhood) from (I think) a 1940s statement of party policy. Inevitably he asked if Dad agreed with it and I looked on in mock horror as he said (after hesitating) 'Basically, yes.' Otherwise Dad was measured and articulate, but repeated his crazy theory about anyone who's gone to university, even in Scotland, being inculcated with Unionism by English staff (he told a Catalan film crew the same thing a few months ago). I hope they don't use that bit. It was a bit weird having Jim Naughtie of the *Today Programme* perched on a table in front of Dad and me, but such is the world of the indyref.

Someone from Iranian Press TV called asking if I was London-based and would I agree to be interviewed for a documentary they're making. Everyone, it seems, is making a documentary. Watched the *Financial Times'* Lionel Barber politely pull apart lots of the First Minister's economic arguments in a short interview on the paper's website (done, presumably, before or after Salmond's speech in Liverpool the other day). 'Is this more happy talk from Edinburgh?' Barber asked at one point, in response to which Alex did his best not to appear irritated. The trouble is, of course, Barber actually knows the economic arguments inside out, unlike most Scottish journalists (myself included). At one point Salmond raised the spectre of Sir Alec Douglas-Home (yawn), to which Barber exclaimed 'I was there!', a reference, of course, to his early career in Scottish journalism.

Sunday, 20 July 2014 (Lewes & France)

Up early to get the bus and tube to Victoria in order to catch a train to Lewes for the Speakers Festival. Displaying an admirably Presbyterian work ethic (we left the house at 7.45am), my brother came too as he had to finish pulling together the House of Lords' annual report; *en route* he explained a bit about the area and given I might end up living there (assuming a No vote), I paid attention.

Luckily, I was in plenty of time for the train and Marc Rattray, who organises the festival, met me at Lewes station and guided me on the short walk to the venue, (Lewes looked charming in the sunshine, a very English market town), a converted church. We had to start more or less straight away with me delivering an edited version of a lecture I'd done (which in turn had been adapted from the conclusion to my book, *The Battle for Britain*) for Five Million Questions at Dundee University earlier this year (or was it late last year? I lose track). This appeared to go down reasonably well, and despite being knackered my delivery was quite fluent.

The audience (surprisingly big for 10am on a Sunday) seemed to engage with what I was saying, which was gratifying, and the questions – all of them cogent and sensible – flowed thick and fast. In fact (as I said to someone afterwards) the quality of questions easily surpassed that at many Scottish events I've done, showing a surprising awareness of the nuance of the debate. It was lots of fun, particularly the Q&A, and afterwards I even managed to shift a few copies of the referendum book (and one short voters' guide). Quite a few Scots expats chatted to me afterwards: one lady from Ayrshire said she'd feel 'really sad' if Scotland voted Yes, but then surprised me by saying in that event she'd move back, for she'd no longer feel happy 'being Scottish in England'. I told her I'd felt something similar when I was living in London, that there was a specific 'being a Scot in London' mindset.

Bit of a travel faff after a quick wander round the town, including Anne of Cleves' old house: the train to Gatwick easy enough (got talking to a Sydney-based English expat who'd been at my event), but then the flight to Paris CDG was delayed and it was also overbooked, so I didn't know until the last moment whether I was going to get on (I did). I then arrived too late to get a train from the airport to Blois, so had to get the RER into the city and managed (just) to make the 7.27pm train via Orleans. The next four days (a gathering in advance of Kath Haddon's forthcoming wedding) had better be relaxing as I'm on the cusp of exhaustion.

Monday, 21 July 2014 (France)

Swam (great pool at the château); ate and drank. There was wifi but not of good enough quality to prevent me (almost) relaxing. Got an email from this chap in response to my *Herald* column:

> 'Governments should always listen to the voices of the people.' And so they should. David Torrance.
> Interesting article today David. Would you therefore encourage ordinary folks to engage with the political elite or would you agree with the majority of your compatriots that this would be beyond them? I refer you to www.freeparliament.org.uk Kind regards, Robert Durward

I had a cursory glance at the web link but couldn't figure out what he was talking about. The château is near Blois, which, by coincidence, is 'twinned' with Lewes, where of course I was yesterday.

Lots of good chat; I grilled Rosie (a doctor) on the SNP narrative about the NHS and she said it was a caricature to suggest the English reforms amounted to privatisation (although it certainly made it easier) or in any way diminished the principle of free-at-the-point-of-use universal service, and of course she's right. Later Greg, her brother, gave me his typically cost-benefit analysis of independence, saying that on balance it would diminish Britain's international standing and therefore he'd rather there was a No vote, while Matt, the Geordie husband of a childhood friend of Kath's, told me he 'loved' Scotland as a result of childhood holidays (his father had also studied in Aberdeen) but said he could understand why many Scots wanted to vote Yes.

The casual terminology of the others brought out my inner Nationalist: references to 'English plugs', the GCSEs we'd 'all' studied, 'English weather' and (more justifiably) 'English architecture' vindicated Jim Sillars' remark about Britain or the UK being simply 'England with bits added' to most of the occupants of these isles. Only Kath, whose late mother was Scottish, was more alert to such things.

Tuesday, 22 July 2014 (France)

Swam, ate and drank (too much).

Wednesday, 23 July 2014 (France)

Swam, ate and drank (some more). President Hollande has apparently made a speech which could be interpreted as opposing Scottish and Catalan independence. Half planned to watch the Commonwealth Games opening ceremony online but a) the wifi probably couldn't have coped with it and b) we were getting cooked dinner by a local chef (fantastic). Thought back to 1986 when the Games were last in Scotland and I was almost nine years old. Afterwards we played a game called 'Mafia', which was surprisingly good fun.

Thursday, 24 July 2014 (France)

Drove to Orleans in the morning then caught a train back to Paris Austerlitz. We had time for a quick lunch near Gare du Nord before the others caught the Eurostar and I made my way to CDG for the late afternoon flight back to Edinburgh, where it was almost as sunny as in France. Caught Jim Sillars on *Scotland Tonight* saying that the Scottish working classes were more politicised than since he first got involved in politics (!); also predicted Yes would win by 55/45 and the proportion would have been greater still had Margo still been alive (he's attempting to raise £50k for a 'MargoMobile'). He did make one good point: that instead of making speeches in Liverpool, Alex Salmond should be speaking in places like Drumchapel ('Alex's great with people when they meet him'), but then the First Minister does seem to like speaking in grand settings, and Drumchapel ain't grand.

Friday, 25 July 2014 (Edinburgh)

Had lunch with a Better Together contact at La Garrigue on Jeffrey Street. He hinted at cash-flow issues and, despite being annoyed at Labour campaigning techniques ('all national in tone, they don't do local as they've never really had to defend many seats'), he reckons Yes will only get 37 per cent of the vote. On the Lib Dems he reckons West Aberdeenshire will fall to the Conservatives though Michael Moore will be harder to budge; Jo Swinson, meanwhile, is probably on a 'shoogly peg' despite ongoing speculation that she'll replace Carmichael as Secretary of State for Scotland. But when? The election is less than a year away and we've just had a reshuffle.

Did a quick TV interview with RTE which was quite good fun, the reporter joked that an independent Scotland shouldn't look to Ireland as a model for a hybrid public/commercial broadcaster. In the evening I went to see *Dawn of the Planet of the Apes* with a policeman friend, which satisfied my desire for apocalyptic (or in this case post-apocalyptic) movies. Over food afterwards he said Police Scotland had been put on alert for 19 September (no leave, etc) as they're expecting trouble if there's a No vote. After a few drinks I walked home on Calton Road and got abuse from a middle-aged guy outside that weird club near the flat, narrowing his eyes as I passed and saying 'Hey, you're that political writer aren't you?' I glanced back but said nothing so he started shouting: 'Not a very good political writer, very poor quality,' (a weirdly specific insult) and, when I continued to ignore him, 'you write shite' and 'speccy bastard'. Charming.

Saturday, 26 July 2014 (Cambridge)

On the move again to catch an early-ish flight to Stansted in order to attend Kath's wedding in Cambridge. More sunshine so I walked from the railway station to Christ's College, where I'd booked a room for the night (and which was also the location for the wedding). This led to the following exchange:

Porter: Which European country are you from?
Me: Well, I'm from Edinburgh, which is part of this country.
Carl (a friend of Greg's): For the time being!

Fnar fnar. The porter looked quite embarrassed.

Also spoke to Greg's step-granny who on discovering I was 'Scots' spoke very animatedly about the independence referendum, saying she 'desperately' wanted Scotland to stay in the UK but if she were also 'Scots' then she'd vote Yes because 'it's exciting and new and England is so stuck in its ways'. The wedding ceremony (civil) also had a Scottish flavour, with the choir singing, barbershop-style, Sir Harry Lauder's 'Keep Right On to the End of the Road' as we walked across the Fellows' Garden for a drinks reception.

At dinner later I sat next to a chap who now works with Greg but used to work in the Prime Minister's Strategy Unit. He reckoned the drive for independence was mainly about 'emotion' but also appeared to buy into the notion that Scotland was a 'social democratic' country whereas the rest of the UK was not.

Sunday, 27 July 2014 (Cambridge)

Had breakfast in the Fellows' Garden (there was a private swimming pool at the back, near Milton's Mulberry tree), which was incredibly pleasant, followed by punting on the Cam, which was also incredibly pleasant. I don't usually enjoy weddings but this one was top notch, and it helped I'd met a few of those present in France last week. After a picnic lunch on the banks of the river I had to scoot off to write my *Herald* column, after which I caught a flight back to Edinburgh. More good weather – perhaps it'll be a nice summer after all.

Monday, 28 July 2014 (Edinburgh and St Andrews)

Met my Better Together contact for tea at Brew Lab in the morning. Like Rob Shorthouse (who'd texted in response to my *Herald* column to say there was a 'very noticeable move to us in pretty much every part of the country'), he was confident the polls were moving in their direction, with the British Election Survey just having published (with incorrect numbers) polling showing the biggest swing to No to date. My contact also said the 'more powers' argument needed more work, not so much on the detail but in terms of convincing some Undecideds it was actually going to happen. Also speculated as to what Yes Scotland had planned to rekickstart the campaign following the Commonwealth Games; he reckoned it would be something big but I've no idea what that could be at this late stage.

Back at the flat Jason told me that at a Tattoo rehearsal (he's directing his school choir) he'd been warned 'as a Tattoo employee' not to say anything about the referendum, and we joked about whether that extended to him having conversations with me. After a quick coffee at Holyrood I caught the 4pm train to Leuchars, intending to cycle to St Andrews (on another nice day) for the second 'launch' of the short independence referendum guide I've written with Jamie Maxwell, although once again I find myself doing it solo. RAF jets roared overhead as I headed towards St Andrews.

The crowd at Waterstones was small but attentive. The questions were quite good although one lady in the front row was just confused and didn't look any less confused once I'd stopped talking. Chatted to a few people afterwards, two of whom – No voters – were rightly sceptical about recent reports that 700,000 Scots would leave the country in the event of a Yes vote. 'Most of them have never even been out of Scotland!' one exclaimed. Another lady, who said her son was a BBC producer, said she had been inclined towards voting Yes on a cultural basis but said having witnessed 'raw Nationalism' and also looking into some of the economic arguments, she was now going to vote No.

Cycled back to Leuchars and an officious East Coast Trains guard wouldn't let me onto the train because the open carriage door wasn't for 'public access', and when I told him my bike folded up he looked dubious and continued to resist. Incredibly frustrating; I then embarked on a Twitter barrage at the East Coast account. They promised to look into it.

Wednesday, 30 July 2014 (Edinburgh)

To the Raeburn Room at Old College for a Round Table to which Professor James Mitchell of Edinburgh University had invited me. There were three speakers, one each from England, Northern Ireland and Wales. Mike Kenny from Queen Mary rebutted the line that the London/English media was ignoring the indyref debate (good for him) and said it was the most comprehensive debate about the UK since the mid-1990s. Also pointed out that gradual shift in English public opinion began before devolution, due to globalisation, rise of the European issue and a significant rise in hostility to London. Later he thanked me for plugging his book, *The Politics of English Nationhood*, in a recent column and was very nice about my book *The Battle for Britain* – said it had been useful preparation for his visits to Scotland. He also expressed sympathy for federalism, so I made a mental note to send him a copy of my recent tract.

Cathy Gormley-Heenan from Queen's University was very funny on Northern Ireland, and later concluded that a Yes vote would be a confirmation that Scotland was different from England, whereas Unionism in the province rests on it being as 'British as Finchley'. Characterised the relationship between Scotland and NI as 'faraway, so close', and also that the province could end up with more devolved power than it could cope with (i.e. when it comes to welfare, which is a historical hangover from the days of Stormont). More widely, she said there was hardly any discussion about the ramifications of a Yes vote in NI, which contradicts what others have told me. Roger Scully from Wales pointed out that the most important relationship in Wales was that with England; also warned that the UK media ignores Ireland (very true) and the same fate would probably befall an independent Scotland, thus making a nonsense of Salmond's 'progressive beacon' claim. Scully also rubbished the post-referendum chances of federalism or even a UK constitutional convention, which was depressing to listen to, but then he's probably right.

During the open discussion I made the point that referendum discourse seemed ignorant of the nature and history of the UK, which was a problem, while highlighting the obvious U-turn in terms of Tory thinking about the Barnett Formula. Also agreed with Mike Kenny about the London-based media, arguing that, on the contrary, the Scottish media doesn't really understand 'English' politics and tends to caricature it while ignoring growing constitutional movement (as charted in Kenny's book). Ended by mounting a half-hearted defence of a federal UK, which seemed to surprise James. Winding up, he appeared to have bought into the Yes line that Better Together isn't holding any meetings (I've been to a few), while 'normal folk' dominate Yes meetings, a phenomenon he reckoned would be difficult to put 'back in the box' in the event of a Yes or No vote.

Some evening escapism by seeing Burt Bacharach at the Playhouse with Mum, which was good fun though let down by the audience who, as she succinctly put it, behaved as 'if they were in their own front room', constantly coming and going from the middle of rows, stomping up and down the aisles (even during quiet numbers) and generally being noisy. Bacharach only sang a few numbers himself, including 'Alfie' and 'The Look of Love': his voice is decent enough, but usefully the lead vocalists were actually quite good. He told the audience at one point that he'd first visited Edinburgh as Marlene Dietrich's accompanist, which must have been a long time ago (Roddy Martine later told me via Facebook that he'd been in the audience). The inevitable encore ended with an audience sing-a-long of 'Raindrops Keep Falling on My Head', which was cheesy but fun.

Thursday, 31 July 2014 (Edinburgh, Glasgow & Dundee

In the afternoon I headed through to Glasgow to soak up some Commonwealth Games atmosphere and visit the Empire Café in the Merchant City, which was great (the brainchild of novelist Louise Welsh). After that I saw the Douglas Gordon exhibition at the Museum of Modern Art, which was also great. Then another train up to Dundee to launch the indyref voters' guide, this time with Jamie Maxwell, at Waterstones; the line from Perth to Dundee, which I don't think I've done before, was really quite scenic, skirting along a river for much of it, and through some great countryside.

There was a good crowd at the bookshop together with some of the usual suspects. The acoustics weren't great so Jamie and I had to stand up and basically shout, and while I tried to play it straight, Jamie couldn't resist a partisan pitch (full of his usual mix of perceptive commentary and leftie analysis), compelling me to make the contrary case, which I didn't want to do. Still, some of the questions were quite good and Chris Whatley, looking relaxed now he's (semi) retired, was on hand to act as compere. I didn't hang around afterwards as I was tired and keen to get back to Edinburgh as quickly as possible.

Friday, 1 August 2014 (London)

Caught the 8.30am train to the Imperial Capital and spent the afternoon cycling between various exhibitions, all of which were interesting in different ways: Sir Kenneth Clark and 'Civilisation' at Tate Britain, First World War art at the recently refurbished Imperial War Museum and finally the architect Louis Kahn (of FDR memorial fame) at the Design Museum. All the while I was fielding calls from RTE, BBC, etc about Tuesday's debate, but nothing too onerous.

Susan Flockhart at the *Sunday Herald* also forwarded me an email from the novelist Alan Warner (who wrote *The Sopranos*, though not, as I initially thought, the HBO miniseries), responding to my pop at him in my most recent column. Headed 'File Under: From "A Creative" to one of "The Chattering Class!"' it was a bit rambly and puerile, basically saying I was a 'Tory' and a 'Unionist' and therefore didn't know what I was talking about. After a couple of drinks with Steve Richmond near the City, I cycled to Aldwych to see the evening performance of Hilary Mantel's *Bring Up the Bodies*.

Saturday, 2 August 2014 (London)

Got up reasonably early and cycled to Sutton House, a National Trust property near where Michael lives in Clapton. It was built by Sir Ralph Sadleir, an aide to Thomas Cromwell who featured (fleetingly) in *Bring Up the Bodies* last night. Nice enough house, but a curious jumble of Tudor, Georgian and Victorian architecture. Interestingly, in 1547 Ralph became ambassador to Scotland and one of the last things he did in public life was act as a judge at the 'trial' of Mary, Queen of Scots.

Michael's barbeque in the evening was fun, even though I wasn't imbibing. James McGachie, who'd come down from Edinburgh, got merry quite quickly and ended up spreading Yes propaganda to anyone who'd listen, while Michael and I chatted briefly to an interesting Czech girl who said she still didn't consider herself 'different' from a Slovak; she added that independence in the early 1990s had been a political rather than a popular movement. Got another long email from the writer Alan Warner, but it was slightly friendlier this time.

Sunday, 3 August 2014 (London & Edinburgh)

Caught the train back to Edinburgh at 12.30pm and bashed out my *Herald* column on the First World War and the Commonwealth Games. In the evening caught up with Richard Pyle for a drink, who was on typically engaging form. He's so unlike his brother (Colin) politically that it's hard to remember they're actually brothers. Told me he'd largely tuned out of the referendum debate and couldn't wait for it all 'to go away'.

Monday, 4 August 2014 (Glasgow & Edinburgh)

Up uncomfortably early to get through to Glasgow for the First World War service at the city's Cathedral. Bumped into David Ross from Better Together just after leaving Queen Street Station and he agreed with me that tomorrow evening's debate would most likely be a damp squib. We were both amused by the sight of large Union flags (and, of course, Saltires) in George Square.

Despite all the flummery and 'security', getting into the Cathedral was straightforward enough, although I arrived far too early and ended up twiddling my thumbs for about an hour and a half. An historical note by Sir Hew Strachan was on each seat and it was quite striking to read that in the months preceding the outbreak of war on 4 August 1914 Irish Home Rule had dominated the domestic news agenda. I sat between Auslan Cramb from the *Telegraph* and Stephen McGinty from the *Scotsman*, which was convivial enough.

Things finally got moving at around 10am and the media row at the back provided a good view of the dignitaries as they filed into the church: the Prince of Wales in all his finery, Ed Miliband, the First Minister, etc. Amid the pinched and serious faces of local Glaswegian worthies, the Commonwealth delegates added some much-needed colour; the row in front of us was occupied by a splendidly attired delegation from Lesotho, including one jovial looking chap in a magnificent green uniform.

The service itself was brisk, sombre and ecumenical (Iain Torrance was in the procession, as were Anglicans and Roman Catholics). Some good music and readings that ranged from so-so to genuinely quite moving. It also felt very colonial, the Governors-General of Australia and New Zealand and the High Commissioner for Canada and India all taking part. The Prime Minister read a portion of St Mark like a political speech, adding a random 'amen' at the end. Sir Trevor McDonald and Kate Adie added some televisual glamour.

When the service ended the initial procession included members of the Armed Forces walking two by two with young schoolchildren, which was strangely affecting, and as we filed out of the Cathedral (David Mundell nodded at me on the way out) all the flags of the Commonwealth were lined up in front of us. I wandered down to George Square with Stephen McGinty but ended up catching the 11.45am train back to Edinburgh, where I bumped into Jim Sillars. Said he'd just been through to get pictures taken for his MargoMobile tour, which kicks off tomorrow. I asked if he'd had a similar bus in Govan in 1988 (not to mention Alex Neil's 'Snappy' bus in 1989) and he said yes, but this one would be 'much classier'. He repeated his belief that Yes would win and that socialism was undergoing a revival. Glimpsed Ian Rankin at Waverley Station, I think with his son.

Later I saw *Matt Forde: 24 Hour Political Party People* at the Pleasance and he touched on this morning's events and the stooshie over Ed Miliband's wreath (although he appeared to think this had taken place at the Cenotaph in London). He was generally very good on UKIP *et al* (a fine mimic too) but less certain when it came to Scotland, which occupied a few minutes, just some tired old stuff about Cybernats, although his line about admitting to being British was like coming out in the 1960s was quite funny. Just before we went in one of the guys flyering outside asked if I was the 'journalist and writer in the No camp', to which I replied that apart from the last bit, yes. He confessed to being a political junkie and said he was nearly finished Gordon Brown's book ('he makes a solid argument') and planned to read mine (*The Battle for Britain*) next. Good for him! He even looked relatively normal.

Spent the day fielding calls from radio and TV producers ahead of tomorrow's Great Debate (which I doubt will be that great). Later, RTE texted jauntily: 'One more question – are you a Yes or a No for independence?' Whatever happened to professional neutrality? I (almost) give up. Popped into Holyrood a couple of times and at one point passed Kenny MacAskill (currently under fire for wanting to arm some Scottish police officers), but when I said 'Hi Kenny' I got barely a grunt in response; weird to think I first met him as a kid when he would turn up at the house wanting to speak to Dad about SNP stuff.

Tuesday, 5 August 2014 (Edinburgh & Glasgow)

Up just before 7am to speak to Nicky Campbell on BBC Radio 5 Live about tonight's debate. Bumped into Jim Naughtie at The Tun, who'd just finished telling *Today* that the SNP might consider a second referendum as some sort of game-changer (he conceded both on air and to me that this wasn't likely). I had an hour to kill before doing another interview (on the same subject) for RTE so I went to Foodies for some tea to read the papers. The only other people inside were Nicola Sturgeon and Peter Murrell, also going through the papers and presumably planning their day. Final interview of the morning was with Ciaran Jenkins from Channel 4 News, who said he'd had flak on Twitter yesterday for doing a Scottish story as 'North of England correspondent'.

At around noon I got to St Andrew Square to take part in one of David Greig's 'All Back to Bowie's' shows. It was all very Natty, and just before I gave my 'provocation' on the 'idea of Britain', the blogger Andrew Tickell said to me: 'Ah, you're the designated bastard.' To be fair, there was no pretence as to balance (it was five to one against, including the chairman Peter Arnott, who kept shooting me pitying glances). I thought my pitch was quite good (David later said as much), i.e. the idea of Britain lived on because the SNP had requisitioned it, but none of the panellists bothered addressing the point, instead making the usual woolly arguments conflating independence with protecting the British welfare state, how 'they'd left us behind' rather than the other way round, etc. Step forward James Robertson and Neal Ascherson, the latter sacrificing facts and solid analysis for a nice turn of phrase (as someone later remarked to me, Neal and Isobel Lindsay – another panellist – were much more interesting 30 years ago). Basically they justified everything I'd written two weeks ago in my *Herald* column. Tickell was at least funny, but kicked off an incredibly patronising discussion about how Yes should be more understanding of No people and 'Britishness'. They all nodded in pompous agreement. I

The author taking part in an All Back to Bowie's event during the Fringe festival.
(Photo: Alex Aitchison)

kept catching Alex Massie's eye in the audience and he looked askance at the madness emanating from the platform. Mum and Dad had claimed my two complimentary tickets and seemed to enjoy it. A chap called 'Wounded Knee' performed two terrific renditions of Hamish Henderson songs, while a West Coast poet called Jim Monoghan was also good. At the end they read out audience attempts to complete the sentence 'Britain is...' which, of course, had produced predictable bile as well as more thoughtful contributions (probably from Alex Massie).

After that I caught the train to Glasgow to do a pointlessly brief interview for the BBC News Channel with Iain Macwhirter, immaculate as ever in a suit. Afterwards I chatted to Bernard Ponsonby outside the Royal Conservatoire and he promised to give me a 'blow-by-blow' account of the negotiations leading up to the debate once the referendum was over; he said both sides were extremely sensitive, even questioning him on the angle of the lectern. He agreed when I said Salmond would be trying hard not to be aggressive and would therefore end up being boring. Managed to spend a couple of hours shopping for clothes (a rare treat) and having something to eat before the madness ensued. Baroness Warsi has resigned from the Government in protest at its stance on Gaza. Not quite sure what to make of that.

I arrived at the venue as the audience was making its way in, and after much toing and froing Howard Simpson (from STV) finally agreed to let me into the theatre space itself rather than watching the debate on a flat-screen television in the 'spin room'. I'm glad I did because the atmosphere was electric inside, though not initially. Darling's opening statement was dreadful (no idea who wrote it) and he was clearly quite nervous, while Salmond's opening pitch was quite nicely crafted ('within 10 miles of where I'm standing in Glasgow there are 35 food banks... within 25 miles of where I'm standing there is Europe's largest concentration of weapons of mass destruction') and he was much more poised. Bernard, who did a typically superb job, tripped Darling up over more powers, which was weird – though evidence that Alistair simply doesn't get that aspect of the campaign.

Things only really got going during the cross-examination section, particularly when Darling got stuck into Salmond on the mooted currency union, and the FM was surprisingly ineffective in response, just burbling on in his usual way. And when the tables were turned, Salmond wasted loads of time banging on about Unionists warning about alien attacks and driving on the opposite side of the road (as I tweeted during the debate, 'Salmond loves quoting newspaper cuttings – with off-the-record quotes – as if they're killer debating points. They're not. They're cuttings.'), which just came across as frivolous. Having rediscovered his Mojo, Alistair had some good (obviously pre-prepared) one-liners, such as 'I didn't vote for you but I'm stuck with you'. On the other hand, Salmond monstered Darling over David Cameron's statement that an independent Scotland could be a 'successful' country – did he agree? For some reason Darling felt unable to answer, though surely an obvious retort would have been: 'Yes, but I believe it could be even more successful as part of the UK.'

The audience, meanwhile, was a bit feral, repeatedly booing both participants and yelling 'Answer the question!' Bernard even had to intervene at points and ask for some decorum, but it was great fun (goodness knows how it came across on television). I snuck out of the theatre towards the end of the Q&A (in which Salmond was better than Darling) in preparation for giving my response from the 'spin room': I just said it was difficult to identify a clear winner, although Darling had done well on currency but he'd missed an opportunity to set out a positive vision, etc (usefully, my pre-debate analysis on the *Telegraph* website had been broadly accurate). Pat Kane was on after me and just spoke nonsense about Salmond and Darling working together to achieve social democracy. Yawn.

After that was a bit of a whirlwind. Gave some brief reaction to Mark MacKinnon of the Toronto *Globe and Mail* then leapt into a cab to Pacific Quay to do *Newsnight* and then *Scotland 2014*. I assumed the former would be a well-oiled machine, but far from it. There was no meet and greet, while the newsroom camera didn't have a feed from London, so I couldn't hear what was going on (nor did I know who I was appearing with). As it happens, it was Lesley Riddoch and Isabel Hardman (in the studio) from the *Spectator*. Kirsty Wark (the presenter) then introduced me as a 'No voter', which was irritating; I toyed briefly with saying something on air but decided against it. Interview was fine, though the audio feed was still terrible. By contrast *Scotland 2014* with Sarah Smith was a breeze. I was on with Alex Bell, who told me I was having 'a good referendum' before we went on air (is that like having a good war?), which was nice of him. Also said he had a book pending from Luath about the SNP's referendum strategy, which should be interesting.

Scotland 2014 finished later than usual so they laid on a driver back to Edinburgh (god bless the licence fee). David Greig (and Bella Caledonia) tweeted asking if I'd been 'outed' by *Newsnight*, so I was quick to put them right. A producer from the *Today Programme*, meanwhile, sent me a snarky text to say they couldn't use me on tomorrow's programme because I'd been on *Newsnight* and they have a policy, etc. Earlier, the *World Service* had also dropped me because I wouldn't let them describe me as a No supporter (still, it would have meant getting up at 6am). Got home at 12.30am knackered but feeling fulfilled.

Wednesday, 6 August 2014 (Edinburgh)

Up at just before 7am to do another interview for BBC Radio 5 Live on the debate with Nicky Campbell, and then another one with RTE (this time over the phone) at 8.45am. Felt exhausted so went back to bed, waking up a couple of hours later to an email from Liz Rawlings at *Newsnight* apologising for Kirsty Wark introducing me as a No voter. It was thoughtful of her to do so, but a bit late. I made a point of tweeting at David Greig and Bella Caledonia to mention this, as they'd both referred to my 'outing' the night before.

Today's papers have all decided that last night was really bad for Alex Salmond, which I think is overstating things a bit, although there's probably the usual gap between how it came over in the hall itself as opposed to television, the latter of course being the more authentic experience, given the viewing figures of 1.7 million (around half a million of whom were online only, so probably not voters); i.e. Darling appeared to me very nervous while Salmond came across as the slicker of the two, the exact opposite of how it was reported to have come across on the box. Allan Massie emailed to say that ITV Border hadn't shown the debate, instead screening Alan Titchmarsh's *Love Your Garden* ('Candide's response to politics, after all.').[3]

---

3 Actually, ITV Border did show it, only it seems many viewers in the region were unaware of how to see it.

On the phone to Mum (who'd only seen bits of it) I overheard Dad saying that he'd watched it in a pub with his SNP mates and they'd booed when I came on from the 'spin room', although he then grudgingly added that what I'd said was fair (this always surprises people, for some reason). I tweeted about this (for a laugh) and Brian Wilson, being uncharacteristically rude, added a comment on Facebook: 'So they should. You were talking uncharacteristic crap. Hope you're not taking the groat.'

Still, the wider point is that the usual duff expectation management from the SNP helped create the impression that their man had lost badly. As in the Euro elections, he and they raised expectations, saying Darling would have the 'heebie jeebies', Wishart invoking Bannockburn, etc, so come the crunch – when Salmond didn't completely balls it up – he came off looking much worse than the reality. In the afternoon I went to review the Scottish Youth Theatre's referendum show *Now's the Hour*, which was actually quite enjoyable and then gave Nick Lester and Sam a brief tour of the Scottish Parliament, chatting to Alex Neil ('Eee, Salmond won!') and Ruth Davidson ('Salmond didn't do as badly as people say') *en route*. Back at home I did a Skype interview for CNN (lots of dumb questions) and then a radio interview at Hemma with a delightfully scruffy Swiss journalist called Andrea Netzer.

Saw a couple of mediocre shows in the evening with Lewis, one about the Toronto mayor, Rob Ford (weird, but with flashes of inspiration) and another featuring the journalist and stand-up comic Viv Groskop, who I remember from a press trip to Moscow back in 2000 (she recognised me, oddly, but then there were only four of us in the audience). I was quite tired so was home by 11pm, where I caught up with some articles online, including this from the delightfully batty Robin McAlpine:

> You wake up to the phone app that gives you your morning radio show covering the news the way you want. By lunch you get a digest of the most important things happening around the world that day. Perhaps you get a summary of the best of the day's blogs in the mid-afternoon. Regular high-quality essays, articles and analysis are a rolling feature. When you get home your evening newscast is waiting for you. Just in time to grab tea and pop out to your local Common where you'll take in a really interesting political talk, catch some music or a comedian and then talk until late with new friends about land reform or the citizens' income or political lobbying or whatever catches your mind tonight. You go to bed with schemes and plans and hopes and ideas. You are ready to organise. And this is your day. Every day.

Good grief, talk about being trapped in a middle-class bubble. I'm not sure I'd want to live in a Robin McAlpine theme park.

Thursday, 7 August 2014 (Edinburgh)

Today's my 37th birthday – as I tweeted last night, how the f*** did that happen? Went for a swim then met a friend for a late breakfast at Hemma. He's now properly working at the Foreign and Commonwealth Office, thus why he was in attendance at Glasgow Cathedral on Monday morning (he told me a very funny story about a DCMS (Department for Culture, Media and Sport) official asking Theresa May which country she was from).

Headed to Holyrood just before noon to catch First Minister's Questions, the first after a mini recess, and of course the first since Tuesday's big debate. Predictably, Salmond had toughened up his line on the currency union (in as much as he could), saying several times that 'it's our pound and we're keeping it', which isn't even a very good sound-bite, let alone a convincing policy. Also repeatedly referred to page 110 of the White Paper, which of course didn't actually cover what he claimed it did.

Apparently the media briefing afterwards was a bit of a car crash. They really have boxed themselves into a corner on this point. After a quick (and small) lunch the SNP MSP Christian Allard (charming, as usual) asked if I'd do a quick interview with a visiting French radio journalist, and of course I said yes. Also bumped into Murdo Fraser, who said he was thinking about applying for funding (possibly from Joseph Rowntree) to launch a federalism campaign.

After that I had to meet a PhD student from the University of Oregon who's studying referendum campaigning techniques. He didn't take many notes as I rambled on, which clearly meant I wasn't saying anything he hadn't heard (or read) before. At one point Anas Sarwar popped over for a chat, no doubt pleased about that day's *Daily Record*, which splashed 'OUCH' underneath a length quote from a 'senior' SNP source slagging off Salmond's performance in the debate. In the afternoon I caught Alan Bissett's play *The Pure, the Dead and the Brilliant* at the Assembly Ballroom (Ricky Ross from Deacon Blue and the playwright were also in the audience), which was as bad as the preview at the SNP conference suggested it would be. Well performed with some nice lines and comic moments, it just didn't convince as political 'satire' – too black and white, no nuance, etc.

In the afternoon Peter (a friend who now says he's a 'soft' Yes voter, having watched the debate last night) and I wandered up to the Old Royal High School (great birthday weather) to see an exhibition in the Edinburgh Art Festival. To be honest I really just wanted to see inside the old Scottish Grand Committee chamber (as kitted out for the aborted Scottish Assembly in the late 1970s), and it was quite atmospheric. We then climbed Calton Hill where I had, for the first time, a proper look at the Parliament vigil memorial.

A birthday meal with the parentals, Sheila and Raymond at Zizzis just after six. Raymond had written me a birthday poem incorporating the names of all my books, which was nice of him. I did a referendum straw poll and found Dad for, Mum and Sheila against and Raymond in favour (though he might have been joking). He also claimed Geoffrey was a 'Yes man' while Alan, a creative type, was leaning that way too. That means the Dickson/Torrance clans are majority Yessers.

In the evening Jason (my flatmate and landlord) took me to see a show for my birthday, *Margaret Thatcher: Soho Queen*, which was obviously well chosen. After that we hung around George Square for a bit (where I bumped into Neil Mackinnon, head of press at the Fringe) and then caught a cab to Hemma for the tail end of a friend's leaving do, so tail end that he'd already left. Everyone extremely lively. It was fun chatting to Ruth Davidson (who said I'd been too 'kind' to Salmond after the debate) and her new partner, as well as an old colleague from STV, who reckoned Salmond had been 'found out' (a good way of putting it), i.e. trying to debate FMQs-style in front of an audience of 1.7 million. She'd heard that the FM was very nervous beforehand, which was interesting.

Friday, 8 August 2014 (Edinburgh)

Mercifully, a quieter day. Got up late, went for a swim then caught up with this diary, wrote up some reviews of referendum-related Fringe shows for the *Herald* and generally mooched. In the afternoon I walked to the Traverse to see *Spoiling*, a play set after a Yes vote and featuring the Scottish Foreign Secretary-designate preparing to make a speech with her British counterpart. For some reason I messed up the booking and it turns out my ticket was for yesterday: only some sweet talking of the press office got me in.

I'm glad they did because it was a good little play (only 45 minutes), certainly much better than the reviews thus far, even though the playwright appeared not to understand the difference between a party political special adviser and an impartial civil servant. The main protagonist, a Foreign Secretary-designate called simply 'Fiona', was (to me) a cross between Christina McKelvie and Fiona Hyslop, but utterly believable. 'Oh Plan B!' she exclaims at one stage, 'there's finally a fucking Plan B,' which got a knowing laugh from the audience. The premise was tension between her and the British Foreign Secretary ('the Eton Mess') just as the 'settlement talks' were drawing to a close, which was a much more interesting dynamic than that explored (or rather not explored) by Alan Bissett *et al*.

Later I met Pablo Rodero, a freelancer working for newspapers in

Madrid, who told me the Spanish state was still very Francist (or was it Francoist?) when it came to dealing with Catalonia, and we agreed the Spanish government's strategy in this respect was nuts. Just after that I bumped into Ian Robertson near the Festival Theatre, the erstwhile Lib Dem by-election candidate who's now teaching in Beijing, having married a Chinese girl. Said he'd met a couple of Scots working at the British Embassy (in Beijing) who reckoned it was going to be a Yes vote.

En route to the Sweet Grassmarket (a Fringe venue) someone yelled 'Vote Yes, Torrance' from a moving car, which was a pretty direct campaigning method. Reviewed *3,000 Trees*, one of two plays about the SNP activist Willie MacRae, where I attempted to smile at Joyce McMillan but she just ignored me – so much for commentariat camaraderie.

Saturday, 9 August 2014 (Edinburgh)

Cycled to St Andrew Square after a swim to take part in another *All Back to Bowie's* event, this time on 'Tory Scotland' with Alex Massie and Lindsay Macintosh from *The Times* and with David Greig in the chair. This turned out to be pretty good. I managed to cover some of the history while Lindsay talked about future prospects – there was broad agreement that the party was buoyed up by the referendum and could hope for a modest recovery.

In the queue for Iain Macwhirter at the Book Festival later on, Brian Cox asked me quite abruptly if he was in the right queue (I should have said no), then I heard him chatting with someone behind me as we moved into the main tent, mainly speculation that Sir Tom Devine would declare for Yes at his event with the First Minister on Monday. Iain was a sellout, which is a testament to his pulling power.

Under questioning he tried to draw a distinction between journalists declaring for a particularl party during a General Election campaign and the referendum (which, bizarrely, he elevated 'above politics'), but of course that's bullshit. Also said he'd be voting Yes ('there's no doubt about that', cue smattering of applause) and went on to say that anyone writing day-to-day on the referendum (i.e. me) should do likewise as 'people should know where they're coming from'. Not sure why he feels he's in a position to tell other journalists how to conduct themselves.

Sarah Smith was excellent in the chair, asking all the right questions and referring at one point to the shift from 'could to should' in terms of independence, which was spot-on. Other Macwhirter nuggets: 'People keep telling me there'll be a federal UK after a No vote' (who?), 'We'll just be a tartan theme park' (he was probably joking), and speculation Salmond will have to resign if there's a No vote. Today there's a pretty devastating poll in the *Scottish Daily Mail* that shows Salmond was perceived by viewers to have decisively lost last Tuesday's debate (also conducted by Survation, which usually *overstates* pro-indy support).

In the evening I heard Holst's Planets with Sheila at the Usher Hall, which was easily digestible and brilliantly performed. Left early (much to Sheila's understandable irritation) to attend the Book Festival opening party in Charlotte Square. This was quite good fun. Chatted to Mark from Cargo who published Iain Macwhirter's *Road to Referendum* and also Susan Deacon, who was very nice about my output. Saw Nick Barley briefly and he said my event (with Henry McLeish) next Saturday was selling well.

Sunday, 10 August 2014 (Edinburgh)

After writing my *Herald* column in some haste I caught the end of the First World War parade as it made its way down the Royal Mile (Magnus Linklater, whose father Eric fought, waved at me); also bumped into Ruth Davidson. Otherwise the day was dominated by *The James Plays*, a trio of historical plays by Rona Munro at the Festival Theatre. The first, *James I*, was terrific, and in the interval I bumped into Quentin Letts from the *Daily Mail*, who'd come up for a few days to review a few different productions. 'Salmond's going to lose this thing isn't he?' he asked at one point, chat having inevitably turned to the referendum.

James II, unfortunately, didn't quite live up to expectations, not least because its predecessor was so good. It also wasn't really *about* anything, which is a bit of a problem considering it was supposed to be a drama. In the longer interval between that and *James III* I chatted to Mure Dickie from the *Financial Times*, who as ever questioned and probed everything I said (in a good way); he's probably the most scrupulously balanced observer of the indyref there is. Also saw Kenny Farquharson and John McLellan, who were sitting near me in the stalls. Met Keith Bruce and Neil Cooper from the *Herald* for the first time and the former urged me to do more reviews, which is good.

James III also felt a bit flat, although the Danish actress from *The Killing* made it quite watchable, very good as the real power behind the Scottish throne, and with a good closing speech which is sure to annoy Joyce McMillan ('You've got fuck all except attitude'). In my head I was constantly comparing it unfavourably with Hilary Mantel's *Wolf Hall* and *Bring Up the Bodies* which I'd seen in London the previous month: Rona Munro doesn't strike me as a top-flight playwright (especially compared with Mantel) and this trio – naturally hyped up as the theatrical event of the Festival – was probably a little over-ambitious. I also couldn't get the old Channel 4 sketch show *Absolutely* out of my head, for Gordon Kennedy was part of the cast and adopted a similarly whiny Scottish accent. Remember Stoneybridge?

Monday, 11 August 2014 (Edinburgh)

Went for a swim and then headed to Charlotte Square to see Sir Tom Devine and Alex Salmond do their double act at the Book Festival. There was an amusing moment in the authors' yurt as I dropped off my bike in the cloakroom. As I made my way back out the First Minister and his entourage swept in and Moira, who trailed in its wake, did a double take as I walked past. Former Archbishop of Canterbury Rowan Williams was also bumbling around, which added an even more surreal air.

The session was convivial enough but it wasn't really clear what the point of it was (and Sir Tom did not, as Brian Cox predicted last week, use it to come out of the Nationalist closet). Devine made several references to 'Scotia' (yuk) while Salmond reminisced about the minuments library at RBS. There were, however, an interesting couple of biographical tit-bits: the First Minister recalled seeing a John McGrath play called *Border Warfare* (which, at its end, invited the audience to vote for or against Union), and when Devine asked how the SNP had gone from a 'sect' to where it was now Salmond replied 1) the SNP has changed fundamentally, embracing a broader spectrum of Scottish opinion and 2) Scotland's changed and, on balance, that was the most important: 'My mother's attitudes were moulded by the Second World War so she was more British, while my father's were much more Scottish.' Devine also asked about 'devo-maximus' (double yuk) and Salmond was surprisingly upfront in admitting he 'would've preferred a second question on the ballot'. He also came close to dismissing Yes Scotland's 'grand claims' as nothing more than campaign posturing, but then drew back.

After that me and Kath Haddon, who's up for a few days covering the referendum for AFP, went for lunch at Gusto and I did my best to bring her up to speed on everything, although of course she's sharp enough to have a firm grasp of it anyway. In the evening I went to an Edinburgh People's Festival referendum debate at the Carlton Hotel on North Bridge. The Labour MSP Kezia Dugdale did her best to get a largely hostile (and left-wing) audience on side but it was no use; John McAllion was rhetorically impressive ('There would be no independence referendum were it not for the SNP') while the Labour MP Gregg McClymont hit them with a coldly logical argument which, being Trots, there wasn't much room for. At one point he said Scotland had been able to leave the UK at any point since the universal franchise and the creation of the SNP ('Rubbish!' 'What about 1979?'), and that in Euro elections a third of Scots had voted for UKIP or the Tories ('Absolute nonsense!'). Elaine C. Smith rattled through the usual stuff: 'I'm an internationalist', 'it's not about identity'; 'it's us in Scotland who are desperately trying to hold onto British values', 'elites' and so on: she even quoted Ralph Miliband. Mind you, at least she was honest: 'It's a neverendum for me, even if we lose it.'

The whole thing, however, wasn't very edifying, with anything Dugdale or McClymont said – however reasonable – denigrated and heckled, while everything uttered by Smith and McAllion was taken at face value. The chair did her best to keep things balanced while I could hear Colin Fox at the back audibly warning people against heckling and generally trying to lower the temperature. At the end Elaine led (almost) everyone in a singalong of Hamish Henderson's 'Freedom Come All Ye'.

Afterwards Gregg and I had a quick drink at the Scotsman Hotel across the road. His father had died recently so he was obviously a bit distracted by that, but his chat was typically engaging; also interesting on why Darling had failed to advance a positive vision of the Union in last Tuesday's debate. Back at home I watched a rerun of the debate on STV (complete with sign language) and, interestingly, Darling came across much better on telly (and Salmond less impressively) than he had in the hall itself.

Tuesday, 12 August 2014 (Edinburgh)

Another day of Book Festival events, both on cultural themes, and both predictably woolly. Alan Riach from Glasgow University opened his (alongside Sandy Moffat) by stating the importance of the 'cultural case for independence' but, as usual, didn't actually say what it was (I later pointed this out and he did his best, reading a couple of woolly paragraphs from the preface of the book: 'Through independence that process [the arts and public money, natch] can be regenerated,' the operative word being 'can').

Riach blamed it all, naturally, on the media, citing the decline in book reviews (!). Moffat, meanwhile, burbled on about the Lander in Germany ('but Germany's one country,' murmured a chap in front of me). Stuart Kelly chaired it well and challenged various points, saying at one point that by elevating the views of writers and artists above everyone else then surely they risked playing into celebrity culture ('to an extent we are' conceded Riach, 'but hopefully backing it up').

Later, an event with Robert Crawford and Paul Henderson Scott was pretty dreadful. The latter opened with a 'statement', which was in fact the usual potted history of his remarkable life, but he kept skipping pages by accident, which wasn't very helpful, and anyway it had little relevance to the discussion at hand. Crawford was more interesting but it still wasn't really clear what the event was supposed to be for. 'Writers live by risk,' he observed, 'so they're not inclined to be frightened of personal or political independence' (as good an explanation as any). Also pointed out that there are no 'English' novels set in Scotland or preoccupied by Britishness, which has always been more a Scottish preserve (he also called England a 'stateless nation'). Crawford also ventured some criticism of Salmond, saying he could be 'too blustering', while he preferred Nicola Sturgeon's 'Borgen Nationalism' to 'Braveheart Nationalism'. Crawford's best line: 'In terms of creative imagination it [Unionism] has no great songs.'

With my commentator hat on I met Andrew Osborn (Chief UK Political Correspondent) and Guy Faulconbridge (UK and Ireland Bureau Chief) from Reuters at Gusto to give them a sort of informal briefing about where things are at in terms of the indyref. Later I reflected that this put me in quite a powerful position with folk like them, coming up from London for a few days to gauge the temperature. Obviously, and probably not entirely successfully, I tried to be responsible and balanced, doing my best not just to give them the Torrance view of the world. They said they'd spoken to Blair Jenkins and Stephen Noon in Glasgow but had got the impression they were regarded as 'the enemy'.

I continue to get pelters from Unionists for my verdict on the first televised debate. Mark Hogarth posted on Facebook: 'Hope your [sic] ok David, Brian Wilson and I a bit concerned after that Manchurian Candidate performance of your last week?' I thought my response was quite witty: 'What, did I accuse the Scottish Government of harbouring known communists?' Popped into the Q Store just off Broughton Street to get supplies and the guy serving me ('You look taller on TV') said that Salmond's performance had shifted him from an intention to vote Yes to not caring/No. Said his mother agreed. 'We're all sick of it,' said another guy in the shop, rhetorically, adding, 'aren't we?'

In the evening I saw the *other* Willie MacRae play for my next batch of *Herald* fringe reviews, George Gunn's *3,000 Trees*, but it wasn't a patch on the one I saw earlier this week. Spotted the SNP MSP Rob Gibson in the front row, who probably knew MacRae. Caught most of Andrew Neil's documentary, *Scotland Votes: What's at Stake for the UK?*, in the evening and although very Establishment it was decent enough, as you'd expect from Neil, who's generally a class act on such things. His conclusion was basically a federal UK, although of course he didn't use the 'f' word. Rounded off the day with a compellingly awful play/farce/musical called *Snow White: the Whole Grimm Affair*.

Wednesday, 13 August 2014 (Edinburgh)

Saw David Hayman's *The Pitiless Storm* at the Assembly Rooms, about a veteran trade unionist who switches from No to Yes as he prepares a speech about his recently-awarded OBE. Like Bissett, it was preachy stuff and therefore not terribly interesting. Lunch with Martin Hogg afterwards at Café St Honore (lots of referendum chat, inevitably) then along to Charlotte Square to see Gerry Hassan and Lesley Riddoch at the Book Festival; the former was good as ever but the latter too inclined to tell audiences what they want to hear.

Usual complaints from the audience about the wicked meeja yet despite despising the mainstream media they also idolise Lesley (who, after all, is a product of the 'MSM' or mainstream media). They're also vehemently anti-politics yet, weirdly, exempt Salmond *et al* from their cynicism. A lady sitting behind me ticked me off afterwards for looking at my phone too much (which I was) and also for how I'd chaired the Five Million Questions Q&A with Douglas Alexander. She didn't really have a substantial point but it was clear her implication was that dreaded four-letter word 'bias'.

Had dinner with Darren Hughes from the Electoral Reform Society at Gusto later on and the chat was typically wide-ranging. I joked that 'Journalists for Yes' ought to register with the Electoral Commission. Afterwards I had a few drinks with Kathryn Sampson and Joe Pike (ITV), Claire Stewart (STV) and the Andrews Browne and Kerr (BBC Scotland) at Hemma on Holyrood Road.

Thursday, 14 August 2014 (Edinburgh)

In the morning I met a kid from Barcelona called Andreu McGurk who, despite his name and Glaswegian accent, grew up in Barcelona (his father is Scottish). He was doing a high school project comparing the independence debates in Catalonia and Scotland, so just asked me the usual stuff, although he seemed under the impression Westminster was engaged in covert operations to scupper independence (no doubt because in Spain that's precisely what Madrid is up to). He was very interesting on the unfolding financial scandal involving Jordi Pujol, said it's been very damaging for pro-independence campaigners in Catalonia (his son is also implicated) but of course the timing is suspicious – the authorities in Madrid probably knew about it for a long time but sat on it until now for obvious reasons. Andreu also said *Homage to Scotland*, the Catalan documentary I took part in, made a big impact in Catalonia with more than a million viewers – funny to think so many people watched me talking to Dad about politics.

After that I popped into Holyrood to see First Minister's Questions where Salmond was tying himself in more intellectual knots over the currency union stuff. In response to another statement from the Bank of England Salmond again tried to claim Carney as an ally while laying the blame for financial uncertainty at Better Together's door. This was nonsense on so many levels that even normally loyal SNP backbenchers didn't quite know how to take it (and generally they can tolerate quite a degree of logical contortions). Currency continues to be a problem though, and the more its contradictions are aired like today, then the more damage it does. Interestingly, meanwhile, a survey shows an increase in the proportion of Scots identifying as 'British', an inevitable side effect of such a polarised debate I guess. Caught up with Neil Mackinnon on George IV Bridge for food in the evening.

Friday, 15 August 2014 (Edinburgh)

After a morning swim caught Owen Jones, the poster-boy of the British Left, at the Assembly Rooms talking about the Establishment. It was all a bit undergraduate politics, but he still made some incisive points, although on the referendum he was unduly cautious: 'Our enemy has no borders' so 'stay united', or something. 'Is that a fudge?' he asked after; 'I don't care...'

Back at Charlotte Square I overheard Paddy Ashdown joking in the authors' yurt about Ming Campbell making a good president of an independent Scotland (apparently this had come up at a recent event). Historian Linda Colley's session was excellent, full of interesting nuggets (Victorian Scots fetishising the Magna Carta and Victorian English the cult of William Wallace); said, rightly, that it was wrong to see the Scottish referendum in isolation given challenges to the UK were much more widespread. More to the point, she repeated her book's conclusion that the aim should be a 'much more explicitly federal state' and a 'wider political and constitutional renovation of the UK'. Magnus Linklater, who chaired the event, made the usual comment about federalism being 'alien' to the 'British tradition', which Colley didn't rebut properly, although at one point she said: 'When people say "we couldn't do it", are people in these islands really that stupid?' This got a reasonable round of applause, which was heartening. She was good under questioning, effectively taking apart a question from (as I later learned) Allan Cameron, editorial director of publisher Vagabond Voices, who said the UK had a 'political divergence' unlike the Iberian peninsula or Scandinavia.

Later I spoke to Cameron at some length in the authors' yurt, but it didn't exactly go well. He came out with some phenomenal nonsense (the devolution referendum, for example, had taken place in 1999 rather than 1997) and just regurgitated standard Yes Scotland lines on the NHS etc. I decided to correct factual errors and rebut woolly arguments point by point, which seriously pissed him off. At one point he remarked that I fell into the 'category' of people who based their views on what the media said rather than what was happening 'on the ground', which I found a bit patronising. Went on to say, of course, that streets he'd canvassed in and around Glasgow were solidly Yes, which was hardly scientific.

Stayed at the Book Festival to see Gordon Brown, although I've seen him in action too often recently to find it interesting any more. However, he used the 'f' word (federalism), saying the UK could come 'as close in a year or two to a federal state as it's possible to be', that the British constitution was 'broken' (which I thought a bit strong), and that disputes between governments within the UK were 'resolved in the courts as if in a federal constitution'. The audience clearly liked him and he told his usual anecdotes about Einstein and JFK. Strong on more powers ('There is no choice; there's no alternative to going ahead for further devolution') and said talks to that end should begin immediately after 19 September ('Can't we have a couple of weeks off?' asked Alastair Moffat, who was in the chair).

Cycled home and then nipped over to Holyrood for a reception to mark the beginning of the Festival of Politics, at which Tricia Marwick (Presiding Officer of the Scottish Parliament) made a mercifully brief speech. Chatted to Darren Hughes and another chap from the Electoral Reform Society, the latter of whom acknowledged weaknesses in the independence proposition but said he'd still vote that way because he thinks too big a No vote means nothing will happen in terms of more powers (he might well be right about that, but then a large No vote seems unlikely). Finally, cycled to the Usher Hall to see the German singer Ute Lemper, who – backed by the Scottish Chamber Orchestra – was fantastic. Saw Ming Campbell, destined to be an independent Scotland's first president, wandering around during the interval.

Saturday, 16 August 2014 (Edinburgh)

Another long and interesting email from the novelist Alan Warner, this one making much more sense, but I just don't have time to respond. Sorted myself out before cycling to Charlotte Square to see a Whitehall contact shortly before my event at the Book Festival. He reckoned the Yes vote could be anything between 38 and 43 per cent, while observing that what Alex Massie calls 'Journalists for Yes' are getting rattled and loopier because they know they're going to lose.

As ever, he was fascinating on behind-the-scenes stuff. On the currency union strategy ('We nearly fucked it up'), he blamed a Downing Street colleague for the presentation of the line (i.e. George Osborne laying down the law), as he insisted on the Chancellor doing a big speech and co-ordinating Ed Balls, Danny Alexander *et al* to agree thereafter. My contact and others were of the view that the veto should have been allowed to 'emerge' from a wider interview, i.e. allowing journalists to 'find' the story themselves and then extract agreement from other players more in sorrow than anger. Of course the UK Government can't allow the currency issue to be framed as them versus Scotland, which is why they're happy Darling did so well on that issue during the televised debate. Meanwhile Salmond simply repeats 'Osborne, Osborne, Osborne' to play the messenger rather than the ball. My contact agreed that Yes had played the currency very badly and that they should have prepared the ground for a Plan B two years ago, fleshed it out with a Fiscal Commission paper and so on. He also reckoned it crystallised the perception that Salmond is running out of steam; this was his big moment and he blew it (while his performance might have meant as much as 4–8 points in polling terms). Darling, of course, will go after Salmond again in the next debate, 'punching the bruise', as Mandelson put it.

My contact had also heard from at least two diplomats that Salmond is going around saying he expects to lose, which seems an odd approach to take, however private the remarks. More widely, we agreed that if we genuinely believed independence would make us richer, fairer etc then a Yes vote would be a no-brainer, but of course not only does that not necessarily follow from independence (indeed the reverse could be true), and nor does it follow from the SNP's specific vision of independence.

Chatted to Henry McLeish before our Book Festival event and he made it clear he wasn't going to declare for Yes (I got the impression Gordon Brown had been phoning him a lot), but at the same time he clearly enjoys keeping people guessing. Richard Holloway chaired the event really well (he had a nice opening section about political heretics) and I read a section from the conclusion of *Britain Rebooted*, while Henry spoke (very well), without notes. The discussion was also quite stimulating although the questions were mixed (the usual nonsense about Ireland rejoining a British federation). Afterwards we even sold a few books with one elderly lady proclaiming 'I've been a federalist since before you were born!'

Had food afterwards with the family, including my brother and his girlfriend Laura, although I felt a little frazzled. Later I went to the Tattoo with Neil Mackinnon, who had his usual VIP seats, although it was as dull, pseudo-colonial and patronising as I feared. Left early to see the *Very*

With Henry McLeish at the Edinburgh International Book Festival. (Photo: James McGachie)

Best of the Fest at the Assembly Rooms with a raucous James McGachie and some of his unlikely collection of friends. It was, of course, a mixed bag, although Brendon Burns literally got booed off stage, not necessarily because he was bad but because he failed to get into a comedic groove.

Sunday, 17 August 2014 (Edinburgh)

Another early start, and a particularly difficult one given my exertions the day before: stupidly I'd agreed to take part in a panel discussion about broadcasting at the Festival of Politics (at Holyrood), although it actually went relatively well. In between his usual script Iain Macwhirter had a nice line about 'blowjob' newspaper headlines, i.e. everything being presented as a 'blow' to Salmond or the Yes campaign. There was the usual nonsense about the licence fee take in Scotland being much larger than the BBC Scotland budget (which of course is dodgy accounting – what about our share of the network spend?), while a lady in the audience (laden with badges) complained at length about Jackie Bird's 'tone' in interviewing Alex Salmond; I told her (very politely) to get a grip. Paul Henderson Scott was also in the (modest) audience, as he was at my Book Festival event yesterday: well into his 90s and still so active. At one point Iain claimed that the BBC network virtually 'ignored' Scotland and the referendum, which is just nonsense (Andrew Marr's series on Scottish writers started last night on BBC1). Afterwards Ruth Wishart (who spoke well and sensibly) told me she'd concluded from Henry McLeish's comments yesterday that he intended to vote Yes, which is interesting as I concluded exactly the opposite. Rounded off the day with Shostakovich's Leningrad Symphony at the Usher Hall. Terrific (if challenging) stuff, and proof, I guess, that nationalist propaganda can also be great culture.

Monday, 18 August 2014 (Edinburgh & Dundee)

Today is exactly a month to go until the referendum. Woke up to several tweets and texts from people who'd heard me and Dad on the *Today Programme* and *Good Morning Scotland* in a trail for Jim Naughtie's Radio 4 documentary *Don't Mention the Referendum!* Thankfully, they'd focused on Dad's more coherent comments – a few people said he should have his own show! Dad's response to Jim's question about what he'd do following a Yes vote was textbook stuff ('the hard work starts then', etc). Later I asked Dad what he thought of it and he texted back: 'Yes it was OK, I sounded most statesman like, not normally me but I will stick to retirement no new careers thanks, it's always interesting to see how they edit it.' Salmond was also on GMS making it quite clear the referendum ballot was 'on the White Paper' and therefore, as Gary Robertson put it, the 'sovereign will' of the Scottish people was actually that of the SNP.

Had a swim and ran some errands before heading to the Book Festival. Stuart Kelly was very complimentary about my *Herald* column, which was largely a response to Sir Tom Devine's rather contrived reasoning in support of independence (not, in any case, new; a few years ago he more or less admitted as much at a Jimmy Reid memorial event). Sir Menzies Campbell also made a point of telling me he'd enjoyed it in the authors' yurt. 'I think it's annoyed some people,' I replied (though that of course was the point), to which Sir Ming retorted: 'If you cough in this debate you annoy someone.' And of course he's right. By contrast, meanwhile, Iain Macwhirter issued a rather patronising tweet calling me a 'brave boy' for questioning Devine's historical judgement. I responded saying I thought the age of deference had long passed.

Caught most of a session with James Robertson chaired by Allan Massie, who was a great foil and very subtly questioned a lot of what the novelist said. Robertson read from a new novel (*The Professor of Truth*) inspired by the events in Lockerbie; this sounded good (though he appears to be with the conspiricists) although he remarked that independence would provide an opportunity to revisit Scots Law, when surely that is already the case? They also discussed *And the Land Lay Still*, although Robertson just reiterated the standard script (now blessed by Devine) that Scottish and UK political 'culture' diverged in the 1980s, so the former has to be independent. Massie pointed out that in some ways Scotland had become less distinct due to decline of the Kirk, while the Empire had perhaps been more important to Scotland than England, both points Robertson didn't really disagree with, thereby tying himself in logical knots. Massie also made a great point about Scotland being 'heavily involved' in first phase of globalisation (which of course has also made Scotland less distinct). Robertson looked increasingly uncomfortable.

I ducked out early to see an *All Back to Bowie's* session on the media. Derek Bateman gave me a friendly wave before ripping into the 'MSM' in his 'provocation'. 'Nuggets of genius stand out because of the mediocrity around them,' the MSM had 'failed' the Scottish people, media is 'on a bended knee to a London hegemony' etc; just his usual bile and of course included a pop at his old employer, from whom he draws (one assumes) a handsome pension. Ross Colquhoun from National Collective just indulged himself and moaned about being 'ignored' by the MSM (odd that they denigrate the MSM while also craving its blessing). Iain Macwhirter said he 'subscribe[d] to a great deal of what he [Derek] says' but basically repeated his script from yesterday. There was the usual fantasy politics when Derek painted a rosy picture of the Scottish media post-Yes, with embassies, more direct flights and media outfits compelled to cover the EU (eh?), which he claimed – UKIP-style – was 'responsible' for 80 per cent of legislation in Scotland/ the UK (!).

I also ducked out of this early to get to Dundee to chair a Five Million Questions session with Danny Alexander. Texted my Yes Scotland contact *en route* to ask for good questions, to which he replied: 'Did Alistair Darling receive a copy of Nick Macpherson's statement before the chancellor? Yes or no. And can he confirm what the prime minister was doing in Shetland. Exactly.' Good grief, a bubble quibble and a conspiracy theory, not a good sign, though he added in another text 'I've not given up'. Also bumped into my Better Together contact on arriving in Dundee, who seemed quite gloomy about a few recent polls; said they appeared to show movement towards Yes and that the NHS privatisation line (however woolly) might be having an impact.

At the Dalhousie Building Danny was personable and friendly (and sporting Union flag cufflinks). Said he'd read my *Herald* column on Devine. Someone later told me he'd had training from Colin Firth's sister and indeed he was quite good, both in Q&A with me and also under hostile questioning from members of the audience (though they appeared to quite like him nevertheless). One questioner raised the Clare oil field (conspiracy theories again) which he dealt with quite well, while a chap at the back muttered about paedophiles at Westminster and then walked out, still muttering.

Preparing to interview Chief Secretary to the Treasury Danny Alexander at a Five Million Questions event in Dundee. (Photo: Dawn Campbell)

My favourite exchange came when two ladies referred to the House of Lords 'taking powers away' from Holyrood, but when Danny asked which powers they meant they looked embarrassed and said 'Ah dinnae ken'. Severin Carrell from the *Guardian* gave me a lift back to Edinburgh and we 'gamed' various Yes and No outcomes, which was good fun; also explored SNP leadership scenarios.

Watched Salmond do a very slick interview on STV's *Scotland Tonight* following his contrived 'Declaration of Opportunity' in Arbroath; very self-indulgent. He was wearing a white tracksuit top, having been playing a game of bowls, which unfortunately made him look like Frank Sinatra *c*.1973. Interestingly he said the NHS had emerged 'as single key issue' of the campaign in terms of converting people to Yes, which was of course nonsense given they'd only just started raising it. Sam Galbraith has died, a couple of decades after he was expected to, quite remarkable; the *Herald* has my obituary on file so it should appear in tomorrow's paper. A friend who works for Danny Alexander was very funny by text: 'Tell me Mr Alexander, why won't you just admit a unicorn will be delivered to every Scot on Independence Day. Isn't your denial a cynical campaign tactic?'

Tuesday, 19 August 2014 (Edinburgh & Glasgow)

Started the day by having breakfast at The Raeburn in Stockbridge with my Yes Scotland contact. He was typically chipper, saying he was confident Salmond would turn things around (in terms of his performance) during the second debate on Monday. Also said if they'd gone down the route of a currency Plan B then by this stage there'd have been people queuing outside banks trying to clear their bank accounts.

Then cycled to the Carlton Hotel on North Bridge to do a long (and quite detailed) interview for Craig Williams at BBC Scotland for a documentary to air after the referendum, called *How the Campaign was Won* (which of course applies either way). At this point I had a bust up with my flatmate, which kept going while I struggled through a live interview on the *John Beattie* show on BBC Radio Scotland about head versus heart in the referendum campaign, and by the time I'd retreated to the Book Festival for soup I offered to move out and he had said yes. So that was that.

The rest of the day was, unsurprisingly, acutely stressful, but somehow I got through it. A session at the Quaker Meeting House on 'Being a Man' was awful, not least because I wasn't in the mood to bare my soul about masculinity and a noisy (not to mention very rude) old couple at the back clearly hadn't understood what they'd bought tickets for ('We came to hear about the referendum and all you're talking about is masculinity.'). Once I'd managed to escape from that particular form of torture I caught the 5.15pm train to Glasgow to chair a republic-organised debate on the monarchy at a drab office building in St Enoch Square. Had a quick coffee with the photographer Keiran Dodds beforehand and he said he was still genuinely undecided about how to vote.

The debate was actually quite interesting but again my mind was on other things. Robert Brown (a former Lib Dem MSP) made a good job of defending a constitutional monarchy in an intelligent way, while John Mason (the SNP MSP) presented the contrary case and I played the sceptical chairman. Interestingly, John said he'd voted No in 1979 as he believed the promise that 'a better Bill' would follow (he wasn't in the SNP at the time). Afterwards I got bought a steak and white wine at the Wetherspoon's pub near Queen Street Station, which was much needed. Some good banter as well.

Wednesday, 20 August 2014 (Edinburgh)

David Ross from Better Together texted about last night's debate and John Mason's throwaway line about Alex Salmond not being SNP leader for much longer, as did Colin Mackay later on, although I wasn't much use as I couldn't remember exactly what he'd said. Spent the morning moving all my stuff out of Jason's flat, with Dad helping me drop off the books ('Where the f*** have all these come from?' he asked incredulously) at the Brunswick Street flat and the rest of my stuff to the parentals' place and some in the car to go to the Green activist and translator Dominic Hinde's Leith Walk flat later in the day. At my flat I retrieved Murray Ritchie's diary of the 1999 Scottish Parliament election campaign, which includes this opening entry:

> Harry Reid and I take Tasmina Ahmed-Sheikh, the Tory candidate in Govan to lunch… [She] is presented to us by Conservative Central Office as typical of the new breed of Scottish Tory, young, talented and determined, the type on whom the party's future depends after the slaughter of the General Election. She certainly makes a change from tweedy old colonels.

Ha!

Did an interview about Alex Salmond for a chap from AFP outside Holyrood then spent an enjoyable afternoon with Haydn and Harriet (who I'd met at Kath's wedding in Cambridge) watching his brother's play *Outings* (guest starring Simon Callow) and then lunch near Teviot. Also slept through a weird Italian production with Neil Mackinnon before moving into Dom's cosy boxroom. Another phone call from a *Newsnight* producer about my possibly appearing on Thursday night to discuss culture and the referendum, but when I made it clear I wouldn't be happy to be introduced as either a 'No voter' or a 'Tory' I could tell from the tone of her voice that I'd just disqualified myself.

Later on I cycled up Leith Walk (bloody good exercise) to see Fred MacAulay's *Frederendum* at the Assembly Rooms, which wasn't really about the referendum at all. Most interesting were the snatched conversations from a couple behind me. 'The thing that really scared me about the debate,' said a lady, 'was when Darling said there would be no going back.' Her husband then chipped in, saying, 'Generally we're more federalist,' mentioning English regionalism etc. Although it's easy to get carried away, the referendum can't have done awareness of federalism any harm. Intriguingly, a recent survey of English public opinion has produced – for the first time – a clear majority in favour of an English Parliament.

Late dinner with one of my publishers, Hugh Andrew, who's now vehemently anti-independence (despite his brief dalliance post-2007) and absolutely scathing about certain Yessers. Several whiskies afterwards, ensuring I was so drunk that I couldn't actually remember cycling home.

Thursday, 21 August 2014 (Edinburgh)

Battled a modest hangover to attend the last First Minister's Questions at Holyrood before its second referendum recess. Salmond actually did quite well in the inevitable exchanges about Sir Ian Wood's intervention on North Sea oil (chiefly that the Scottish Government has overestimated reserves by about 60 per cent), partly because Sir Ian was guilty of rhetorical inconsistency on the subject, but also because Salmond knows his way around the politics and economics of oil pretty well. Joe Pike from ITV whispered to me that it might very well turn out to be Johann Lamont's last ever FMQs, or indeed Salmond's depending on the referendum outcome. The FM was also pitch perfect when questioned about Ferguson's shipyard.

After that I spent the next couple of hours in the Garden Lobby catching up with myself and others. Campbell Gunn told me he thought the debate – despite the 'fringes' on Twitter – had been good and relatively civilised; I suppose he has a point but it's still not been particularly edifying. Also saw Douglas Pattullo, who said further telephone canvassing of Undecideds in working-class areas had convinced him it would be a big No vote. Finally, spoke to Glenn Campbell ahead of Monday's debate. He seemed a bit vague as to the format (there was a Twitter spat between Rob Shorthouse and Kevin Pringle about the allotted time for cross-examination) but he said questions would mainly be driven by the audience. Also had an email from a BBC producer saying that there would be 'five different' results programmes coming from Pacific Quay on referendum night. Five!

Cycled to Charlotte Square to see Jim Sillars and Gavin McCrone at the Book Festival. The latter made a compelling point that only in the last 20–25 years has Scotland become one of the wealthiest parts of the UK – until then it was one of the poorest (why haven't the No campaign made more of this?), and if any part of the UK was radically different from the rest it was London rather than Scotland. Sillars, meanwhile, was more engaging but just read from his usual script about socialism, how the referendum had led to the 'rebirth of an old idea', 'stirring up the working classes', etc. He also got very emotional when he quoted Margo at the end of his speech.

Under questioning, Sillars had a nice line about Sir Ian Wood saying he was worried about his grandchildren: 'He's a multi-millionaire, his grandchildren are alright, I'm worried about everyone else's grandchildren.' There was a deluge of summer rain halfway through which made it quite difficult to hear what anyone was saying, and even thunder (Jim: 'That's Alistair Darling!'). McCrone spoke about more powers ('Pish! Read a history book,' said a chap near me), which allowed Sillars to drone on about 1979. He also said he reckoned that by 2016 a majority of Scots would regret voting No ('We had our chance and we blew it'); lots of mad Nats muttering throughout.

A brief break in the rain enabled me to cycle up to the Quaker Meeting House for a session with Alex Bell (substituting for Jamie Maxwell), who was a typically good chair. He puffed me up by saying I was the 'star journalist' to have emerged over the last few years, then we sort of meandered through a discussion about the voters' guide, my federalism book and his recent publication, *The People We Can Be*. I told him I'd almost finished reading it and while there's some interesting stuff in it (later picked up by the *Daily Mail*) it was disappointing and slight given how good a writer and thinker Alex is. There were a couple of silly errors (several references to 'Lord' Calman and also the '1978' devolution referendum) but his wider point – that neither the UK nor Scotland is responding adequately to global challenges – is of course true. Also some interesting historical stuff, for example an allusion to talks with Westminster on devo-max which fizzled out in the summer of 2010.

During our discussion Bell rubbished my federalism chat but did agree there was movement in England as well as a sincere commitment from Westminster to devolve power to cities and regions. Otherwise there was a mini debate between Michael Gray from National Collective and Professor Tom Gallagher, both blinkered in their own way but a nice microcosm of the debate as a whole. Finally I cycled back to Charlotte Square for the 'Writing the Future' event with Alan Bissett (who waved at me from the stage), Lesley Riddoch, Hugh Andrew and Sarah Prosser (from the British Council in Norway).

Not as lively as I thought it'd be (I wanted blood on the floor) but lots of the usual arguments and lines. Lesley made a weird point about 'two-tier culture in Scotland' which was later taken apart by Hugh ('somehow Robert Adam isn't Scottish... we can't pick and mix our history'), while Bissett went on about the Barnett Formula being adjusted by between £4–7bn (where are those figures from?) and that 'with a No vote we'll be trapped in 2014 forever' while the world will shrug and move on and 'we'll become culturally an irrelevance' (what, like after 1979?). Hugh could barely hide his disdain ('culture is made by people not politics') while Prosser was very interesting on Norway's system of guaranteed income and sales for writers (which sounded generous but scary).

After a quick dinner with Hugh *et al* – and rather too much wine – STV sent a cab to take me to their Edinburgh studio to do round-up punditry with Kevin McKenna on the week's news. Taxi driver told me he'd started off as a No but had moved to Yes because of various statements from Better Together, but at the same time he was 'realistic' about just how transformational a Yes vote would be. Girl at STV told me the Luath *Voters' Guide* had been useful in making up her own mind, which is good, as that was the whole point of writing it.

Friday, 22 August 2014 (Edinburgh)

Despite my intention to make Friday a reasonably relaxed day ended up cycling (after a swim) to Dynamic Earth for what Yes Scotland had bigged up as a major event at 9am. In the event it was a glorified photo call though, I guess, an important one, the announcement that the Independence Declaration had more than a million signatures, conveniently with just a few weeks to go. In the media huddle afterwards Blair Jenkins said each name had been checked against the electoral register but that they wouldn't be publishing it in full. 'So we've just got to take your word for it?' asked Alan Roden from the *Scottish Daily Mail*, which threw Jenkins a little. He murmured something about confidentiality, but in that case why not publish an edited list?

The Proclaimers were also there looking a bit awkward, while Angus Robertson was having fun showing off his German to some European broadcasters. I tweeted a picture from the event with the innocuous observation that the Indy Declaration had been launched more than two years ago. Cue tweets about me 'sneering' etc; so bloody paranoid/hypersensitive – Eddi Reader even waded in in her usual eccentric manner. Dad also brandished the Electoral Commission guidance at me a couple of days ago, something that's perfectly balanced with full-page ads from Better Together and Yes Scotland, but Dad said the fact there was more text on the former ad was proof of 'bias'. I tried to explain that they'd both have been submitted by each side, but he wasn't to be persuaded. Jeezo.

Dossed around in the afternoon catching up with myself and the last few days' newspapers, had lunch with Michael and Laura (who said she hadn't heard a single convincing argument for independence since arriving in Scotland for the first time), and also dinner later on before seeing an outdoor screening of *Ghostbusters* at Old College with Dominic Hinde and Dan Heap, a former Labour activist now sporting an ostentatious Yes badge. It was very 1980s but some much-needed escapism; the rain started and ended with the film, which wasn't much fun and I ended up cycling back to Dom's flat in more freezing rain – it's late August!

ITV's *Good Morning Britain* wants me to do a stint early on Tuesday from Kelvingrove about next Monday's debate. Unlike the BBC, they were more content with my assurance that I hadn't declared my position on independence and nor would I.

Saturday, 23 August 2014 (Edinburgh & Stirling)

Up, reluctantly, to attend a Better Together event at the Macdonald Holyrood Hotel in Edinburgh. A press officer sighed at me on the way in: 'Roll on 19 September; it's just gone on too long.' He was waiting for Lord (Jack) McConnell, who was making the main speech at an ecumenical event with a trio of peers: Steel, McConnell and Goldie. There was a good crowd, not least for a Saturday morning in Edinburgh in the midst of the festivals – mainly middle-aged and elderly though – affluent, middle-class types chattering politely.

They loved Annabel Goldie, of course, who's very funny at such events ('I'm not Baroness Williams'). 'I have many new friends,' she said of campaigning alongside Labour people, followed by a comic pause, 'for the moment.' She did say something interesting though, that with a No vote Scots 'don't just reject independence, we also endorse the UK'. Jack's been conspicuous by his absence in this campaign, and this was only his second speech which echoed some of the first, including some nuanced criticism of his own side, talking of the campaign having been 'polarised' between an 'an old view of the UK and all decisions being made in Westminster and Whitehall and the completely opposite view of independence or a separate Scotland' (ouch).

It was a good speech, though, and a robust defence of devolution; particularly good on NHS nonsense (which was the main news 'line' from the event), saying it's a 'big lie', 'shames the Yes campaign' etc. He made the key point that having used its (the SNP's) record under devolution as a reason for voting Yes they can't then switch to saying it's under threat from a No vote.

Meanwhile another former First Minister, Henry McLeish, has finally confirmed that he'll be voting No in the referendum despite Blair McDougall having tweeted yesterday that he would declare for Yes on Monday; he's now said it several times but still Yessers live in hope of gaining a high-profile convert (not, I suspect, it'd make much difference even if he did).

Caught the 12.03pm train to Bridge of Allan and then cycled to Stirling University for the If Scotland event, which takes place over the weekend, hosted by Scott Hames, who edited that book of writers on Scotland (*Unstated*, which included Alasdair Gray's 'settlers and colonists' essay). I was one of three people responding to an opening pitch from Lesley Riddoch, which was typically wide-ranging and didn't really address the brief, that is Scottish culture after a Yes vote, just her usual Nordic fetishism. I read out a section from *The Battle for Britain* on 2024 and looking back on a Yes vote, critiqued the 'cultural case' for independence then responded to some of Lesley's policy ideas. The other speakers were Aileen McHarg (Professor of Public Law at Strathclyde University) and Kirstin Innes, an arts journalist and Alan Bissett's other half.

Everything Lesley said got a round of applause (it was a bit of a fan club) whereas my contrarian cynicism was met with stony silence – Kirstin even accused me of 'glibly' dismissing Scottish culture, which just wasn't true. One chap asked if it was possible to define 'Scottish culture' and I joked (well, half joked) that to me the most important cultural event of the day was whether and how I'd be able to watch *Doctor Who* in the evening, and in that sense low or popular culture was pretty much the same across the UK and much of the English-speaking world, an obvious point but not one they liked. A lady in the audience likened the SNP to the old Kirk: moralising, statist etc – not a bad point.

At a fringe session later on I sat next to the poet Robert Crawford, who said he'd nearly incorporated parts of my Salmond book into a biographical poem about the First Minister for his recent collection *Testament*. Unfortunately he said it was 'so bad' that it would never leave his desk drawer. Also sat next to him and the writer Jenni Calder (who's done an edited version of Scott's *Waverley* for Luath) at dinner later on, which was good fun. Crawford said university research funding was the decisive issue among his academic colleagues when it came to the referendum. Gerry Hassan had a review of several indyref books in that day's *Irish Times*, including the dismissive conclusion that federal schemes were 'merely liberal-elite wish fulfilment', although surely that also applies to many proponents of independence.

After dinner we watched *Then is the Hour*, a reasonably engaging postscript to *Now is the Hour*, which I had reviewed for the *Herald*. The 'literary discussion' afterwards was pretty turgid: all were Yes for the usual woolly and uninteresting reasons; hardly any intellectual engagement given they're supposed to be writers! I retreated back to my (very comfortable) room with half a bottle of white wine to watch *Doctor Who* on iPlayer, but it was disappointingly (and inevitably) sloppy and self-indulgent, although

In conversation with authors Robert Crawford and Jenni Calder during the 'If Scotland' conference at Stirling University. (Photo: Scott Hames)

thankfully Peter Capaldi was pretty good. 'I'm Scottish,' he said at one point, 'I can complain about things!' There was also a referendum reference when the Doctor speculates about his eyebrows ceding from the rest of his face. (Yesterday Nicola Sturgeon tweeted a selfie of her and Sylvester McCoy at a Yes meeting – two worlds collide!)

Sunday, 24 August 2014 (Stirling & Edinburgh)

Up painfully early to hear Michael Keating kick off the morning session of the If Scotland conference. He was, as ever, very interesting, called Gordon Brown's book the 'most heavyweight intellectual defence of the Union' while noting that until the 1980s Unionists argued that Scotland had done the 'patriotic' thing by joining the Union in 1707. Also said Conservatives would find it easier to devolve more power after a No vote than Labour, which is probably true.

After lunch Ken MacLeod, a sci-fi writer, looked back from 2034 on a No vote and was generally warm and engaging if not particularly strong on the politics. I responded last and did okay, but in the Q&A that followed there was a bit of loopiness when Kirstin Innes trotted out the line about the House of Lords taking powers away from the Scottish Parliament. I (politely) corrected her afterwards, usefully backed up by Aileen McHarg, but she just looked at me blankly as if to say 'Well you would say that, wouldn't you?' No attempt to engage with my point: inconvenient things, facts. Afterwards a Swiss journalist said he couldn't understand why the Scottish debate was all about detail rather than the wider principle of independence.

In the afternoon I went to another break-out session at which Christopher Silver of National Collective burbled on about the usual stuff; weirdest bit was when he quoted from Neal Ascherson's *Stone Voices* about the 1979 referendum destroying many Scots' lives, turning them to alcohol, etc. He paused afterwards to indicate that he believed the same bleak consequences would flow from a No vote this September. What planet are these people on? One of the university catering staff was wearing a small 'No Thanks' badge the whole weekend, which must have broken some rule or other.

It was good to get out of Edinburgh for a day and a half but the conference lacked focus and wasn't very well attended, although it was useful to meet Scott Hames for the first time, who seemed like a good guy. Alex Salmond, meanwhile, has succumbed to the ice-bucket challenge (the video shows him hugging a very wet Nicola Sturgeon after she did it too) and has challenged the 'Scottish press corps' to follow suit, but I've decided, conveniently, that doesn't include me. Had a quiet dinner at a pub in Leith and overheard some surprisingly informed chat about the first televised debate: a chap saying that Salmond avoiding his usual confrontational debating style had backfired, etc. After that I saw my last fringe show with Paul, an amusing enough burlesque show called *Dixey*. I'm glad, however, it's all packing up tomorrow.

Monday, 25 August 2014 (Edinburgh & Glasgow)

Cycled to The Tun first thing to do *Good Morning Scotland* with Murray Ritchie (who was wearing his Yes hat rather than his commentator one). Near the end of the discussion, such as it was, Murray said a No vote would be a 'vote against their country', which usefully backed up something I'd said in my *Herald* column today. Saw Mark Diffley from Ipsos MORI afterwards who said the Yes vote was now around 42/43 per cent although he thought it was unlikely to increase by much more. Interestingly, he also said the major five pollsters were all now within two points of each other, which of course hasn't been the case in the past. Andrew Wilson was also in the studio ('I think it's happening!'), as was Jim Naughtie. Some guy from RIC later tweeted that I was a public-school boy and, when I contradicted this, referred to my 'Anglicised accent'.

Bumped into the Advocate General (Lord Wallace) at Waverley Station, as you do, and asked the obvious question about how he thought things were going. He admitted to being a bit 'paranoid', and when I raised the NHS line he conceded that 'desperation works'. Back at the flat I did a Skype interview for Al Jazeera (on tonight's debate) during which the presenter asked how I was planning to vote. Obviously, I didn't answer. Then I cycled to Hemma to see Èvelyne Brie, a strikingly attractive Québécois political scientist, who's in Edinburgh examining the impact of the two Quebec referendums on Scotland's. Like other academics/journalists from overseas she was surprised not to see more posters and general campaigning activity in Edinburgh; she said Scotland increasingly featured in the media and political discourse in Quebec. Her questioning was good although she appeared to be under the impression the Scottish Government had been shafted in the Edinburgh Agreement negotiations, which of course isn't how the SNP sees it. We chatted about the Clarity Act that followed the 1995 referendum (she said the joke is that it isn't very clear) and her forthcoming duties as an international observer (of the Scottish referendum) for the Electoral Commission.

After lunch I caught the train to Glasgow and then cycled to the West End to speak to Murray Leith and Duncan Sim about my PhD (the former was quite upbeat about when I might hope to complete this). Dropped into Better Together HQ at the Savoy Centre on Sauchiehall Street, a somewhat innocuous setting for the official campaign to save the UK. It felt busy, and slightly odd seeing familiar Tory, Labour and Lib Dem faces working alongside one another (Danny Alexander was there, as was a tired-looking Douglas Alexander, who said he'd heard Dad and me on Radio 4). My usual contact took me for coffee with a Northern Irish chap called Quentin Oliver, who described himself as a 'referendum anorak' (or was it geek?), whose first vote had been in the 1973 'Border Poll' which, of course, established the precedent for one part of the UK seceding. He was quite interesting on the campaign thus far, basically admitted that it had been fought too much as a traditional General Election campaign with Better Together distracted by policy rather than 'prosecuting the case'.

We talked about that evening's debate and my contact was confident Darling was now up to speed on more powers, etc. He said the key word was 'default', in that if Salmond produced his threat not to shoulder a share of UK debt then Darling would go on the attack about defaulting on debt (although of course an independent Scotland couldn't technically 'default' without first issuing debt). Interestingly, he admitted that in planning the first debate they hadn't actually wanted a cross-examination section, even though it ended up playing to Darling's advantage in terms of currency (which they claim is still 'playing big' with focus groups). Neither my contact nor Quentin believed Yes Scotland actually had a million validated signatures to its Declaration, if for no other reason than the manpower required to check every name against the electoral register simply wouldn't have been possible.

Cycled to Kelvingrove to do the top of *Reporting Scotland* with Iain Macwhirter but, annoyingly, this got binned when Iain turned up five minutes later, saying he'd ended up 'in the wrong place'. Saw from Twitter that Alan Taylor had again been introduced on Radio 4 as 'Alex Salmond's biographer' (of course he doesn't correct them!), which was doubly irritating. A BBC producer showed Iain and I down to the 'spin room' (a lot nicer than STV's) and I caught up with this diary, emails and so on. My aunt Frances texted me (with her usual erratic capitalisation): 'WHY AM I scared?'

Lots of people coming and going, including Danny Alexander, Humza Yousaf ('Hair's looking great!') and, of course, fellow scribblers including quite a few I hadn't seen before. Katie Grant asked what was on my T-shirt 'this time'; I said it was a bear but it wasn't significant, to which she exclaimed 'It will be by the end of the night!'

The set at Kelvingrove looked great – very dramatic – but the debate itself was bitty and frustrating. Annoyingly, I had to file 450 words for the *Herald* by 10pm, just before speaking to *The World Tonight* on Radio 4, so I didn't really have time to concentrate on everything that was happening. Salmond, however, clearly duffed up Darling who was pretty awful, humming and hawing his way through most sections, although a pretty partisan audience (a few of whom may have been briefed by Yes Scotland) didn't help in that respect. The main problem was that Darling was stuck too much in the groove of the first debate, while his 'default' line was a damp squib and the currency stuff just came across as hackneyed and tired.

Afterwards Mure Dickie from the *Financial Times* secured a quote (I said Salmond won but it had often been a triumph of style over substance, which thereafter became the main nub of my analysis) and reminded me that I'd given him the 'key' quote prior to the first debate, chiefly that Salmond could often be rubbish in debate. After doing Radio 4 with Joyce Macmillan (who was in Edinburgh) I waited outside for a cab to Gerry Hassan's place in Strathbungo, and as I loaded my Brompton into the boot I saw Paul Sinclair and Eddie Barnes on their way home. Tellingly, they didn't demur when I gave them my verdict, although Paul rather weakly maintained that the lack of a currency Plan B was still 'cutting through' on the doorstep. Neither of them looked particularly happy.

My taxi driver was a Pakistani Glaswegian who said he was still undecided, although he'd seen Salmond speak at a recent Asian community dinner and had been quite impressed (he also remembered voting to come out of the EEC in 1975). When I got to Gerry's place he was still at BBC Scotland doing Kaye Adams' phone-in programme, which was populated by the usual eccentrics (one of whom said 'the referendum is daeing my nut in'). My Yes Scotland contact texted to say 'You'll be writing a lot about that debate in the next edition of your book', while Alex Massie – who I sat next to in the spin room – tweeted: 'Still, we can look forward to @ GerryHassan's essay on how the debate showcased the darkest pathologies of crisis-hit Scottish masculinity.'

Tuesday, 26 August 2014 (Glasgow & Edinburgh)

Up at 5.20am in order to do a radio interview on last night's debate for BBC Radio 5 Live at Pacific Quay. *En route* to Edinburgh BBC Radio Foyle tried to interview me while I was on the train, which just didn't work (I did warn them!), and I then spoke to RTE's morning radio programme from a rather noisy platform at Waverley, just after struggling to file copy for the *Guardian*'s Comment is Free website – oh, the glamour.

Despite this piece repeatedly naming Salmond as the victor and criticising Darling's performance I got the usual flak after the *Guardian* tweeted it (one lady 'wished' her medical condition on me – nice). The trouble is that 'bias' is now defined incredibly broadly and includes any piece of analysis or commentary the tweeter doesn't agree with. After a couple hours' sleep in the box room, Dad helped me transfer my stuff to Hugh Andrew's place in Newington. His (Dad's) verdict on the debate was 'Darling's a tube' (Mum didn't even bother watching it, like the majority of Scots, I guess); part of me wonders why I bother churning out hundreds of words of analysis when he can be so concise.

Had lunch with Paul at the City Art Centre Café before he caught a train to London and, by chance, at the next table was Gavin MacDougall from Luath and the political theorist Tom Nairn, who was surprisingly bashful when Gavin introduced me ('I kent your face from the *Scotsman*'); a bit later on Gavin asked me to sign a copy of the *Voters' Guide* for Tom, which was quite humbling. Talking of Nationalism, that morning I got an email from a Flemish journalist saying the Scottish debate was 'of great importance and particular relevance to us because of our local politics'. He went on:

Yesterday in the BBC debate I again witnessed the same tactics from the First Minister as are common in the polemical arsenal of our Flemish nationalists: that there are two democracies with opposed tendencies. Flemish nationalists hold forth that Flanders with it's [sic] conservative 'natural majority' has had to accept governments with centre-left leanings that obstruct the kind of government that this right wing majority yearns for. Reverse the positions and you get Mr Salmond's main line of attack yesterday night.

While obviously hostile, he makes an interesting analogy. Cycling home later, one half of a gay couple (they were holding hands) crossing Hanover Street shouted 'Well done on Five Million Questions!', which was a slightly unexpected bit of feedback. After attempting to relax in the afternoon I cycled to the National Galleries for an RSA lecture by Professor Joseph Stiglitz. Chatted to an academic beforehand, who said he was embarrassed that the rest of the UK (and indeed the World) had seen Monday night's debate as he reckoned it projected an unflattering view of Scotland (he had a point).

Inside the lecture theatre I sat, by chance, next to Noel Dolan (Nicola Sturgeon's special adviser) and inevitably we talked about the debate. 'Alistair Darling is not a junior backbencher,' he observed witheringly, and of course he's right. Stiglitz's lecture (on building a 'learning' economy) was overlong and badly structured, although he was a bit better under questioning ('The idea of the US as a land of opportunity is statistically a myth'; 'The reason the invisible hand often seems invisible is because it doesn't exist'). On Scotland he'd basically swallowed the Scottish Government's line that free tuition fees was 'progressive' and that it was committed – via independence – to what Stiglitz termed the 'new Scottish Enlightenment'. Amusingly, a guy in the audience pointed out that the first Scottish Enlightenment had taken place *within* the Union, while more seriously another Fellow challenged him on fees, making the obvious point that outcomes (*vis-à-vis* England) were not progressive at all. To be fair, Stiglitz acknowledged that free tuition wasn't a panacea, but nevertheless he's a powerful intellectual ally for the Scottish Government, no matter how muddled his thinking.

Colin Donald from the *Sunday Herald* (who was chairing the event) encouraged me beforehand to ask about the currency union (which Stiglitz had supported at the Book Festival the day before), but I gave in to fatigue and chickened out (I had scribbled one down: How would the US Federal Reserve respond if California seceded from the United States and then demanded a currency union to prop up its slightly ropey economy?). Professor Joe Goldblatt (from Academics for Yes) fawningly welcoming his praise for Scotland while Douglas Robertson (a former 79 Grouper) asked a rather convoluted question. Susan Deacon, giving the vote of thanks, alluded to 'an interesting time in this shiny wee country of ours'; the word 'wee' made Noel Dolan flinch.

Back at home I texted my Yes Scotland contact saying: 'Perhaps my mind's thinking too much but is there any chance AS was deliberately below-par on 5 Aug so as to make last night all the more impressive?' He responded pretty quickly: 'There is no way I would ever answer that question with a view in writing.' I took that as a yes!

Wednesday, 27 August 2014 (Edinburgh)

Haircut at Ruffians. Stewart (my hairdresser) is still 'probably' voting No. Cycled to City Art Centre Café where I saw Helen Milburn of Twitter fame. She asked if I'd seen the 'patronising' Better Together film featuring a lady explaining why she's voting No ('The Woman Who Made Up Her Mind'); I said I had, although it's not nearly as bad as Twitter chatter (hashtag PatronisingBTLady) would have us believe. Nevertheless, one gets the feeling Better Together is in a bad place post-debate, just as it was a few months ago; a feeling that's it's coasting and on the back foot – not a good position to be in three weeks from polling day.

The City Art Centre Café seems to be quite a meeting place for the (Scottish) great and the good. Yesterday it was Tom Nairn and this morning I saw Richard Holloway and also Sir Peter Housden, who introduced himself to me while I spoke to an Oxford student called James Taylor who's studying 'imagined futures' regarding Scotland and the EU. Sir Peter said my 'voice' was a valuable one in the debate and that once 'all this is over' we should have coffee, which, of course, I'll follow up.

After a swim I cycled – amid the detritus of the Fringe – to the Edinburgh International Conference Centre to take part in a panel discussion about higher education and the referendum at the CASE Europe annual conference. This I'd never heard of but there were hundreds of delegates from around Europe, and we got a good lunch beforehand. The discussion itself was a bit odd: I was sandwiched between Dr Stephen Watson and Professor Bryan MacGregor from Academics for Yes and Hugh Pennington from Academics Together, so I'd clearly been cast as a No person without them being up front about it. Stephen, who I'd met before, is intense and seized of the faith, although Bryan seemed a bit more level-headed. Naturally they banged on about 'evidence-based research' and then proceeded to set out lots of woolly, aspirational stuff; an independent Scotland *would* (not could) mean this and that, inexact language I made a point of picking them up on. In my opening remarks I said the debate in Scotland was obsessed to the point of distraction by the free tuition fee mantra (of which Professor Stiglitz had provided ample proof last night) and that there needed to be a conversation about private education, but of course neither point was addressed over the next hour and a half. The two Yessers were certainly well briefed but also reluctant to concede any points, not least when I raised the potential loss of income from no longer being able to charge students from rUK, assuming a Yes vote. Stephen and Bryan just said it would all be fine, while the former kept quoting Abraham Lincoln, which was a bit weird. Bryan referred to the UK university brand in international terms being 'contaminated', which I called out as extraordinary hyperbole.

In the afternoon I caught up with myself at Hugh's place and then wandered around Newington, which is increasingly like a trendier suburb of London, before heading back to West Newington House for drinks and (Turkish) food with Hugh, Stephen O'Rourke (an advocate) and Alastair Stewart (formerly a Tory researcher but heading to Spain to teach English). It was, predictably, extremely boozy, but also good fun. Frances texted me again: 'Wearing my "No thanks" badge! GOING back South tomorrow. Awful to think that next time I come, it could be to a foreign country. Good luck!'

Thursday, 28 August 2014 (Edinburgh)

Woke up extremely hungover and to the news that the Conservative MP Douglas Carswell has defected to UKIP and wants a by-election (which he'll probably win); talk about shoring up a key Yes campaign narrative, not that that will have featured anywhere in Carswell's analysis. Oddly, the news felt very distant: all the usual stuff about Tory splits, UKIP's rise and the next General Election, though of course it's all incredibly important.

Had lunch with a former Tory MSP on Dublin Street in glorious sunshine. We chewed over Better Together's bad week: the second TV debate, the 'patronising' lady video and so on, but at the same time we found it hard to say precisely what the outcome would be. I ventured that even with a Yes vote in the early 40s it would represent a serious (and lingering) challenge to the UK given that it's not healthy for nearly half of any territory in a multi-national state to want out. I also said, self-indulgently, that the only logical outcome had to be a more federal UK, and he more or less agreed, although now he's in a different line of work he's not allowed to have political opinions, federal or otherwise.

After that I cycled to the Balmoral Hotel for tea with Mure Dickie from the *Financial Times* and his deputy editor, who was visiting from London. They both asked pretty good questions, mainly on post-referendum scenarios and scribbled away as I burbled on. The deputy editor said 'London' (by which I assume he meant the media, financial and political classes) were very alive to what was happening in Scotland and following developments closely. At one point I asked what the *FT*'s 'line' was on independence and he made it clear it was against, although naturally in a questioning way.

Had dinner with with a former Westminster lobby colleague at the Outsider in the evening. Surprisingly he revealed himself to be a soft Eurosceptic and spoke with great passion about 'Britain's best days' being ahead of it, but that meant controlling its borders, immigration and so on. When I pointed out that much of his critique of the pro-independence argument in a Scottish context (unrealistic, out of step with geopolitical reality, etc) could equally apply to his vision of an 'independent' UK, he only half ceded the point.

Friday, 29 August 2014 (Edinburgh)

Woke up briefly at 7.45am to do a phone interview on Nick Ferrari's morning programme on LBC radio about, for some reason, the Prime Minister's appearance at a CBI dinner the night before. After a further doze and a swim I cycled to Holyrood to do a TV interview for Laura Pous Trull, who works for a Catalan television station in London, then gave Tony Grew a tour of Holyrood, which he seemed to like (the security guards were extremely officious about my Brompton, which they said had to go through security each time it entered the building, passholder or not – that isn't even necessary at Westminster!). Popped in to see Douglas Pattullo, who said Better Together's canvass returns from the Lothians were, with exceptions, solidly against (Leith Walk, interestingly, is 50/50). James McGachie texted me, although I couldn't figure out if he was joking or not, saying four previously staunchly No Facebook friends had converted to Yes: 'I really am starting to wonder if we are living in the dying days of the Union.'

Had lunch at Hemma with Daniel Johnson, a bright Labour activist and (no doubt) future MSP. He said it didn't feel close on the ground (the *Scottish Daily Mail* splash today was 'UNION ON A KNIFE EDGE!') and split Yes voters he'd encountered on the doorstep into two categories: the disenfranchised and the idealists, the latter being middle-class, sandal-wearing former Lib Dems who buy all the hopey changey stuff. Pretty horrible weather so hibernated at Hugh's in the afternoon. Papers full of stuff about Jim Murphy getting abuse during his town centre meeting in Dundee. The pictures did look pretty awful, full of Yes campaigners foaming at the mouth, but of course Jim is overplaying it with a view to depicting Nationalists as sinister and aggressive.

In the evening I had a quick drink with Michael (my brother), who was up for a wedding and then had food and drinks with my Whitehall contact at the Filmhouse bar. He said he'd been busy cleaning up the mess after the Secretary of State vowed to join Team Scotland in the event of a Yes vote, and he didn't demur when I said that Michael Moore should never have been ousted from the Scotland Office given that he'd carved out a good and effective niche for himself. He also echoed Daniel Johnson's argument that it didn't feel like a close race on the ground and that most opinion polling was flawed. He wants to do something completely different after the referendum, probably something in the private sector, and I can't say I blame him.

Saturday, 30 August 2014 (Edinburgh)

A relatively quiet day, which was useful. Had lunch at The Dome with several old university friends and their respective partners. Ross's wife (a doctor) said she was voting Yes as she found the 'Scotland will always get the government it votes for' line quite compelling. I pointed out that a) in an independent Scotland Orkney and Shetland wouldn't get the government they voted for (we'd been talking about the Northern Isles) and b) the logical extension of that argument would be for Australian states that didn't vote along federal lines to become independent (she's from Australia). She conceded both points but, as usual, I ended up just appearing a smartarse. Ross (an actuary) said he was still No but wavering, while Al (who doesn't have a vote) said it wouldn't really effect him. Huw (a GP on Orkney), as usual, didn't give anything away.

Matthew Parris has a blistering column in *The Times* about Carswell's defection, fearing a Tory split and imploring One Nation Conservatives to fight back. Spent the afternoon catching up with myself and then saw *Ubu and the Truth Commission* at the Lyceum with Neil Mackinnon, a South African play using animation, puppetry etc to depict the post-Apartheid Truth and Reconciliation Commission. It was good, if a little dated. Cycled home to watch the second episode of the new series of *Doctor Who* on iPlayer; it was better than last week's, although that isn't saying much.

Sunday, 31 August 2014 (Glasgow & Edinburgh)

Up reasonably early to get the train to Glasgow for *Sunday Politics Scotland*, on which I did the punditry spot with Kevin McKenna from the *Observer*. I wore my Beatles Hard Day's Night T-shirt as a subtle reference to Sir Paul McCartney's support for the Union (cue pun-tastic press release from Better Together), but no one got it. On the same programme Gordon Brewer interviewed the First Minister from, as usual, a field near Strichen, and Salmond did his usual 'there's a delay on the line' trick as Brewer beavered away on debt, currency etc. The FM looked quite chipper.

On the way out of Pacific Quay I met Natalie McGarry from Women for Independence, who's good, bright and decent but sees the campaign from inside a rather small bubble. Libby Brooks from the *Guardian* phoned to get quotes for a profile she's putting together of Nicola Sturgeon and as a paid-up member of the DFM fan club I said nice things. She also asked the inevitable question about how things were looking and I replied that despite lots of confusing noise I still reckoned it looked like a 60/40 defeat for Yes (though I have periodic doubts about this). Mooched around Glasgow in the afternoon, finishing my *Herald* column on the Establishment and catching up with Josu, a Basque voting Yes, and Mark, a middle-class Fifer voting No by post (it felt weird seeing his postal ballot two weeks ahead of polling day).

Back in Edinburgh a lady recognised me outside Sainsburys, where I was meeting Kenny Morrison (a friend from London) to get food and wine for the EIF closing fireworks concert: 'You were on TV this morning! Don't listen to them, you looked really cool!' (meaning my T-shirt). The weather just about controlled itself for the concert, for which Kenny and I got reasonably good seats, although with a better view of the orchestra than the fireworks, which kind of missed the point. My obsessive indyref mind read too much into the choice of music, which included one piece about a Spanish 'freedom fighter' and closed with the very jingoistic 1812 Overture, unusually performed in full. I overheard a lady behind me joke with her husband that they might not be speaking to each other on 19 September.

Had a couple of drinks with Kenny afterwards and he bemoaned several friends declaring their support for Yes on Facebook for what he called 'dough-eyed' reasons. He has a point, for I'm increasingly struck how blasé a lot of folk are about incredibly complex things like monetary policy, debt, international markets and so on, a view that they're somehow mere formalities (a view underlined by Macwhirter in today's *Sunday Herald*, his column concluding that voters don't care about currency). Also picked up some mail from Jason's flat including a copy of the Dutch newspaper *de Volkskrant* from last Wednesday, which included a large picture of me in a pub on Cockburn Street – wrongly captioned as the 'trendy' Fruitmarket Gallery Café – and the headline 'Referendum is historical accident'. It still feels a bit weird to be taken so seriously by the Continental media.

Later on I got some Facebook messages from a friend at STV. He asked, as does everyone else, how it's looking and I said, as usual, 60/40, to which he replied that he'd 'bite' my hand off for 55/45 'right now'. He went on: 'Five separate people – nice, middle-class people with good jobs – have all told me they've moved from No to Yes this weekend. "Now that the currency thing is resolved," one of them said to me; "Why not?" another put it bluntly.' When I ventured that it might just be a chattering-class phenomenon he replied: 'I know it's totally irrational but I feel... something. Like there's a majority for Yes on there. Or at least a majority that's not bothered enough about it to turn out and vote.'

I know what he means but at the same time the data from people on the ground tells a very different story. Better Together briefed today's *Sunday Herald*, for example, that undecided voters in the six SNP seats are three-to-four times more likely to back No than Yes, an average of 58 per cent planning to vote NO and only 14.8 per cent Yes. The Yes campaign rather feebly retorted that BT didn't have enough people on the ground to have produced such figures, but it chimes with what Douglas Pattullo (and others) have been telling me. But then the noise – if it is noise – is getting louder.

Monday, 1 September 2014 (Edinburgh, London & Aberdeen)

Got a jaunty text from Karl Turner, the Hull Labour MP, in the morning: 'Hope you're well. How do you see the indyref?' (I replied with my usual caveated line and asked if he was well). 'Yeah good. Won't be if your lot divorce us. Never see the corridors of Whitehall again without our socialist relatives.' Not entirely true but evidence Labour MPs south of the border are alert to the consequences of a Yes vote.

Spent the morning preparing for a very corporate two days: chairing an indyref debate at Slaughter and May in London then a Universities Scotland away-day in Aberdeen tomorrow morning. Makes a nice change from doing a lot of work for very little (or even no) pay – today and tomorrow it'll be the other way round. Bumped into someone from the *Irish Times* outside Waverley, said he would virtually be based in Edinburgh for around six weeks. He reckoned Better Together were right to feel jittery (I'd mentioned recent messages from various people) but said while one campaign was 'dishonest' the other was just 'limp' (I knew which was which), and that if Scotland voted Yes to this particular proposition (as opposed to the principle of independence) then 'this would be one very unhappy country'.

On the train south I read *Time* magazine's rather paint-by-numbers cover story on the indyref (although a piece by Rory Stewart setting out the No argument was surprisingly good), caught up with this diary and also started reading *The Positive* Case edited by Brian Monteith, a collection of 13 essays (including Hugh Andrew, my current landlord) on the 'positive reasons why Scotland should remain a full and active member of the United Kingdom'. One of the contributors is Robert Kilgour, who'll be at tonight's Slaughter and May debate.

Another weird Better Together campaign poster: 'I LOVE MY FAMILY. I'M SAYING NO THANKS.' Er, ripe for parody. Slightly better was a speech today from Darling, including these good few lines:

> If you want to hear the positive case for the United Kingdom it is at the heart of what the nationalists are saying. They say: Keep the pound. Keep the Bank of England. Keep the open market. I agree with them. Those things are good for Scotland. But the only way to guarantee Scotland keeps them is by voting No.

At Slaughter and May in Moorgate it turned out I had met Kilgour before (I should have remembered his tartan waistcoat), in fact I'd been to an event in his Westminster flat when I still lived in London. The Yes speaker was a former Labour candidate called Frank McKirgan who, by his own admission, had done rather well out of London and economic activity being concentrated in the southeast of England. Kilgour's (English) wife was in the audience along with his 16-year-old (Scottish) neice.

She had a vote unlike most, if not all, of those in the audience, which was surprisingly large and included an inevitable smattering of ex-pat Scottish lawyers. The debate itself was good fun; we covered a lot of ground and I enjoyed, as ever, being a professional contrarian. I called out McKirgan on a couple of lines in his opening pitch, the usual stuff about the best people to make decisions about Scotland being those *in* Scotland (what about currency, EU, etc?) and also a weird line about the Union 'dying on the inside'. Kilgour was decent enough but tended to end up arguing against himself on certain points. Like Sillars vs Forsyth in Melrose, in the course of the debate a consensus of sorts emerged, mainly in terms of the low-tax, fiscally responsible Scotland both of them want to emerge on the other side of the referendum. Frank in particular was honest about this not necessarily meaning a social democratic nirvana. McKirgan also likened independence to a 'management buyout', which I thought contrasted nicely with Cameron's CBI dinner line the other evening about the Union being the most successful 'merger' in history. Questions from the audience were all good and intelligent, including one guy who pointed out to Robert that if his most positive argument for the Union was loosening that Union (he'd waxed lyrical about more powers), then where did that leave independence? Quite. One (Scottish) guy came up to me afterwards saying he'd read my Salmond biography.

Afterwards Slaughter and May laid on a driver to Heathrow, which made me feel like a bloody banker, but I sat in the back happily munching on Tunnock's Tea Cakes and Irn-Bru that Paul Dickson's (legal) partner had sorted for me. Getting to Terminal 5 took as long as public transport, which tells you something. London, a city I still adore, suddenly feels distant. I remember the sensation, leaving the Scottish Parliament on its second sitting day back in May 1999, that the centre of political gravity had shifted from Westminster to Edinburgh, and it feels similar now; perhaps just the (extensive) discussion of potential independence makes Scotland increasingly *feel* independent. It wasn't a bad feeling, just disconcerting.

YouGov is publishing a poll tomorrow showing 53/47 against. 'Time to pack that suitcase,' my STV friend messaged me later. 'Panelbase is going to put them ahead tomorrow or Wednesday' (a producer at STV told him as much). Then a Twitter DM from a friend at the *Sun*: 'I'll level with you, I'm now officially pessimistic. They reckon it's not an outlier. Scary stuff.' Later on Facebook Ross Colquhoun posted a link with the comment 'History awaits the bold'... Alan Martin, another university contemporary, picked me up at Aberdeen University, his (very) large car boldly displaying a 'No Thanks' sticker; he said everyone he worked with in shipping was also voting No; his wife Jill was swithering but said 'uncertainty' about the currency would probably lead her to the same conclusion as Alan.

Tuesday, 2 September 2014 (Aberdeen, Dundee & Edinburgh)

Texted my Better Together contact to ask for his thoughts on the YouGov poll, and he replied saying he was 'a bit sceptical' (so am I).

> The distance moved is slightly suspicious... Will wait and see tables but I suspect [Peter] Kellner has eaten a bit of humble pie and may have shifted his weightings. He's been briefing this poll pretty widely unusually. Poll of polls feels right at the moment. 45/55.

Later an MP contact of mine also replied to a similar text, rather jauntily saying he hoped the pollsters were 'right that Don't Knows are overwhelmingly No!

The Kellner analysis accompanying the YouGov poll certainly amounts to a major *mea culpa* given his conclusion a few weeks ago (that No would win big). He said the 'biggest movements' had taken place among Labour supporters, rising from 18 to 30 per cent intending to vote Yes, and number of Lib Dems making same switch now up to 24 per cent; only Tories are consistently against, though three per cent still intend to back independence, though I can't help feeling they're confused and actually think they're voting Yes to the Union rather than independence. Kellner also reckoned the gap in terms of folk who thought independence would improve the economy was narrowing, while the NHS nonsense was also having an impact; although there remained a 'fear factor' driving the No lead 'now, a great many Scots are also beginning to fear remaining part of the UK'. Negative campaigning works! 'If the final vote is anything like our current poll figures,' concluded Kellner, 'I would not bet much against a second referendum being held within the next 10–15 years.' When I spoke to Mum later on the phone I mentioned that the polls were narrowing (not being in the bubble, she hadn't heard about it, like the majority of Scots) and she sounded horrified.

I get the overwhelming impression Westminster is a bit complacent about all this. Today's *Financial Times*, for example, record's the PM's spokesman's reaction to what might happen in the event of a Yes vote, chiefly that 'no such work is being undertaken', a line that might come back to haunt them. The YouGov poll reminds me of what happened during the 2011 Holyrood election. For once I had some sympathy with a tweet from Iain Macwhirter: 'R4 leads with a report about London airport rather than polls showing union on knife-edge. I'm not complaining. But rather sums up problem.' (To be fair, someone from Radio 4 later told me editorial policy was not to lead bulletins on polls, which would usually be fair enough.) To underscore the complacency point, Quentin Letts texted to say he'd found my Salmond biography at Foyle's (as I'd suggested) but that it had taken 'some hunting' because the girl on the front desk had 'never heard of Alex Salmond'; she told him to look in the 'Scottish history section' so Foyle's, quipped Quentin, 'has already decided it is an independent country'.

There are two letters in the *Herald* in response to yesterday's column about the Establishment. The first, from a Yes supporter, expresses hope I'd be 'sincere' enough to acknowledge independence as the answer (thus confirming my argument), while the other is from John Edward at the Scottish Council for Independent Schools more or less accusing me of indulging in 'us and them' politics but not actually engaging with the point, which is as depressing as it is predictable. Got a more thoughtful response from Daniel Johnson, who ('as a self acknowledged product of the system') said Edinburgh was run by an elite but that it 'is not often spoken about' and that 'elite has withdrawn from public life'.

Got a cab to Robert Gordon University for a Universities Scotland principals' 'away day', which provided a fascinating insight into the academic Establishment: Sir Tim O'Shea, Louise Richardson and Pete Downes were all there. I spoke for about half an hour (from notes, which I find best) then took questions, which seemed to go down quite well (I'd done my homework on Sunday, which was useful). Only one principal (from Robert Gordon University, I think, he'd outed himself at an SNP conference fringe meeting two years ago) was declared. I joked that a full report of proceedings would appear in the following day's *Scotsman*, while the key point I made was that most post-Yes scenarios assumed a benign economic climate, which seemed unlikely no matter what the outcome of negotiations.

En route to Aberdeen railway station I grilled my taxi driver about his voting intentions and he seemed happy enough to talk, saying he would be voting No mainly because of economic uncertainty ('I'm not really a risk taker'); he said an English guy working in Aberdeen had done a poll of 15 cabbies (including him) and only one was voting Yes (and he was Latvian). Still, he added, he'd probably engaged more with politics over the past two years than ever before. Aberdeen was drenched in sunshine and the east coast looked captivating as I skirted down the coast by train; it reminded me of being a student – before the Scottish Parliament even existed.

Before speaking to students at Abertay University I had lunch with yet another university contemporary who's now lecturing (part time) there and I hadn't seen in about a decade. She looked exactly the same and was as rational and level-headed as ever. Said she would definitely be voting Yes because 'England is right wing and Scotland is (more) left wing'. I pointed out all the problems with this and she listened politely, but she knew what she was doing. Said her husband would cancel her out as he works in oil industry and they're all voting No. My Dundee taxi driver had a prominent Yes sticker in one of his windows. Can't help feeling I've been a little slow on the uptake on all of this.

At Abertay University one guy read straight from the Wings Over Scotland script about foreign-owned newspapers, BBC bias etc, and in response I gave him rather short (but polite) shrift; another, a nursing student, said she was voting Yes because Scottish NHS funding was 'directly linked' to English NHS funding and was therefore 'synched in a downward spiral'. She looked at me smugly afterwards as if content she was in full possession of the facts but I couldn't muster the energy to contradict her. Otherwise the consensus was that the debate had got to 'over saturation' point, 'tired', 'not a very good' level of debate, 'too much to handle', and with an overemphasis on currency at the expense of other areas. There was also the usual fantasy politics ('Scotland is verging on being a socialist country'), but one can (almost) forgive that from students.

At Waverley station I bumped into Professor James Mitchell and he made the point that No ought to be 'miles in front' at this stage, and he's right. Walked back to Hugh's to find Dad waiting for me with some mail, although he was surprisingly sanguine about the poll, doesn't quite believe it, said polls are polls, etc. He'd just finished telling Hugh that the Jim Murphy egg attack was co-ordinated by Unionists (apparently footage shows people with 'earpieces'). Once he'd left, Hugh told me he'd spent the previous evening with a friend of his from Better Together and that he'd called it the 'worst campaign he could remember', that most staff are hopeless, Lib Dem activists have been sent out to 'do what they can', etc. Meanwhile a faintly hysterical tone is creeping into Unionist press releases and tweets.

In the evening I cycled to the Assembly Rooms to watch STV's latest debate, this time with three representatives from each side and compered, as ever, by Bernard Ponsonby. It was a nice evening so I was in shorts and a T-shirt, which caused a degree of mirth. Eddie Barnes from the Scottish Conservatives sat next to me and admitted there was 'no point denying' there'd been a shift in the polls, while Mark Diffley from Ipsos MORI (sitting behind me) said he thought YouGov was spot-on and mirrored his private polling. Michael White from the *Guardian* was also there ('We live in lively times!'). The debate itself actually very good, particularly the audience (selected by Diffley). Colin McAllister, a Scottish Government spad (special adviser), said to me that STV 'know how to do punter' and he's right: STV's had a pretty good referendum, and has certainly put the (much better resourced) BBC Scotland to shame. The news about a hostage from Perthshire filtered through during the debate, which put everything in perspective.

We all got a bit pissed afterwards (the free bar helped) and an old colleague from Grampian told me the Aberdeen newsroom was probably majority Yes. Also saw Stephen Townsend, STV's main politics producer, who said 'I know you've been having fun' (meaning my casual dress during TV punditry) but that I had to wear a suit for the STV/ITV coverage. Later on Fran sent me an email she'd sent in response to a plea for pro-Union arguments from Charles Kennedy:

Keep the Great in Great Britain! Truly we are GREAT together! Rich Cultures, diverse Histories. Sporting Rivals, but amazing ALLIES!, The Union we have works.

Flawed? Always room for progress and improvement, Political tweaking absolutely necessary, but truly Better Together!.

Do we want a Border? Controls? Unable to pop back and forth as we do now? Do we want different Currencies, Passport checks? Layers of Bureaucracy, Obstacles? FRUSTRATIONS in our daily lives?

Grandchildren, sons and daughters living in different Countries when we've all grown up in ONE?

Let's celebrate our differences, Introducing more Powers to reflect where we vary in outlook, attitude and priorities, building on the Parliament we already have in Scotland, Be patriotic, love our rich Scottish Heritage, but PLEASE let's Stay Together, as ONE Country, unified in the ways that truly matter. All we have achieved together as a Nation is surely too precious and valuable to toss away with one small cross in a Heady moment on a Sept. night in 2014. Seductive that brief moment of Power may seem, but PLEASE truly reflect on Everything that will be thrown away in that fleeting second, with no chance 'tae think again'!.

Amazing how the same parents produced both a vehement Unionist and an ardent Nationalist.

Wednesday, 3 September 2014 (Edinburgh)

Got up late with another hangover. After getting my Brompton sorted at a local bike repair place – it not working always makes me feel a bit lost – I retreated to Apiary (across the road from where I'm staying) for a restorative lunch and coffee. Rattled through a bit of work and also put in some phone calls. My contact at Better Together told me their initial reaction to the YouGov poll on Monday night was 'oh for fuck's sake' but that they were now 'in a pretty good place', heartened by 'good' canvass returns and an expectation that Undecideds opting for No would soon show up in polls, just as those opting for Yes had done in the YouGov survey (mmm). He agreed with me that lots of voters are tuning out of certain aspects of the debate, not least technical stuff on currency and debt (the latter still being halfheartedly pushed by No). He said they couldn't walk away from making 'substantive' arguments ('we can't cede that stuff') and admitted it was difficult given the Yes's framing of monetary policy etc as somehow straightforward issues. 'If you don't know, vote no.'

My contact also said he thought there was 'strength' in the line that independence would mean 'getting the governments we vote for', no matter how many holes we could pick in it. Superficially, England does look more right wing, not least when it's obsessing over Clacton, UKIP, Boris, etc. He was, however, very happy about last night's STV debate, noting that Nicola was increasingly focused on Tory-bashing (thus her opening statement name checking 1979 and the Poll Tax). At some point, he mused, there has to be a genuine opening of discussion about 'what we're doing here, not just what we can do to get through this'. I asked if the will still existed at Westminster and he wasn't sure it did (nor am I, frankly). He said Alex Massie's recent blog had been 'spot-on' (which it had).

Also spoke to my Yes Scotland contact, as cool and collected as ever. His take on the YouGov poll was that it was playing 'catch up' with what was happening on the ground and that most polls would soon end up showing 50/50 (mmm); said he didn't know anything about a Panelbase poll. Said it 'feels like 2011' (although I pointed out that in 2011 polls hadn't so much been inaccurate, just a bit slow to pick up a switch in voting intention), in that there was great disparity between polls then they all settled in roughly the same place. I guess it vindicates the Stephen Noon prediction that once voters started to think properly about independence (as in 2011) they'd move in favour of Yes, indeed I remember him saying a couple of years ago he'd never seen people as open to the idea of doing so, and it seems he was right.

In the evening at Hugh's there was a launch for Brian Monteith's latest publication *The Positive Case*. This includes lots of good, stimulating stuff (including by Monty, Hugh and Adam Tomkins) but struck me as much too late, with only two weeks to go. The main speaker, who shall remain nameless, made quite an amusing speech, saying that initial indications from postal votes were encouraging and observing that his 'new best friend' Jim Murphy had been shielded by a bunch of 'Tory ladies' at a recent appearance in Edinburgh. The 'fundamental problem', he argued, was that Better Together had 'too many Labour people in it', so that Darling's approach to Salmond in the debate was to agree that 'Britain was crap' but that a Labour Government would put that right, thus reducing it to a Labour/SNP debate and undermining the broader case for the Union (on this he had a point). 'If any of you aren't working your fingers to the bone over the next two weeks,' was his parting shot, 'you damn well should be.'

It was a very Bufton Tufton gathering, complete with chaps in blazers and pink (and even green) trousers, all harrumphing that Salmond was a cad and why weren't people like me (i.e. journalists) exposing what a charlatan he was, etc. I gave one or two short shrift and implied they didn't live in the real world (which of course they don't). Even Sir Michael Hirst was there. Had a long chat with Ian Smart, who seemed under the impression devolving Inheritance Tax was the answer post-No vote (!), although he made the interesting observation that the exact form of 'more powers' depended (as ever) upon an internal Labour Party debate (sigh), not least those who resent any further erosion of their status.

Escaped from the launch to have a couple of drinks with David Melding, the Deputy Presiding Officer of the National Assembly for Wales, who didn't bat an eyelid at the rather loud music in Holyrood 9A. He was, as ever, engaging and frank about the constitutional situation and particularly the Conservative Party. He reckoned Plaid Cymru – however weak – would get a fillip from a Yes vote in Scotland, not least because it would legitimise their own (less developed) independence project. I could tell he despaired of recent Tory developments, i.e. Douglas Carswell, chatter about withdrawing from the ECHR ('We bloody wrote the thing!') and so on, and of course he's right about that too. We discussed the 'f' word, positing that the period following a close No vote would be the most fertile ground in which to develop a properly federal UK, though of course we both acknowledged it still wasn't likely. I mentioned to him Murdo's nascent plans for some sort of federalist campaign.

Thursday, 4 September 2014 (Edinburgh & Glasgow)

Text from Gerry Hassan: 'Is all getting a bit exciting and close. Still think no. But yes could just do it.'

Extraordinary story in the *Daily Telegraph* about Salmond offering Ben Riley-Smith (a reporter at the paper) a bag of sweets, and trying again even after Ben made it clear he thought it was patronising (which of course it was). I texted Ben saying that if it was any comfort the FM could be as condescending to journalists ten years his senior. I tweeted a link to the story and got the usual crap about me attempting to 'denigrate' the leader of the nation – extraordinary how blinkered some people can be. If the story had concerned David Cameron, you can imagine what the reaction would be, but then Salmond is subject to different rules on several different levels.

I discussed this later with Douglas Alexander, who was doing an event at the Grassmarket Community Centre with Andrew Wilson, when he recounted an anecdote along similar lines. He thanked me (ironically) for a tweet on Tuesday night pondering what the No campaign would have looked like under his leadership ('That'll help my relations with certain people'). He was, as ever, frank and engaging. Admitted they had their 'work cut out' and said 'if we want to keep Britain together we've got to vote for it', etc. He was quite pleased at having challenged Humza Yousaf to give examples of the SNP's 'redistributive' policies on last night's *Scotland 2014* (I watched this online later and Humza didn't come out of it well). On the YouGov poll he didn't dispute its central conclusions but argued it could have a useful motivating effect on the No side; thought it might be the result of a post-Commonwealth Games swell in pride (that seems unlikely). In short, Douglas still holds to the view that the vast majority of Scots don't want to make the rest of the UK a 'foreign country' but at the same time want Scotland 'to move forward' and if that can be 'resolved' then everything will be fine (federalism!). Said he might be making a speech at Edinburgh University over the weekend on more powers and some 'unexpected' things (such as, one suspects, a UK-wide constitutional convention). At one point Andrew Wilson joined us. 'Welcome to the Unionist conspiracy,' said Douglas. 'He's voting Yes,' replied Andrew, pointing at me and without missing a beat.

The event itself did its best to be polite but inevitably slid into pure politics. Robin Harper was there ('Hi David!'), as was Susan Deacon, who said she liked my casual punditry look. A lady at my table was wearing a very loud blue Yes hoodie. Douglas, who's incapable of saying anything that isn't interesting in some way, said the referendum had liberated us from the view politics 'doesn't matter' and that politicians 'are all the same', while it had both energised and divided Scotland. He also quoted Michael Ignatieff about politics being reduced to a 'battle of standing', an attempt to deprive one side of 'legitimacy' in talking about the future. Wilson, meanwhile, said (interestingly) he reckoned the outcome of the referendum would be the same either way, basically a recasting of the UK with decentralisation (particularly in England) but that the 'quickest route to getting there' was through a Yes vote: 'But I can see a similar route to getting there through a No, it would just take an awful, awful long time.'

After hanging around in a couple of cafés pretending to be hip and 20 I caught the train to Glasgow for the *Herald* indyref debate at Òran Mór which was, predictably, heavily oversubscribed and, equally predictably, stuffed full of Yessers (all credit to them for being so motivated, unlike their opponents). During drinks beforehand a lady came up to me and, whispering, said she read my stuff and was glad someone was 'thinking' and making 'reasonable points' etc. Also chatted to one of the Scottish Government spads beforehand (Ross?) and he said momentum was clearly with them, it was just a question of whether it'd be enough.

At the end of Fiona Hyslop's opening statement (which was so-so) I almost found myself joining in the rapturous applause before checking myself. Alistair Carmichael in his (well-crafted) opening comments joked it was clear there were 'a lot of Undecideds in tonight', which got a laugh. He said the UK was 'not some awful country from which we should escape' and reeled off a list of what made Britain great, much more convincingly than some of his colleagues. I later made the mistake of telling one of his advisers that I thought her boss had done quite well and before I knew it I had a text from my Whitehall contact saying it was a 'road test'. I replied, retracting and saying it was clichéd and dull, to which he texted back: 'Excellent, needs to fit the BT mould.' The crowd was feral, loudly applauding anything said by Patrick Harvie and Fiona (even when it was contradictory, i.e. on oil) and noisily deriding anything said by Alistair or Johann Lamont, however reasonable. One guy behind me was munching on crisps as if he was at his local multiplex. Afterwards I had a drink with Magnus (Llewellin) and David Thompson, who recently left the BBC to work at the Scotland Office. Fiona Hyslop joined us at one point and asked what I was up to ('Er, I'm a journalist.') before appealing to our 'enlightened self interest', just as the FM had done at the first SPJA lunch a few months ago. Had a long chat with Tom Gordon about how things were looking.

After slightly too much to drink I somehow found my way to Pacific Quay in the dark, although it was a lovely mild evening. Lord Robertson was also there and asked with faux outrage if I was planning to go on TV 'dressed like that' (I was wearing my now favourite Gillian Kyle Tunnock's Tea Cake T-shirt). I said I was (he was wearing regulation navy blazer and slacks). The programme itself (*Scotland 2014*) was a good example of village Scotland. First, Sarah Smith interviewed her sister's father-in-law (her sister is married to George's son) then her co-presenter Jonathan peered at me before his segment and said 'Weren't we at university together?' (We were, direct contemporaries, though I don't remember him.). Entertainingly, the last bit of the punditry section, which I did with Susan Stewart, was on Joan Rivers, whose death was announced towards the end of the *Herald* debate. Afterwards Susan and I hung around to do 'referendum radio' with Graham Stewart, although God knows who listens to that. Graham introduced me as being 'in the No camp' which I swiftly corrected, to his obvious surprise. Later saw a tweet from someone called Calum Findlay: 'Fuck sake... David Torrance on again. Is the greasy weasel never aff the telly?'

Friday, 5 September 2014 (Edinburgh & Dundee)

Up late due to late finish last night and cycled down to the City Art Centre to meet Lucy Hunter, an ex-civil servant who now picks apart Scottish Government/SNP claims on tuition fees and university access to great and uncomfortable (for Mike Russell) effect. She was a breath of fresh air: rational and fascinated by the gap between rhetoric and reality when it comes to tackling inequality. Then met Marc Van de Weyer, a reasonably switched on Flemish journalist, who's over for a few days to cover the referendum. He was (intimidatingly) well versed in my various utterances and he seemed genuinely surprised when I was willing to admit to having

A portrait of the author with his Bromptom taken for a Flemish newspaper.
(Photo:Tom Palmaers)

got various things wrong. Afterwards his photographer (also from Brussels) took pictures of me practically hugging my Brompton on the News Steps.

Got an email from Douglas Pattullo saying that all Better Together canvass returns 'suggest it is substantially less close than the YouGov poll suggested', which is interesting, although I guess those canvass returns could predate any shift in public opinion. My Yes Scotland contact texted to say BT were indulging in 'amateurish and transparent' expectation management tactics by putting it around that the Panelbase poll (still to surface and not in today's *Daily Record* guest 'edited' by Alex Salmond) shows Yes ahead, proof, he added, they were 'rattled'. But at the same time why not just publish the bloody thing? My contact at Better Together said they were doing no such thing, while Gerry Hassan later phoned to say he'd heard there were no fewer than three polls pending, all of which show Yes in the lead. That, I think, seems unlikely. I texted Angus Robertson to remind him that he'd promised me the ambassadorship to Croatia. 'I'm intrigued by the timing of this reminder,' he texted back. 'Feeling the momentum?' 'Purely coincidental,' was my response.

Caught the 4pm train to Dundee for what Patrick Harvie called a 'light grilling' on Twitter, cue lots of jokes about grills, sautéing etc. It was actually one of the best Q&As I've done at the University because Patrick engages with points and doesn't indulge in too much bullshit. Of course as one of only two MSPs he has the luxury of doing so but still, he consistently refused to overstate the advantages of a Yes, particularly in environmental terms. The audience asked decent, sensible questions, including one guy who pointed out the curious desire to leave one Union (the UK) but stay in another, arguably less democratic one (the EU). Patrick, to his credit, agreed it was a 'paradox' (in that the direction of travel within the EU gave less independence to individual member states). I indulged myself at the end by speaking about *Doctor Who* for a few minutes but it kinda worked and got a laugh, particularly when I asked him if casting a Scot in referendum year was a 'BBC conspiracy' (he pointed out that McCoy was Yes, Tennant No and Capaldi undeclared). A few folk said afterwards that they'd enjoyed all the events, and indeed so have I. One Yes activist asked for my prediction but I declined on the basis that it would only be wrong, like my previous call of 60/40 against.

Caught (just) the 7.33pm East Coast train back to Edinburgh and then got a taxi to Area C coffee house (covered in Yes posters) near the bottom of Leith Walk for the launch of Dominic Hinde's *Scotland 44* book. It was quite good fun if only because it was full of people I wouldn't usually speak to – Green activists and National Collective types – and therefore quite revealing. Try as I might no one was getting carried away at the polls, but at the same time they're quietly confident. Had too much wine at one of the nearby Swedish bars but lots of good chat. Outside I bumped into a guy who used to work as a security guard at the Scottish Parliament and a lady academic we were with asked how he was voting. 'No,' he said, 'because I feel British.' The chief driver was military service, which he and two generations of his family had in common.

I wandered up Leith Walk at just after midnight in search of a taxi and stopped in at Eatalia for some chips and ice cream (I was that drunk). The

Scottish-Italian lady who works there remembered my brother and I from regular visits when we both lived in the area a while back and naturally chat turned to the referendum. She was voting No mainly, interestingly, as a result of the recent STV debate ('too many unanswered questions'). A colleague (also Italian) was also No because he feared foreigners would be compelled to 'go home', but they all thought (including an Eastern European girl) that it'd be a Yes vote on the day.

Got home at about 1am to see I'd featured in one of David Greig's Yes/No Play tweets:

> Yes: New jumper?
> No: Mm.
> Yes: Colourful...
> Yes: New hair?
> No: Mm.
> Yes: Perky...
> Yes: (eyes narrow) Are you copying David Torrance again?

Saturday, 6 September 2014 (Edinburgh & Glasgow)

Woke up late to an excitable tweet from my contact at Yes Scotland: 'Looking like my reading of polls was spot-on. Trend too!' I asked him to elaborate and he replied:

> Two tomorrow. Please do not tweet or any other chat. I don't have all the details but my points to you days ago remain. YouGov has caught up, it's basically 50/50 or thereabouts and trends underneath the headline average is what matters. Difficult to stop the underlying trend with ten days left even if headline numbers vary day to day. There is one poll out tomorrow which I don't know about but if it's yes over 50 I'd rather that was a bit later than tomorrow! I will take it of course but later would have been ideal. Late fourties with yes underlying momentum is perfect right now.

I replied (jokingly): 'Of course I've always supported independence, etc,' to which he replied: 'Ha. This could go either way. It's fun! Kenny F[arquharson] has been tweeting all week about a Panelbase poll saying Yes ahead obviously on back of No spin. Put it this way, I doubt that's the case. Like I said, they are consolidating. Poor Peter K[ellner]!'

Nick Wood (from Political Tours) phoned (twice) in a bit of a flap about tonight, mainly because we can't get the group access to the Sikh temple for a debate between Nicola Sturgeon and Anas Sarwar. I texted Anas asking if he could twist some arms and he duly did so, digging us out of a rather big hole; I texted him to say I'd buy him lunch once Scotland had voted Yes. Over lunch I read Douglas Alexander's speech at Glasgow University this morning, which he'd suggested would contain some surprises, i.e. a call for a UK-wide constitutional convention after a No vote. It included nothing of the sort, just a rather flat 'Nats bad, more powers' pitch, which suggests the usual internal Labour nonsense compelled him to pull back. I'm struggling to understand the Labour mentality (propagated by both dinosaurs and others who should know better) that places internecine strife above securing a No vote – it'll hardly matter if around 40 Scottish Labour MPs don't have seats in a couple of years' time!

Got the 3.45pm train to Glasgow to join the Political Tour group at the Grasshoppers Hotel near Central Station and then headed to the same Sikh temple we visited last year for a rather lengthy debate between Nicola Sturgeon (wearing a headscarf) and Anas Sarwar. Surprisingly, Anas did extremely well; a strong opening statement followed by deftly handled questions and various well-targeted digs at an obviously worn-out Deputy First Minister. I got the distinct impression the predominantly Sikh audience wasn't at all enamoured with the independence project.

Just as I was gearing up for my peroration at dinner afterwards, news started filtering through about tomorrow's YouGov poll. 'I will take 51pc,' texted my Yes contact, and then: 'Trend good for yes but anyone's game. UK offer of "federalism" is a mistake on their part.' This was a reference to the front page of the *Observer*, which used the 'f' word, although when I read on this seemed to mean simply more devolution for Scotland within the UK, which of course isn't federalism by any stretch. The 'briefing', such as it is, started just after 6pm ('Jim McColl got a call,' he texted, 'Desperate stuff.'). He also flattered me by saying 'You of all people should have been briefed?' (But of course I hadn't been.) The Palace has also told the *Sunday Times* that the Queen is 'horrified' at the prospect of independence, etc. 'Feels like 2011 again,' observed my contact. 'No all over the place. No one channel or direction.'

Intriguingly, he then suggested that Marcus Booth (who I'm due to have lunch with on Sunday) was 'influencing' Rupert Harrison and George Osborne, 'who does the thinking for the government'. 'He tells me they wouldn't even put detailed proposal in reserve.' Even more intriguingly, when I later tweeted about it ('Whatever this is it isn't "federal"; the word "panic" strikes me as a better description…') Marcus responded several times in a manner that implied he *did* know what was going on ('Why class as panic, listening to what people clearly are calling for?', 'should give it a fair hearing, at very least' and 'Union needs radical renewal and reform – drib drab reforms will land us in same place as we are now in a few years time'). Maybe so, but it still isn't anything approaching federalism – if it was I could claim to be a constitutional visionary!

Anyway, all of this contributed to a rather charged atmosphere at dinner, which was great for the political tourists but at points a bit much for me to handle. Robert, a retired *Observer* journalist, had bought completely into the line about Scots wanting to reject the neoliberal status quo. I did my best to point out the likely gap between what's promised and what's deliverable while Jamie Maxwell deployed some Marxist analysis (the poll showed 'working class' and Labour voters shifting to Yes). Nick – who really feels *British* – looked engaged but rather gloomy.

Ended a memorable day rather incongruously watching *Doctor Who* with a girl who worked at the hotel on her desktop iPlayer, not that I ended up paying much attention. She thought the poll news was 'great' although she was also worried about losing £20 she'd bet on a No vote.

Sunday, 7 September 2014 (Glasgow & London)

Terrible sleep but got up early for breakfast and then to watch George Osborne (curious choice of messenger) on the *Andrew Marr Show*, looking sinister but striking more or less the right tone. Beyond that he simply reheated the carrot-and-stick strategy, more powers being the carrot ('a plan of action' within days he said) and a currency veto (yawn) the stick.

'You panicking yet, Torrance?' texted a friend from the *Sun* (I replied saying 'neutral' journos had nothing to panic about and asked what Mr M was planning.) 'Last I heard was that they were staying neutral,' he replied. 'Now? Who knows?' Later Mr M tweeted: 'Salmond's private polls predict 54/46 Yes. Desperate last ten days ahead for both sides. Most powerful media, BBC, totally biased for No.' That suggests to me he's toying with revisiting the *Scottish Sun* circa 1992 and backing indy, but we shall see. The interesting thing is that I don't really feel anything at all, certainly not panic.

Took the Political Tour group to Baillieston to witness some Better Together campaigning on the ground. We spoke at length to a textbook Yes voter, every answer considered, thoughtful and straight from the Yes Scotland playbook. Also managed to grab Blair McDougall for a quick chat (much to the frustration of a Better Together staffer) and – to his credit – he was happy to take questions for a bit. He looked surprisingly cheerful.

After that we drove to Govanhill Baths for Gerry Hassan's Festival of Ideas, at which I was taking part in a panel discussion about the 'future of the UK'. This was long and very badly chaired, although I got to kick off on federalism etc, which wasn't so bad. Also on the panel was Iain

The 'Political Tour' group questioning Better Together's Blair McDougall in Bailliston.

Macwhirter, Madeleine Bunting from the *Guardian* (whose nuanced points about Britishness clearly didn't go down well with the audience), the economist Jo Armstrong and James Foley, an earnest young left-winger who made predictably superficial points. Questions ranged from batty to quite sensible, though most sprang from a belief (and no doubt intoxicated by the polls) that all this is some sort of game with clear winners and losers, predictable outcomes and everything ending in the spirit of comradeship. The setting, however, was great: the crumbling surroundings of an old Victorian bathhouse, which I joked might be taken as an analogy for Britain.

I then cycled (in beautiful sunshine) from there to Queen Street Station. For some reason things felt different; noticed lots of Yes posters and even a poster advertising Wings Over Scotland's 'Blue Book' outside a derelict pub. Ben Riley-Smith from the *Telegraph* texted to ask: 'If you had to call it today, gun to head, which way would you go?' I didn't really answer. At Waverley I bought a late lunch from M&S and then caught the 3.30pm to King's Cross. Felt slightly melancholy.

Hugh emailed me a couple of hours later saying my biography of Alex Salmond was now out of print and 'very dated' given events since 2011. He added that 'if they win' then we'd need to consider an updated edition. 'This is one commission,' he added sadly, 'I sincerely hope not having to make a quick decision on.' Stephen Daisley was very funny on Facebook, posting: 'We cross now to Scotland, where economic reality has been suspended, and to David Torrance in our Edinburgh studio. David, how are Scots reacting to the First Minister's announcement of free unicorns for everyone?'

After a really bad (and expensive) meal with Michael and Laura at a place near King's Cross Michael and I got a cab to Millbank so I could do an interview near the top of the *Westminster Hour*. This went reasonably well (I followed pre-recorded interviews with a gloomy-sounding Anas Sarwar and Pete Wishart repeatedly using the royal 'we') and was followed by some chat with the Tory MP Mark Field (who dismissed YouGov as a 'rogue poll') and Labour's Alison Seabeck, who was pretty hopeless: she had an A4 sheet of paper in front of her headed 'Scotland', while she implied independence-supporting Labour voters were emotionally 'volatile'. Oops.

Monday, 8 September 2014 (London & Edinburgh)

Up at 7.30am after a very sound sleep. Sky News sent a cab at 8.45am (Laura hitched a lift) but the traffic was so bad there was no way I was going to get to Millbank for 9.30am and a producer asked me to head to the Gherkin, but by the time I made it up to their studios on the 15th floor the slot had gone – slightly frustrating. After that I cycled around the City (where the pound was busy losing one per cent of its value) and then in the direction of Waterloo; it was a gorgeous day and it felt good to get out of the political hothouse that is Scotland. London felt different somehow. Lots of flapping in today's papers, mainly from Buckingham Palace; someone remarked this morning that the panic rather shored up the frequent Nationalist claim that Britain was 'broken'.

After coffee and emails I caught the train to leafy Barnes and then cycled to St Paul's, George Osborne's *alma mater*, where I'd agreed some time ago to give a talk to its 'Polecon' about the referendum. It struck me *en route* that everything I saw might be wielded in a support of a Yes vote – expensive London suburb and exclusive boys' school – but then of course both those things exist in parts of Scotland too. I just ad-libbed the talk, which worked surprisingly well, and then I took questions. There was one Scottish kid in the audience and also a Scottish-born Latin teacher, both of whom made good points. In fact, all the questions were good. Then we had lunch in the canteen and several boys bombarded me with questions. Later I asked if they'd be bothered about Scotland becoming independent and one guy said he'd be sad from a 'patriotic' point of view but happy politically (actually his father's view) as it'd increase the chances of Conservative governments in future. St Paul's was actually rather drab aesthetically – a mix of 1960s

The Brompton meets Jim Murphy's Irn-Bru crates.

brutalism and contemporary steel and glass. 'Thanks for the talk!' said another pupil chirpily as I unfolded my Brompton.

Cycled all the way to King's Cross, which took about 50 minutes, but it was an easy and pleasant journey (despite several terrifying roundabouts) and I fielded calls from *Newsnight* ('We're having a discussion about what a federal UK would look like' – my time has come!) and *The World Tonight* (what impact will the royal baby have on the vote?). Chris Deerin tweeted a link to his typically excellent *Scottish Daily Mail* column, which included a reference to 'that nationalist fantasy',

> soundtracked and scripted by middle-class musicians, playwrights and actors, urged along by disenchanted, superannuated newspaper columnists, gleefully led by a pied-piper politician as cynical and self-interested as any of those he castigates at Westminster. Everything will be fine, the detail doesn't matter, we'll cross each bridge as we come to it, it'll be alright on the night. Let's just *get out*.

Absolutely spot-on, not that anyone's listening. All discussion is now couched in terms of campaign tactics, not what's realistic or desirable;

grand principles have been sacrificed to chatter about presentation and framing. Somebody from the *Daily Record* called to discuss some copy Jamie Maxwell and I are providing for a special indyref supplement later this week; he said he was 'still hoping for the best' as if someone had a terminal medical condition.

Lots of crazy chatter on Twitter about the UK Government's 'more powers' offer being 'illegal' because voting has already begun, while Buzzfeed reports that a majority of Scots believe ministers have hidden new oilfields from the Scottish people because of the referendum, and a quarter believe MI5 has been deploying the dark arts and a fifth think it's likely the result will be rigged. This referendum has extended SNP paranoia to the population at large!

Gordon Brown is making a speech (another one) setting out a clear timetable for 'more powers', building on his call last week for a Commons debate straight after the referendum and then legislation targeted at St Andrew's Day and Burns Night next year (sigh). This, on reflection, was quite extraordinary – a former Prime Minister announcing Government legislation at a miners' club in Midlothian. I wracked my brains for a constitutional precedent but couldn't think of one. But will it work? 'Realistic. Not enough,' was my Better Together contact's verdict, and when I asked if Wednesday's announcement would flesh it out further he said: 'It may. Depends on how rapturous the media get. This is a media litmus-test moment. You must do your duty.' (I replied saying my *Herald* column probably hadn't quite done that.) 'Yes,' he texted back, 'MI5 have been informed.'

A TNS poll due tomorrow, meanwhile, puts Yes and No at level pegging at 50 per cent excluding don't knows. Brian Wilson had a blistering take down of George Monbiot in today's *Guardian*, including the opening paragraph:

> Other people's nationalism tends to look cuddlier from afar. Those on the left who would be horrified by association with the version on their own doorsteps fall over themselves to find progressive potential in movements they do not have the inconvenience of experiencing at close range. Balladeers who have strummed righteously to songs of solidarity and working-class unity become cheerleaders for the destruction of these very values. Convoluted theories are constructed about how dividing people will actually unite them through some mysterious process of inspiration and example.

Of course he's right, Chris Deerin and I having made similar points in our respective columns. Meanwhile there's continued pressure on sterling and stocks in firms like RBS and the Weir Group are falling, not that anyone seems to care. Increasingly part of me wants independence to happen simply so that the SNP is confronted with the reality of everything they appear to consider so simple and straightforward. Lots of emails from foreign journalists asking, inevitably, lots of questions, some good, some bad.

Dad picked me up at Waverley, gave me some mail and then drove me down to the Shore in Leith where I was meeting Neil Mackinnon for dinner. Full of interesting chat as ever and understandably smug at having said all along the result would be close. He pointed out that it was difficult (and had always been difficult) for Better Together to sell the UK when they didn't have a shared view of what it actually was (true). Labour, he added, was being punished in Scotland for appearing to collude with the Tories over austerity, whereas south of the border they were suffering for not being seen to collude enough. We also discussed the likely shape of Anglo-Scottish negotiations in the event of a Yes vote: Neil predicted an early statement (certainly by 8am on Friday 19) to calm the markets, then a pause over the weekend before the talks started in earnest on Monday. A delayed General Election seemed likely, which would avoid awkwardness with Scottish MPs, who'd simply leave in 2016 once everything had been sorted out. We agreed the talks would be reasonably amicable, that EU membership and a currency union would be agreed but not necessarily with great terms and conditions.

The very fact Neil and I were discussing this seriously spoke for itself. He pointed out, shrewdly, that columnists like me, Fraser Nelson, Iain Martin and Chris Deerin, who'd all worked in London (or abroad) for prolonged periods naturally had a different perception of Britain and the UK than most Scots, who of course haven't. At the same time (I pointed out) I felt attached to Liverpool and Manchester too, so the London dimension can't be the whole story. We also touched on the class dimension (I mentioned that Jamie had been banging on about this on the tour), and Neil broadly agreed with my (uber-cynical) assessment that the 'working classes' (whatever that means these days) were basically being used as lobby fodder to deliver a Yes vote while, if anything, they stood the most to lose if things got difficult in the short term. After all, it's worth remembering that until three years ago the SNP hadn't thought about welfare, currency or any number of important policies because they hadn't had to.

I got home just in time to catch most of Bernard Ponsonby grilling the FM on a *Scotland Tonight* special, and of course he did a good job on Income Tax, the NHS, Corporation Tax, etc. 'Give me three tough decisions an independent Scotland will have to take?' he asked at one point, to which Salmond replied: 'We'll move out of austerity.' (I rest my case.) If Yes wins, the FM concluded, 'then we'll be hoisting a Saltire a week on Thursday'. I thought it wasn't about 'flags or anthems'? When I tweeted approvingly about the show an SNP councillor in Aberdeenshire replied snidely that it had been a 'shocking' interview and we'd see 'your [i.e. my] friend' the following night, meaning Darling.

Of course one side effect of the referendum has been to delegitimise the media, so perfectly justified but robust questioning is now seen by otherwise sensible people as 'biased' or pushing a Unionist agenda. Of course no one could argue that the press is perfect, but there's now a widespread view that almost everything journalists in Scotland write or report is a tissue of lies, which hardly bodes well for democracy. Dominic Hinde messaged me on Facebook to say he was concerned about the anti-journalist sentiment among the Yes camp (!). Chatted to a few folk online and several were moving from No to Yes, one because of the NHS and the prospect of Boris Johnson becoming Prime Minister, although he at least conceded that 'difficult decisions' lay ahead no matter what.

Got some texts from Karl Turner, a Labour MP in Hull: 'This might well be an absolute disaster. Very concerning.' I replied saying his party hadn't covered itself in glory, to which he replied:

Dear me... This getting rid of Tories forever is an attractive proposition to younger electorate and the negativity of the campaign was inevitable in my view. I definitely believe we are better together but matter for Scots at the end of the day. Let's see but it looks dreadful from where I'm sitting.

He then added, apropos of nothing: 'Disastrous. Truly disastrous if it goes belly-up.'

On *Newsnight* Douglas Alexander pointed out that Scotland had gone from one of the poorest parts of the UK to one of the wealthiest in 30 years, a factoid I flattered myself he'd remembered from my conversation with him a few days ago. Later in the programme (which I'd been lined up for earlier in the day) there was an entertaining battle of egos between Sir Tom Devine and Niall Ferguson (from the US). Devine, in pompous overload, said he'd only come out in support of Yes 'reluctantly, if you will', added that independence would contribute to a 'sense of leaving a very good and old friend' and then burbled on about the social union being strengthened. He also said the Union was now a 'destabilising factor on this archipelago', which didn't really make any sense. More generally, Devine just quoted straight from the Yes Scotland playbook, while Ferguson (equally puffed up) just made a fool of himself. The briefing against Douglas Alexander continues. Apparently he's known as 'Rainman' in Labour circles (not my experience), but more to the point what does blaming him at this stage, even if justified, actually achieve? It just highlights how dysfunctional the Labour Party really is.

Tuesday, 9 September 2014 (Edinburgh, Falkirk and Perth)

Awoke to the usual tranche of emails, tweets and texts (I'll be glad when this is over), including one from a junior diplomat in Washington who was in touch a while back. 'Washington,' he said simply, 'is definitely paying close attention now...' As I got ready to head out for a swim I texted a mate of mine at the Scotland Office, who I've not seen or spoken to in ages, just asking for his thoughts. 'Well, imagine a political has-been in the Labour Party announcing govt legislation on, say, welfare policy or tax policy,' he texted, 'and you'll see how much of a mess the pro union parties have got themselves in.' Quite.

He added that at the same time they 'should and could' have set out the timetable 12 months ago as doing so now looked 'extremely panicky' (which of course it does). I asked if anything was happening tomorrow. 'Who knows?' was his weary response. 'The reverse of the fag packet might get something scribbled on it for tomorrow too.' Indeed, when I got to Dynamic Earth after a swim, it did look kinda hasty, a bunch of ostentatious Tory activists standing with 'Best of Both Worlds' banners and waiting for the three Scottish Unionist party leaders to turn up and say how amazing Gordon Brown's plan was. Halfway through a senior Tory contact of mine texted me: 'Is this as unconvincing as it looks?' 'Yup,' I replied, 'crowd behind them predominantly & ostentatiously Tory.' 'Fuck,' was his one-word reply.

The Westminster Lobby, however, looked as if they were enjoying themselves, particularly Quentin Letts, who was leaping around in his usual impish way. Needless to say most of them were playing catch up, something reflected in the rather witless questions lobbed at Davidson, Lamont and Rennie. When one asked about federalism Johann responded with a dig at constitutional anoraks, at which point Ruth caught my eye and looked as if she was trying not to laugh. One girl from Better Together remarked to me that Yes must be unhappy at having lost two days' of newspaper headlines (an interesting way of looking at it), while afterwards I caught Jim Gallacher just before he gave some background to the gathered hacks. 'You remember the press notices the Russians put out during the Second World War?' he said to me when I asked how it was going. 'We're advancing on all fronts!' I also spoke to someone from Scottish Labour about George Osborne's telly turn on Sunday morning. 'I've always assumed there were smart people running things down there,' he said wearily, 'but they're not.' The main problem with the Chancellor's remarks hadn't been their tone, he added, but the vague impression that the devo offer would go much further than that already set out in the various party commissions. Jack

The three Unionist party leaders tell the media why they're supporting Gordon Brown's timetable for 'more powers'.

Blanchard (now at the *Mirror*) texted me wanting to arrange dinner: 'Mr Torrance. It appears Westminster had [*sic*] noticed that all that stuff you've been banging on about for the past few years is actually a story after all. I'm therefore being sent North forthwith.' He's not the only one.

I emailed another Tory contact to ask what he made of it all. 'There is a sense of panic and desperation,' he said. 'I still think we will be okay on the night but not thanks to the campaign...' I suspect he's right, a narrow No will be in spite of Better Together, not because of it, but at the same time the trouble goes much deeper than simply 'more powers', which the Westminster bubble has convinced itself is both the cause and the cure. As the polling makes clear it's now about trust and legitimacy, and that of course can't be put (fully) right in just a few days.

After that I caught the train to Falkirk to meet the Political Tour group at one of Jim Murphy's '100 towns' tour stops. His voice was hoarse and the crowd more benign than usual (the attack dogs have clearly been called off), but I admire him enormously for putting himself through such a punishing schedule. Afterwards he sat in a café and chatted with the group for around 15 minutes, which was good of him considering none of them have a vote. His lunch appeared to consist of a sandwich (to go) and several bottles of Irn-Bru. Sheila texted, clearly quite exercised by events, asking if I knew where David Cameron would be the following day (I didn't) and when I replied asking what she made of it all, she left me a voicemail saying she hoped 'it' (the Brown plan) worked. Had a brief chat to someone at Downing Street and asked him what the PM's plan was and he said it would be 'central' but beyond that he still wasn't sure what form it would take. They really are making all this up as they go along.

My Better Together contact phoned and texted several times asking if I had the result of the next Survation poll but I didn't (he promised to keep it very 'tight'). He then gave me a typically thoughtful survey of where things were at and didn't spare his own side: it was a 'wake-up call' to Westminster and its view of the world, but where it all ended up was another matter. I asked if he knew what was happening tomorrow and joked that they must be running out of fag packets. 'Behave,' he replied by text. 'This is politics. And don't imagine it is ever any different.'

Willie Sullivan from the Electoral Reform Society emailed asking me to put my name to a letter he (and others) planned to place in Thursday's *Times*, basically calling for a UK-wide constitutional convention no matter what the vote. After some reflection I agreed, not only because the text was ecumenical in tone but it was more or less consistent with my position on federalism. Vernon Bogdanor had also signed it, so it had an Establishment seal of approval. *The Times* also contacted me wanting a profile of Alex Salmond, which will basically write itself, while I fielded about half a dozen emails and calls from international journalists. A bored sounding girl also called from the BBC News Channel wanting a 'No voice' but immediately lost interest when I said I didn't have a declared position. The irony of all these claims the BBC are biased is that armies of producers are spending their lives trying to 'balance' panels and content exactly between Yes and No, and not just with politicians. After dropping in on the Strachans (veterans of last year's Political Tour) at their home in Perth, I cycled to the railway station and got back to Edinburgh in time to change for the Chancellor's dinner at Holyroodhouse.

This was quite good fun and, more or less, a referendum-free zone, that is after Andrew Kerr and I had a long and entertaining chat with Jim Naughtie. When I complained to him and Andrew about BBC producers requiring commentators to have a 'position' he murmured that it was the official campaign period, which I suppose is true, but still. Before we ate Princess Anne was guided around certain guests by the Principal, but HRH didn't make it to the media corner (Sheena McDonald added to our trio), which was probably just as well. I sat next to a constitutional lawyer called Jo Shaw ('I follow you on Twitter!') who said lots of rational things about the likely status of an independent Scotland in the EU (in short, it'll be fine).

Caught a cab home and the driver said he probably wasn't going to vote as neither side had convinced him, although he made a point of flagging

The author with his dad. (Photo: Calum Cashley)

up Better Together's recent thing on supermarket prices as evidence of their 'bullshit'. He also didn't believe there'd be more powers after a No. Alex Massie has declared himself as a No, which is unhelpful, though he's done so in a typically well-written piece. When I tweeted a link it generated some predictable flak about my 'dishonesty' in not also saying how I planned to vote, including a tweet from Rory Ford, a former colleague at the *Edinburgh Evening News*, who said, snidely, 'If you think you're fooling anyone that you're neutral, you're only deluding yourself – and the BBC. Good luck with that.' Actually, now the polls have narrowed I'm even more convinced I've made the right decision.

Wednesday, 10 September 2014 (Edinburgh & Barcelona)

Woke up late-ish (well, 9.15am) and a bit hungover after last night. Absolutely crazy day but warm and sunny, which helped; cycled to Piershill (near where I grew up) to see the MargoMobile (finally) together with Salmond and Sturgeon (the indyref could even bring together sworn enemies Jim and Alex!) and a reasonably big crowd had turned out to see them, though I recognised most as local activists. Indeed, Dad was there wearing a loud blue Yes T-shirt so I got someone to take a (as it turned out, really nice) picture of us standing together. Later I tweeted it and it got retweeted nearly 200 times.

Toni Guigliano was there, pouting and looking utterly superior, but others (like Calum Cashley) were their usual down-to-earth friendly selves. It was basically a glorified photo call, but the logic of doing it in a working-class area like this was clear: not only shoring up local campaigning but keeping hold of 'soft' Labour voters. Spoke to Michael Gray and Cailean Gallagher who were friendly but clearly swept up in it all (entirely understandable in the circumstances). One guy recognised me from the *Herald* and started telling me how he'd 'burned' the previous day's *Times* because of the 'language' used; when I explained that the majority of *Herald* columnists were pro-independence it appeared to take him by surprise. And after doing a quick interview for Martin Geissler at ITV an incredibly rude guy barged in between us (introducing himself as 'a Common Weal author', which is a new one) and attempting to remonstrate with both us about what I'd said (which, incidentally, had mainly been complimentary about Salmond and the Yes campaign). As I cycled away a passing motorist yelled, rather feebly, 'Vote No!'

I got to Scottish Widows on Morrison Street just in time for the Prime Minister's visit, which was an interesting contrast with the Salmond event in Lochend: while the FM engaged with activists in a working-class area, Cameron addressed a bunch of over-paid suits in the heart of Edinburgh's financial district. Tonally he was fine, contrite and even quite emotional. Admitted that if Scotland voted Yes then he'd 'help make it happen' (a point he repeated several times), while cautioning against supporting independence just to punish the 'effing Tories'. All the questions were good ones and not necessarily helpful. Finishing up, he announced that Lord Hill had been made the EU's financial services commissioner, although that's hardly going to win over wavering voters. Craig Oliver was there looking (for some reason) rather pleased with himself, as were half the Westminster Lobby, still furiously playing catch up with a story that took them, like the PM, completely by surprise. One of my tweets, Cameron's comment that 'you cannot hold people in the UK against their will... we are a democracy' was swiftly translated into Catalan and Spanish and did the rounds in Iberia on Twitter.

After that I cycled down to The Tun to do a discussion on the *John Beattie* show about the visit of the 'three amigos' (Cameron, Clegg and Miliband) and the campaign more generally (I was on with Andrew Tickell and Duncan Hothersall). Also spoke to someone at the *Daily Record* (which ran the supplement by Jamie Maxwell and me today) who had details of the most recent Survation poll. All he'd give me in advance of the 10pm embargo was the headline finding, 57/43 in favour of No, and asked for 200 words of analysis for tomorrow's paper. When I asked him to email me the full dataset he basically refused as polling data is now market sensitive. Indeed, he said various financial outfits had spent the morning trying to get information out of him, while my Better Together contact told me later that someone at their HQ had been tasked with monitoring the dollar online. This is all getting a bit weird. Later Standard Life said it was making contingency plans to move south after a Yes vote and Salmond said they were bluffing. I wonder if he thinks the financial markets are bluffing too? Chatted to a few people in the No camp and they remain quietly confident about a narrow win.

After lunch at Hemma and a quick interview for *Voice of America* I cycled up to St Giles' Cathedral to do another interview (I've no idea who it was for) and then home, briefly, to change and pack stuff for Barcelona. Dad then gave me a lift to Waverley, complaining that the Edinburgh Southern Yes office had been defaced overnight with 'NO' in large letters and Nazi imagery. At the Balmoral Hotel bar I spoke to Konrad Kramar from an Austrian newspaper and he asked relatively sensible questions about what was going on. Did a quick phone interview for a CBS radio station in LA, during which the best question was: 'So, David, will the Republic of Ireland be next to seek independence from the UK?' Good grief. They also asked if Scotland would want to become a US state, but that at least was tongue in cheek. Caught a bus to the airport and nearly missed my flight to Barcelona, which would have been an absolute disaster.

I've never been so relieved to get on a plane. After checking into my hotel on Las Ramblas I faffed for a bit online before heading to Fossar de la Morreses to catch the end of a pre-Diada rally at which various shouty Catalan politicians were speaking. I arrived just in time to hear Liam O'Hare, a Radical Independence Campaign activist who was there with fraternal greetings (secessionists of the world unite!), and his speech was translated into Catalan every few paragraphs or so. It was generic left-wing stuff, but quite good fun: 'Just as we're going toe-to-toe with British state, you're going toe-to-toe with the Spanish state, but here's the good news – we have them on the ropes!' 'We stand on the verge of history comrades,' he concluded, 'let's make it together.' I said hello afterwards and we agreed to meet the following day (or on Friday) for a drink.

Thursday, 11 September 2014 (Barcelona)

Up at 8am and after a failed attempt to get breakfast (despite having full board the computer said no) I caught the Metro to the Generalitat for Artur

Catalan president Artur Mas (left) during an international press conference in Barcelona.

Mas's international press conference (I very nearly ended up in completely the wrong place). This was pleasantly straightforward and I ended up sitting next to Liz Castro, an American journalist whose name I knew from a book on Catalonia I'd bought a while back (which included a particularly bad chapter on Scotland). She was very friendly and took obvious pleasure in telling me the nuances of Catalan politics and the proposed referendum. Mas himself was handsome and slick, and proceeded to answer questions (fluently) in four different languages (Catalan, Spanish, French and English). He was cautious, obviously keen to do things 'by the book' and, if possible, reach agreement with Madrid, which of course isn't going to happen. I asked him about the likely effect of a Scottish Yes vote on both Madrid and Catalan public opinion and he gave a reasonably expansive answer saying he was confident the EU would accept the outcome and that negotiations between Brussels, London and Edinburgh would take place swiftly thereafter. In fact Scotland came up in other questions too, but then it wasn't difficult to understand why.

After that Liz and I went for coffee before getting the Metro to Plaça de les Glòries to collect my pass for the 'Catalan Way' (or Diada) itself. There Liz seemed to know everyone and I bumped into Marc Vidal from the *ARA* newspaper, who I've seen around in Edinburgh. He was heading back into town so we got the Metro back to Las Ramblas and agreed to maybe meet up later on. Back at the hotel I transcribed the best Mas quotes and also bash out a skeleton of my *Herald* piece for later on. At about 3pm I walked from there back to Glòries (as Marc had urged me to do), which was useful in terms of getting a feel for the day and the sort of people taking part. At the press room I bumped into a guy from *The Times* who I'd chatted to briefly at the press conference. This time he asked if I'd written 'some books' because my name seemed familiar, but otherwise seemed quite bitter. 'What on earth is happening to Scotland?' he asked incredulously at one point.

As I made my way over to the viewing platform (such as it was) a local television journalist smiled and said, 'You're the Scottish guy from the *Guardian*!' (well, sort of) and the three of us (the third being his cameraman) eventually found our way to the bottom of the 'V' formation. In fact, for a few minutes a gaggle of journalists milled around in front of *lots* of people (the 'official' estimate was 1.8 million, though I'm innately suspicious of official figures) who were about to move forward, as indeed they did. We were then ushered back, somewhat chaotically, and we watched as a 15-year-old girl (who'll turn 16 on 9 November, the date of the referendum) cast a symbolic ballot. After that, frankly, it got a bit tedious, so I sat on a kerb in the shade and started writing my *Herald* article. As the crowd (all well behaved and upbeat) dispersed I made my way back to the press room and finished it there, although the wifi wasn't the best. At about 8.30pm I caught the Metro back to my hotel for a free (and extensive) dinner complete with a whole bottle of white.

Someone from the *Daily* and *Sunday Politics* finally got back to me to say they won't be using me on Sunday after all: 'It's nothing to do with you – but [the editor's] decided to go with journalists who have allegiances to the campaigns rather than a neutral voice.' Good grief. The media's already in great difficulty and now this: everyone pigeonholed, everyone declared officially biased, journalists debasing themselves and their profession. Even more depressingly, Salmond was in full condescending mode ('I know some of this might be news to the metropolitan media') at an international press conference earlier today, slapping down Nick Robinson and, bizarrely, getting a round of applause from some sycophants in the audience as he did so. When Robinson (who admittedly didn't do himself any favours) tried to respond Salmond accused him of 'heckling' and moved swiftly on to 'our friends in the international media,' who of course don't do him the discourtesy of asking difficult (or detailed) questions. Nick Wood, who was there with the tour group, said it was clearly 'rent a crowd'. Drunkenly, I texted my Yes Scotland contact saying (rather pompously) that I didn't want to live in a country where sycophants applaud politicians at press conferences. He replied (feebly): 'It was intl press that clapped too.' And?

Friday, 12 September 2014 (Barcelona & Edinburgh)

Slept in late and had as late a breakfast as possible while catching up with the newspapers on my iPad. The *Herald* included my report on yesterday's Diada ('Catalonia pays homage to brave Caledonia' – good headline) and a bit later a reporter called from *Le Figaro* to ask some questions about Alex Salmond for a profile he was writing. I made all my usual points which I doubt will endear me to the First (soon to be Prime) Minister, but hey ho, it needs to be said. Someone also called from the *Daily Mail* saying, frankly, that he'd been asked to do a hatchet job depicting Salmond as a left-wing radical republican, so I pointed him to the relevant section of my biography (which he had in front of him). Eventually, he ran an intro by me that was factually accurate if very *Daily Mail*.

After tapas for lunch I spent half an hour looking round the Sagrada Familia, which is still unfinished but still quite remarkable (I first visited about a decade ago). When I was finished there I met Liam O'Hare for a wander, only 25 but among one of the more sensible RICers I've come across (he said he'd had to convince several Catalans that Scotland wasn't oppressed by Britain). He argued the recent movement in the opinion polls had coincided with the Yes campaign doing what they'd (the Scottish Left) argued for all along, i.e. a 'critique' of the British state and the dangers of staying in the Union. Now although he might not have been happy about how that manifested itself (i.e. the nonsense about the NHS) it had nevertheless worked. I asked if he thought they'd win and he said yes, and when – this was a crucial test – I asked how he'd have responded if I'd asked him that a few weeks ago, he admitted he thought they'd lose. I asked what RIC would do in the event of a Yes vote and he said the plan was to hold a big conference before issuing a list of 'demands', which he told me half smiling at how absurd it sounded. He conceded points (always a good sign) but reckoned I was too harsh on the SNP (which perhaps I am), and I also did my best to defend the 'British media'. Ironically, he's thinking about going back to university to study broadcast journalism. 'If you can't beat them,' he remarked laconically, 'join them.' We had a couple of beers in a courtyard near the church Liam had spoken at on Wednesday night (after looking at the El Born ruins, a result of the 1714 bombardment by James II's illegitimate son), relaxation interrupted only by a chap from Reuters wanting quotes for yet another Salmond profile.

Barcelona really is a terrific city, particularly in mid-September sunshine, so chilled and architecturally interesting. More to the point, these two days (even though yesterday was quite flat out) have been a much-needed tonic amid general indyref madness. I can't help feeling the Catalans, in many ways, have a stronger independence argument than the Scots, not only because it has clear majority support but because of Madrid's inept (not to mention insensitive) tactics and the clear cultural (chiefly linguistic) distinction between them and the rest of Spain. There's also the economic dimension, which is much clearer cut than in the UK. Of course the Diada was covered – at length – in all today's newspapers and Marc Vidal had quoted me in his report for *ARA* (he's also promised to secure me a red '*Ara És l'Hora*' T-shirt). At El Prat airport another journalist called Jordi Caixàs tweeted a picture of me waiting to board and he ended up sitting behind me on the flight. CNN also emailed wanting a Skype interview at 7am on Monday morning, but when I asked if there'd be a fee the producer said it was 'CNN policy not to pay for interviews'. I replied, slightly cheekily, saying it was my 'policy' not to get up early in the morning to do free interviews.

The *Economist* has devoted its front page and most of its 'Britain' section to Scotland, including a thoughtful editorial and a column by Bagehot which, though a bit over the top in places, was a pretty cogent analysis of how the Yes campaign had succeeded in tarring all Unionists with the Tory brush and depicting journalists as similarly duplicitous agents of the broken British state. A *Guardian* editorial stating its position (a qualified No) has also gone online, and is much better written than the *Scotsman*'s rather plodding front-page effort the other day.

The Scottish Free State felt much chillier than Barcelona, and when I got back to Hugh's I saw that he'd fastened Scottish Lib Dem-branded 'I'm voting NO' posters to three of his street-facing windows.

Saturday, 13 September 2014 (Edinburgh & Dundee)

Met the Political Tour group at their hotel near St Andrew's House before heading down to the Meadows to watch the Orange March, although before that kicked off I had to do an interview for a *Panorama* programme Allan Little was putting together for Monday night. The march itself was oddly impressive, a working-class subculture I'm almost completely ignorant of: around 12,000 Scots – mainly from former mining communities – saying in an almost dignified way they want to remain part of the United Kingdom. Of course this was a generalisation but at the same time it was largely benign despite the presence of a loony fringe: one old guy told the group that God would 'deliver' a 65/35 result on Thursday. Another guy in a kilt taunted the marchers that they wouldn't be doing it again in 2015 (meaning after a Yes vote), but a couple of coppers politely bundled him away. As I later half joked to someone from Better Together, the visuals might have been bad but the votes hardly unhelpful.

Orange Order march in Edinburgh.

We had lunch with Peter Geoghegan at Hemma afterwards and he gave them a typically interesting insight into the historical and social background to the march. Later we had coffee and he gave my confidence a boost by saying he thought I'd done the right thing by not declaring a position (there aren't many of us left). When I popped into a newsagent to get some papers a voice said 'Boo!' in pantomime fashion (it was Peter Murrell). After that I had just about enough time to cycle home and change into a suit for the Five Million Questions event at Dundee University.

This, despite me having done absolutely no preparation, went quite well, an amiable discussion with Peter, Laura Pous (a Catalan TV journalist) and David Patrick, an amusing west coast guy now based at the University of the Free State in South Africa. The latter was interesting on press bias (and much more rigorous than Professor Robertson of the University of the West of Scotland), saying that in general terms Scottish newspapers (particularly the *Herald*) had been pretty balanced in their referendum coverage in stark contrast to London-based titles, which have been generally blisteringly anti-independence in tone and content. At the same time he appeared not to understand (along with Prof Robertson) how editorial decisions were made, which is pretty fundamental to any analysis of press 'bias'.

After that the Political Group had a final dinner in a restaurant near the Dalhouse Building to digest the week and give some concluding thoughts. I was pretty exhausted but it was genuinely interesting to hear them all reflect on what they'd seen and heard. Jamie Maxwell and I ended up having a pretty animated conversation which explored all the usual territory. The drive back to Edinburgh took forever as the Forth Road Bridge was closed for fireworks to mark its 50th anniversary. I then rocked up at The Tun to do BBC Radio 5 Live's midnight newspaper review, although this got cancelled because news had come through that ISIS had killed the Scottish hostage. This I understood completely, but not the 50 minutes it took to get me a taxi home. For the first time in my life I emailed the BBC to complain, although of course the only possible motivation for doing so was to make me feel better.

Sunday, 14 September 2014 (Edinburgh)

Over lunch at Indigo Yard Douglas Pattullo told me he thought having the Prime Minister do a big speech in Aberdeen just days before the referendum was a mistake. 'It should be,' he observed, 'Gordon Brown, Gordon Brown, Gordon Brown, not David Cameron.' That said, I suppose if he doesn't show willing then it'd look odd too. Spent the rest of the afternoon speaking to more Catalan/Spanish journalists about the indyref and fielding yet more calls from BBC producers. 'Can I ask what side you're on?' 'No,' I replied, 'you can't.' Later an odd Russian girl quizzed me about Scotland's 'upper classes' and where, even more weirdly, she'd 'find' them.

Had an early dinner with Kath (from AFP) at the Filmhouse café. She was, as ever, a tonic, and typically well informed about recent developments despite dipping – like other London-based hacks – in and out of the referendum debate. After that we wandered over to the Usher Hall for 'A Night for Scotland', a very National Collective evening of song, poetry and general hip-ness. There was, it has to be said, an extraordinary atmosphere, with lots of trendy young Yessers getting high on the excitement of it all. I'd given Dad my spare (purchased) ticket and I bumped into him *en route* to the rather sombre press room, which was full of bored-looking Spanish journalists. Otherwise all the Nationalist glitterati were in attendance: Duncan Hamilton, Andrew Wilson and, of course, the FM and Nicola. I spent most of it gossiping with Joe Pike and Kathryn Sampson from ITV Border.

In one of the intervals I bumped into Blair Jenkins who asked if I'd 'changed my mind yet'. Once I'd figured out that he didn't mean my vote but what I thought the result would be, I cheerfully admitted I'd got it wrong by predicting a 60/40 No vote (though not, mercifully, publicly). He seemed *very* confident (indeed I think he'd briefed journalists to that effect earlier that day) and told me a turnout above 80 per cent would be 'good for us', although the modelling on that can't be very scientific. Also saw Colin Pyle from Yes Scotland, who looked a bit overwhelmed by it all, and Jennifer Dempsie, who gushed that all the performers had refused payment because they were 'doing it for love'. As I left early with my bike I had to squeeze past the First Minister posing for selfies with excitable teenage girls.

At about 9.30pm I cycled down to The Tun to do Radio 4's *Westminster Hour* for the second week in a row, one of the only programmes that doesn't demand to know how I plan to vote in what is, after all, a secret ballot. During the interview I inadvertently gave away the location of the Prime Minister's rally in Aberdeen tomorrow (the AECC), and while I was still on air I was inundated with text messages and phone calls from Downing Street. 'Did you just reveal venue of PM speech tomorrow?' texted someone from Number 10. 'We are getting angry calls.' It was, of course, a genuine mistake, but remarkably no one appeared to notice. When I got home I searched Twitter a few times and found general chat about it being in Aberdeen but nothing beyond that. Still, it wasn't rocket science, only one venue in Aberdeen would support a rally of any size and it's the AECC. Downing Street's pointless flapping was quite revealing and frankly, they have bigger things to worry about than a few protestors turning up to boo the Prime Minister.

Monday, 15 September 2014 (Aberdeen)

En route to Aberdeen I bumped into the *Guardian*'s Nick Watt at Waverley. He still reckoned the final result would be 60/40 against, regardless of what Peter Kellner said. 'Who's that handsome chap?' he said, pointing to my picture byline on the front of the *Herald*; later the historian Tom Holland tweeted that it was 'depressingly good'. I joked to a colleague at the *Herald* that I wouldn't be able to write any more columns from the re-education camp and he replied: 'Indeed. Last chance to write that one, I fear.' Everything's just too weird at the moment.

In Aberdeen I had lunch with the always entertaining Jack Blanchard from the *Mirror*. He seemed to be enjoying his Scottish foray but also told me he couldn't envisage any scenario under which Ed Miliband *wasn't* Prime Minister next May. He might be right but at the same time I find the General Election almost impossible to read with any degree of certainty.

After lunch (and an ill-judged bottle of wine) we walked through town and all the way to Old Aberdeen, which Jack seemed to enjoy. From King Street we caught a cab to the AECC and I was amused to see the driver had been reading Wings over Scotland's *Wee Blue Book* (he also told me he read newsnetscotland almost every day). At the conference centre there wasn't a single protester. When I texted someone at Downing Street to point this out (partly out of relief) he replied saying that somebody had told him my mentioning it on Radio 4 had been 'a deliberate bluff'. 'I suspect,' he added wryly, 'the same person will be carrying their own pen to the polling booth.'

Inside I saw Quentin Letts, clearly still enjoying himself, and bantering with other Lobby journos about Aberdeen, whether there were good reciprocal clubs, etc. He said the last time he'd been this far north was in 1983 when he tried begging a girlfriend to take him back. David Mundell told me he still anticipated a double-digit margin of victory (55/45?) as he couldn't see where the Yes votes 'would come from'. The PM's speech was preceded with a no doubt hastily assembled video extolling the virtues of Britain, complete with archive footage of Churchill and the Queen. It was all a bit *Daily Mail* (or even *Children of Men*) but it seemed to get the ageing Tory crowd aroused. Cameron practically begged Scotland to stay and although it was a reasonably solid speech, the very fact he was making it at all betrayed the extent to which he'd allowed the No campaign to let its lead slip. An hour or so later there was a 'Let's Stick Together' rally in Trafalgar Square, which could easily have been a damp squib but actually looked quite busy. All very last-minute, a bit like Quebec in 1995, together with the last-minute hardening of the 'more powers' offer. Fascinating that Better Together studied all things Quebec, determined not to make the same mistakes but going on to make them anyway. I missed the train I intended to get home so Ben Rose, who now works for Ian Duncan MEP, gave me a lift home in pouring rain.

Tuesday, 16 September 2014 (Edinburgh)

Early start down at the media village for the BBC News Channel. The presenter tried to pigeonhole me as being in the No camp so I responded by blethering about federalism. 'I know I'm supposed to be focused laser-like on the future of the country,' texted Douglas Alexander afterwards, 'but WHAT WAS THAT T-SHIRT? As the Proclaimers might say #jumpersnomore'.

At Costa on the Royal Mile I bumped into one of the First Minister's advisers who, despite clearly being busy, joined me for a longish chat. He was very upbeat and said their supercomputer (the same one used in 2011) currently puts them ahead, although he was careful to add that on the day the fear or 'fuck it' factor could push it either way. When I said I didn't think the 'Boss' (as he calls Salmond) had had a very good referendum he half conceded there'd been a couple of 'scratchy' interviews but otherwise launched a robust defence: 'make no mistake, all this is down to him', 'he's a f***ing master at riding two horses at once', etc. I raised the recent agro with certain journalists and he just said the FM was irritated by 'metropolitan' journos coming late to the Scottish debate (I know what he means actually, not least the constant invocation of 'devo-max'). When I made my usual points about the Yes campaign overpromising he said the Scottish Government had been careful not to (I disputed that), and that people had said they wouldn't deliver in 2007 and they had (a fair point, although hardly comparable). He said, and I agreed with him, that they'd successfully separated voting Yes from supporting the SNP.

After a quick chat with Gavin MacDougall at Luath about various projects I cycled back to The Tun to do an interview on the *John Beattie* show (with Iain Macwhirter, in a reasonable frame of mind) about the 'Vow' (on the front of that day's *Daily Record*) and then cycled down to Leith to have lunch with David Grossman from *Newsnight*. He was smart and pragmatic, but – like everyone else – genuinely scunnered by anti-media atmosphere in Scotland. After interviewing me about the role of the Conservatives in all of this he asked me if anyone mourned *Newsnight Scotland*. I said no, far from it. Received an email from a battle-hardened veteran of the 1997 devolution referendum and he predicted that No would win by 55/45, a ten-point lead, 'less than the 14 points I thought three weeks ago but more than the current narrow margin of the polls'. He also reckoned turnout out would be higher than he previously thought, at 80–84 per cent. He neither thought Yes would be 'crushed' nor 'win narrowly'. 'I think the line was stabilised last week and since then pushed back,' he added. In a spare moment I googled my foreign media presence, not that I could understand most of it; I was in *Le Figaro* talking about Alex Salmond and also a German newspaper: '*Schottlands Jedermann ohne Ideologie*' was the headline, followed by '*Der Journalist David Torrance sieht den Regierungschef als Karrieristen*'.

Given they were heading southwest to Moffat, Grossman and his crew dropped me off in Newington and later I caught the train to Glasgow in time to watched the FM be interviewed by Sky News' Adam Boulton, after which I was to do a turn on the man and the wider campaign. As Tom Gordon and I waited for our slots Salmond (with Duncan Hamilton and Ewan Crawford in tow, the latter, as ever, looking like a frightened poodle) chatted as if we were long-lost friends; when I mentioned squeezing past the rock-star FM at the Usher Hall on Sunday night he said 'Why's that odd?'

The First Minister waiting to be interviewed by Adam Boulton of Sky News.

(jokingly), adding that 'Mrs Salmond' had 'liked Franz Ferdinand'. He also said he'd met Dad, and that although he hadn't let on he had 'recognised him', later in the conversation he quipped – looking at me – that political beliefs didn't necessarily 'run in the family'. Mercifully, as he launched into a lengthy racing anecdote a Sky producer summoned him to be grilled by a Buddha-like Boulton. I'd never seen him so charming and relaxed. (Later I texted Dad asking if he'd met the FM and he said no, so goodness knows who Salmond was talking about.)

Boulton was good, pushing Salmond on foreign policy (on which he was typically weak) and, less effectively, attempting to pin the Edinburgh tram fiasco on his first administration. Salmond pointed out that he'd actually opposed them and, during a commercial break, looked over at me for confirmation that it'd been their first lost vote in 2007 (I said it had, although in truth I didn't know for sure). Interestingly, the FM also repeated the line that the referendum being a once-in-a-generation thing was merely his 'personal view'. Just before I went on Boulton was merrily retweeting various insults directed at him during his 'disrespectful' (natch) interview with Salmond.

Afterwards I cycled to Better Together's rather ramshackle offices on

Sauchiehall Street, mainly to steal their wifi in order to do a Skype interview for CNN (later aborted due to poor bandwidth), but ended up staying for a bit to chat to various people. There was almost a party atmosphere, late-evening pizza and it was odd to see posh Tory girls rubbing alongside hardened Labour apparatchiks. 'We're going to win this,' Douglas Alexander said to me earnestly. I asked him why and he said the momentum was now back with them and canvass returns showed Undecideds splitting 2-1 for No, although he admitted it was difficult to predict what newly-registered voters would do. He also reckoned the recent 'mob' stuff looked bad and was damaging, i.e. protests outside BBC Scotland.

Blair McDougall was chuffed that Bill Clinton had just put out a statement ('he delivers our lines better than we do'), something sorted out by Tony Blair and Alistair Campbell, the latter of whom had been in the office a day or so earlier. At one point Rob Shorthouse also informed Douglas that the *Scottish Sun* wasn't going to back independence. Alluding to my globetrotting Douglas turned to me and asked: 'What country would you rather be in right now?' A bit OTT but he's right, I wouldn't miss this for the world. Had a quick drink with my usual contact in an Irish bar nearby and I made the point that a final split of 55/45 would look better than it actually was given the narrowing of the polls, while for Yes to win it'd have needed a larger and more consistent poll lead, which of course it doesn't have. He also said he didn't think Better Together had been too negative, rather forming a positive case had been the job of Labour, the Tories and Lib Dems and they'd failed to do it. Three more polls, meanwhile, have all shown Yes on 48 and No on 52.

On my way home I got a text from David Mundell: 'Emily Maitlis thinks you look like Matt Damon. Think that's a compliment.' (Grossman's report on the Conservatives had gone out on tonight's *Newsnight*.) Despite me getting back to Edinburgh well after midnight Mum agreed to meet me to drop off mail and give me a lift home. She was appalled by what she called the 'thuggery' of some Yes supporters. Dad, on the other hand, didn't care, holding to his belief that it was all orchestrated by the No campaign. 'But we live in a democracy!' she'd said to him, to an incredulous roll of the eyes.

Wednesday, 17 September 2014 (Edinburgh)

Another early start to do a phone interview for LBC at 7am, then *Good Morning Wales* at a church café on George Street and, finally, another interview for RTE, although this one was in a BBC studio rather than over the phone. Cycled back to Hugh's to have lunch with John Bannon, a delightful old Australian guy who used to be the Labour Premier of South Australia; he'd made a point of being in Edinburgh just to soak up the pre-referendum atmosphere. On our way to the restaurant we passed the Newington Yes 'shop' and an old guy accosted me to evangelise about how he used to be a trade unionist, Labour Party member etc and now he was voting Yes. I asked if he believed independence would deliver socialism and he practically exploded: 'Yes! It's got to! Scotland's a socialist country!' Eventually one of his fellow Yessers prized him away from us. Lots of geeky constitutional chat over lunch. Our waitress said she'd probably only make up her mind which way she'd vote at the polling station tomorrow.

Cycled to the Point conference centre on Bread Street to do a short slot on BBC Wales' main evening television news programme, which was fun. The make-up lady said she was voting Yes and teased me about my intentions. 'Your hair's hot!' she exclaimed as she gleefully plucked a grey hair from the side of my head. At one point the presenter alluded to me having lived in Cardiff, which I thought wonderfully parochial.

Texted Douglas and he said he was confident there'd be a 55/45 split on the night, citing 'shy Nos' (just like 'shy Tories' in the 1980s and '90s). Later I phoned my Yes Scotland contact who, when I asked what was going to happen, said Yes would win. 'Is that what you have to say at this stage or what you actually think?' I asked him. 'It's what I think,' he replied, echoing the FM adviser's claim that their computer says Yes, as well as his gut. Also bumped into Alex Bell and Morag (his wife), the latter of whom was gloomily expecting a No vote. There was an odd atmosphere in Edinburgh and I was aware of lots of flags (mainly Saltires, but some Union Jacks too) being displayed from cars and flats. Having launched a Twitter appeal for a lift to Perth for the SNP's eve-of-poll rally (although I couldn't quite figure out why they were wasting campaigning time holding one), I got a lift from an Israeli journalist called Anshel Pfeffer, who writes for a left-wing paper called *Haaretz*. He told me he was currently being deluged by requests for interviews (in Israel) about Scotland, and that although Hebrew was better for news writing, English was better for commentary as it was a richer language, although translations from the former into the latter always ended up 30 per cent longer.

The atmosphere at the Perth Concert Hall was giddy, and on the way in I reminded Stuart Nicolson that I'd been promised the ambassadorship to Croatia (he just laughed). When Nick Robinson appeared on the balcony there was general booing while one lady yelled 'Hang your head in shame, Nick!' It wasn't very edifying, although to his credit Robinson showed no reaction and only backed away once it had died down. Weird that a bunch of activists (apparently) on the cusp of a remarkable victory could think that was a good idea. I got a random Facebook message from a Catalan just before things kicked off: 'Good luck tomorrow! Best wishes from Catalonia! We envy you so much...'

Once things got under way there were lashings of sanctimony. Elaine C. Smith quoted Vaclav Havel, much to the obvious chagrin of Anshel, while she then introduced Nicola Sturgeon as 'our very own Borgen'. Disappointingly, Nicola's speech was all a bit platitudinous, while to say Alex Salmond got a good reaction would be an understatement: he could have read out sections of a telephone directory and got the same reaction. Chants of 'Yes we can!' punctuated the proceedings but he looked tired (although it'd have been a surprise if he hadn't). Not Salmond's best speech, but not at all bad in the circumstances. 'We can write a new chapter,' he said at one point, 'in the history of this ancient nation' (Nicola had also stressed Scotland's age). When it was all over some activists walked out chanting 'Yes we can!' before someone else began singing 'Flower of Scotland'. Outside it was all a bit tacky: flags, kilts and bagpipes.

Had a quick drink with Jamie Maxwell and his girlfriend (she also remarked on the tackiness) before catching the last train home. John Swinney had just told him that they'd based the Yes campaign on his late father's book (Stephen Maxwell, who wrote *Arguing for Independence*), so he was understandably thrilled about that. On the train back I sat listening to some Sinatra, catching up with Gordon Brown's (pretty good) speech from this morning and drafted some indyref articles while Kath Haddon filed some copy for AFP (most of the other seats in the carriage were taken by bored-looking international journalists and Yes activists, one of whom recognised me just as we arrived in Edinburgh). It was late but Kath was keen to have a drink so we ended up at the City Café on Blair Street. Afterwards a guy from National Collective recognised me and came up to have a chat (it'd been him who'd asked me to pose with an NC sign at the Common Weal event in Glasgow a few weeks before). He asked me if I'd come to my senses yet. Cycled home at about 1am – Edinburgh was very atmospheric, foggy and dark.

Thursday, 18 September 2014 (Edinburgh & Glasgow)

Got up at about 11am and saw that Michael (my brother) had posted on Facebook: 'Having a strange out-of-body experience today as a disenfranchised London-based Scot.' Got ready and cycled to the Traverse Theatre to see David Greig's Yes/No plays, which provided me with some much-needed light relief on polling day (we also got a pie and drink

Contrasting messages on polling day.

beforehand). One of the characters, 'devo Max', was very funny, although the whole thing – based on Greig's Twitter plays – was smart and insightful. After that I cycled to Brunswick Road in order to vote. For some reason I expected to be seized by the enormity of it all, but in fact it just felt like every other occasion I've voted at the same polling station. After a quick chat with a French PhD student called Cyril Trepier (another referendum tourist) I cycled home to get changed for tonight. Allan Massie called, saying that his polling station in the Borders had been 'quiet as the dead'.

As I cycled to Ruffians to get my referendum haircut, I was again overly conscious of the number of Saltires and Union flags on display, but I guess that makes sense. Sky News' Faisal Islam was also at Ruffians, although I didn't figure that out until after he left. On Princes Street I saw a motorbike with a sidecar and 'No Thanks' sign racing towards Charlotte Square while someone shouted 'Vote No,' passing a Yes van as they did so where someone was urging people, of course, to do precisely the opposite. After that I met Martin Kettle from the *Guardian* at Café Royal for an early dinner of oysters, scallops and (for him) lobster; I joked that it was like being in first class on the *Titanic*. His chat was, as ever, good; I expressed my frustration that Left and Right both caricatured the UK economic model when in fact it was mixed, as it had always been, and he said it wasn't an 'insignificant point', adding that 'neoliberal' was one of those terms that both said a lot while at the same time saying nothing at all. In the bar afterwards I bumped into a typically jovial Craig Harrow (a Lib Dem representative on Better Together) and then Martin introduced me ('he knows lots'), to Anji Hunter who worked for Tony Blair until 2001 – I told her I'd seen Adam Boulton (her husband) on Tuesday in Glasgow. She seemed like good fun but I had to catch the 8pm train to Glasgow.

I continued to be deluged by emails and calls from international journalists, but I just had to ignore most of them, there aren't enough hours in the day, although I did speak to someone from the *Washington Post* (couldn't really say no to that). In Glasgow I stocked up on Red Bull and apples at WH Smith in Queen Street station and overheard two spirited Yes badge-wearing ladies asking the check-out assistant how she'd voted. 'Yes!' she replied, 'I voted Yes!' 'How could anyone not have voted Yes?' she added. I caught a glimpse of George Square as my taxi headed to Pacific Quay and I could see that it was full of flags and high-spirited Yessers.

At STV Bernard Ponsonby implied he thought the Yes campaign might just pull it off, which surprised me. James Mitchell was also there, although he was sensibly keeping his predictions to himself. Peter MacMahon from ITV Border reckoned No, Stephen Daisley Yes. In the make-up room Alex Neil told me his side would be 'very happy' with the result, which of course was carefully worded to mean just about anything (i.e. they could be 'very happy' with a high Yes vote short of a majority). But if it was a No, he added (rather conceding the point) that the in/out Euro referendum planned by the end of 2017 could represent another opportunity; he chuckled when I mentioned the recent Salmond caveat about once-in-a-generation becoming his 'personal view'.

In the studio, and before we were on air, Bernard did his Alex Neil impression as the minister took his seat and said 'Free by '93! Better late than never!' It was all good fun and my suit (three piece, not ideal for a hot studio) seemed to meet with Twitter approval, although given the nature of the programme there was an awful lot of sitting around and trying not to look bored when in shot. By midnight, the counting was, in the clichéd language of election nights, 'well under way', but any actual results – even in local authorities renowned for their speed – seemed a long way off.

Friday, 19 September 2014 (Glasgow & Edinburgh)

The results took a long time to come through, but even from the first (Clackmannanshire) it was clear that Yes didn't have the level of support necessary to pull it off. That said, at about 1.50am I texted a Tory MP asking for his thoughts on how things looked and he replied: 'Too many big urban authorities voting Yes.' He meant Glasgow and Dundee, which of course went Yes, but not by as big a margin as some expected. In Glasgow turnout was also an issue, the low (relatively speaking) level of 75 per cent being, in his terminology, 'helpful'.

Given that the pattern was clear, the night itself became rather dull and anticlimactic. I was also boiling in my three-piece suit, not to mention tired. By around 6am I'd ducked out of the studio – through which I'd seen the noble Lords McConnell and Reid and the former First Minister Henry McLeish, not to forget former SNP leader Gordon Wilson – it was a veritable who's who of Scottish politics past and present. At one point I had to mess around with social media stuff on air, which didn't really sit well with the rest of the programme, while Twitter went into overdrive. My favourite piece of abuse was a guy who said I looked like a 'fuck toad' (whatever that is). In the green room there were general high spirits, and at one point I shouted 'Resign!' at Mark Diffley from Ipsos MORI as he fretted about being one point out in his final prediction.

I stuck around to do the morning results programme at 7am in a different studio upstairs, which included the Prime Minister's statement outside Downing Street. On first impression this seemed quite bold and well pitched, referring to 'millions of voices' in England which needed heard, but also a loaded commitment to pursuing English Votes for English Laws. Bernard Ponsonby and I then warbled on about that, federalism, etc. I had to duck out to speak to RTE about the result, where I saw Kevin McKenna and Alex Massie (who exclaimed 'Victory!'). Also had a good chat with a friendly Shona Robison, who also seemed quite impressed with the PM's comments. She also reckoned the appointment of Lord Smith of Kelvin was a smart move on the UK Government's part, not least because the Scottish Government rated him following his handling of the Commonwealth Games.

I then cycled, despite feeling tired and sweaty, to Queen Street station in order to catch the 8.15am train back to Edinburgh, on which I did a phone interview for ABC radio (in Australia), no doubt pissing off my fellow commuters and lost the signal just as the host was thanking me, which was fortuitous. My Yes Scotland contact, clearly frustrated and disappointed, texted to say:

> You'll hate this attitude from me but you can quote me as an unnamed source if interested: 'I can't be in an SNP which if "federalism" isn't delivered and if Cameron is re-elected is not then willing to push for another referendum in 2016. Without a referendum in our manifesto I'm out. Labour promised the people they would get back in. They won't. With Miliband as leader it's as certain as night follows day and deep down everyone in politics knows it.

I was too tired to figure out what any of this meant, let alone use it in anything I was (or rather wasn't writing). All I had time to do on the train was 600 words for the *Herald*'s supplement using the 1992 General Election as a hook.

Edinburgh was wet and miserable, so I cycled to Brown's on George Street to get coffee and breakfast before the First Minister's press conference at 10am, although a text from Stuart Nicolson confirmed that wasn't happening. I overheard one of the waiters expressing dismay at the result, only to be contradicted by his colleague, but neither sounded overly fussed, just treating it as one of many things they had to consider that morning. Indeed, I was struck by how normal everything was: most folk I saw in Glasgow and Edinburgh were just getting on with their lives, as of course they should. On my way back to Newington my taxi driver noticed someone taking down a Yes poster. He said he'd voted No as there were too many 'unknowns', mainly regarding currency. Once again I was struck by my own emotionless response. I just felt tired.

I had been lined up to appear on a special ITV programme lasting from 10am–2pm but I'd got wind the night before that this would only go ahead if there'd been a Yes vote. A producer then called to downgrade this to an appearance on their 1pm news programme, and then again to say they just wanted a prerecorded clip. There, in microcosm, was the waning London-based media interest in the whole thing. At home I showered and shaved, which almost made me feel human again. Dad texted me saying: 'Cameron sounds like a fed'. I replied asking if he meant federalist, to which he replied: 'Devolving powers to rest of UK, that will not be quick. I do not disagree with that, he maybe read your book.' Also spoke to a very gloomy Labour MP ('You had a tremendous referendum.') who lost every 'box' in his constituency, which obviously didn't bode well for next year's General Election. He was about to do a radio interview so I suggested that he point out that a clear majority of Scots had self-determined in favour of the Union. He said it was a good line and I could hear him scribbling it down. I jokingly asked if he'd like me to come up with an election strategy as well and he said please do, please do. Fran texted me: 'Are u happy w. result? We all are, at Malc's. Spoke to yr dad. Sorry he's in pain w leg. Saw u on Newsnt! Interesting Discussion.'

In a blistering piece for *Scottish Review*, Kenneth Roy cheered me up with the following paragraph:

> What was true of the writers of fiction was true with semi-colons attached to the Scottish commentariat, most of whom abandoned any pretence of objectivity. The performance of the *Herald* group of journalists was astonishing: one of its commentators addressed a Scottish republican rally while another became such a cheer-leader for Yes that, as recently as last week, he was advising his Twitter followers how to behave during the party leaders' visit to Scotland. ('No egg-throwing.') How can such people ever expect to be taken seriously again? They have reduced themselves to the abject level of fans with laptops.

I can't imagine whom he was referring to. After doing a clip for ITV they'd probably never use I slinked into a place on Rose Street for lunch and to finish writing a couple of articles I'd stupidly agreed to a few weeks back. At around 3pm a tabloid colleague phoned basically to say that the press conference Salmond was due to hold at 4pm could very well be his last. I struggled to digest this, although it made sense given that a) the time had changed several times throughout the day and b) access was being limited to certain journalists only (I rather feebly emailed two of my usual contacts asking politely to be allowed in). What other head of government, I thought later, holds a resignation press conference and keeps out journalists they don't like?

Back down at the media village there was a slightly heady atmosphere. I bumped into Andrew Kerr from BBC Scotland who told me they were hearing that the press conference wasn't to announce the FM's resignation, which made the whole thing even more confusing (though I guess his people were deliberately briefing that). At one point I called someone at the *Guardian* to ask him what the score was and he ranted, quite rightly, about how it was being handled. As I cycled past a couple of guys hanging around next to Holyrood one of them said, simply, 'Well done'. Eventually I slunk off to The Tun in order to watch the Bute House presser live on the BBC News Channel.

A few minutes into his statement it became clear that Salmond was going to resign. I managed a one-word tweet ('Eek') and then my mobile phone exploded into life with calls, texts and emails, some of them barely coherent, asking (and even demanding) interviews. The *Herald* called wanting 800 words, while the *Scotsman* and *Edinburgh Evening News* wanted the same 500-word piece between them. My Better Together contact texted, rather triumphantly, 'Yyyyyyyeeeeeeeassssssss!!!!!!!!!!!' while Jamie Maxwell, more thoughtfully: 'Seems so unnecessary, politically speaking. Suspect he's physically & mentally exhausted.' He certainly looked it during his statement, although it was also Salmond at his best: elegantly crafted words movingly delivered.

Sensing that I was a bit overwhelmed, a girl from National Collective called Vonny Moyes (not, I think, her real name), who was also at The Tun, offered me a hug, which I somewhat awkwardly accepted. Back in the media village I spoke to BBC Radio 4's *PM* (to be fair, they'd lined this up in anticipation of AS resigning) and then BBC Radio 5 Live, and at one point BBC producers were circling me like vultures as I bashed out articles and replied to emails and texts. As I left the media village to do a quick interview for David Grossman from *Newsnight* Andrew Wilson playfully punched me but I was so tired I nearly fell over. Somehow I managed to form coherent sentences in interviews for Sky and the News Channel. Angus Yarwood texted from Switzerland to say it was a good interview. 'You look much refreshed,' he added, 'You've slept a bit I take it.' I replied saying 'not a wink'. For some reason Dominic Grieve, the Tory MP, was wandering around.

After that I caught a cab to the Mercure Hotel to do a very enjoyable interview with Alex Bell on the rooftop overlooking Princes Street. Jon Snow, who was presenting, said he liked my T-shirt and, on prompting from Alex, revealed himself as a bit of a Salmond fanboy (they'd had breakfast at some point and indeed Snow had been allowed into the press conference). Alex and I made a good double act. Another taxi then took me to the STV studios at Fountainbridge to do another interview – alongside Gordon Wilson – about Salmond and here, at last, I was a bit more balanced about his strengths and weaknesses, having got a bit carried away earlier on.

Finally, I got home to Newington at about 9.30pm and managed an hour's nap before heading out to Duddingston to do the midnight newspaper review on BBC Radio 5 Live. On my way out I encountered Hugh and a friend bouncing around like excited schoolboys; they'd been amusing themselves by looking at the reaction of certain Yessers on Twitter (Alan Bissett had tweeted: 'Empty. Just empty.'). By this point I felt completely spaced out but perked up a bit after consuming some hot chocolate and crisps. Also there was a novelist I'd met briefly during the Edinburgh Book Festival called Sara Sheridan who, once I'd woken up, was quite good fun (she seemed astonished to find herself agreeing with me on certain points). On the way back home there was an incredibly weird atmosphere, although it's difficult to know how much that had to do with my fatigued state rather than any genuine frisson. As I finally drifted off to sleep (not, for obvious reasons, at all difficult) the pub opposite still sounded very lively – or was it the sound of people drowning their sorrows?

Saturday, 20 September 2014 (Edinburgh)

Up early after just five hours' sleep, although I felt immeasurably better for it. Spoke to BBC Breakfast from The Mound with my hair sticking up then went for a swim, which (almost) made me feel human again. Then did Sky News, BBC Radio Scotland, BBC Scotland, RTE and finally the BBC News Channel. After the last gig I got a narky text from a chap who works for Margaret Curran: 'The agreement hasn't broken down. The motion has been signed laying out the timetable we agreed to and will be laid first thing in Monday morning...' I pointed out that it was supposed to be Friday and joked that next he would be telling me there was broad agreement on English Votes for English Laws. He replied: 'There is disagreement on that but it's a different process. PM made that clear yesterday... Motion was signed yesterday by Ed, Cameron and Clegg will be laid first thing Monday and it details the same timetable laid out during the campaign.' But the point, surely, is that the punters won't be able to separate the two.

Today was busy but compared with yesterday seemed almost relaxed. I based myself at Hemma, where I bumped into a very chirpy Stephen Gethins with his family, and also bashed out comment pieces for the *Sunday Express* and *Scottish Sun on Sunday*. Picked up some papers at a newsagent on the Royal Mile and, seeing the front of the *Herald*, the guy serving me gesticulated at a picture of Alex Salmond resigning and told me he 'loved' him. Finally spoke to Dad on the phone and he said, as usual, lots of sensible and not-so-sensible things. Said he was glad the outcome had been decisive as he found that easier to deal with than a much closer margin; I also told him he should feel vindicated that he'd always been cautious about opinion polls showing it neck and neck. He was also surprising, basically declaring that federalism was 'the answer' although he didn't 'believe any of these vows or any of that shite'. 'Basically,' he reflected later on, 'I'm better off under the UK [he meant in terms of pensions] but that doesn't mean I want to keep it.' Said he planned to boycott John Lewis. Also spoke to Mum, who told me that now there'd been a No vote Sheila wasn't interested in getting devo-max any more.

In the afternoon I spoke to Hugh about doing another edition of the Salmond biography and perhaps even a standalone book (he used the term 'pendant') on the period 2011–14. After catching up with more newspapers I dozed for an hour or two. In the evening I did my bit for national reconciliation by watching *Doctor Who* with two Green activists, one of whom was the always engaging Dominic Hinde. Afterwards we chewed over the result, and the likely reaction from the Left, over some food at a good Italian place on Leith Walk. I cycled past Gerry Hassan on the way home and we discussed the crazy stuff flying around on Twitter, calls for a judicial review of the referendum result, recounts, etc. I always predicted that a No vote would lead to lots of silly people saying silly things and so it has come to pass.

Sunday, 21 September 2014 (Edinburgh)

Up early (again) to burble nonsense at BBC Breakfast outside St Giles', where a service of reconciliation will take place later on. Still feeling half asleep, I went for a swim and then grabbed breakfast at Café Nero on the Royal Mile. Not a bad day – the sun continues to shine on the Union – so sat outside. Lindsay McIntosh from *The Times* stopped to chat, as did James Cook from the BBC, whom I joked was an 'approved' journalist (he'd been at Friday's press conference). We then wandered up to St Giles' together, unintentionally following in the wake of Alistair Carmichael *et al*.

Inside, the relief on the faces of the Scottish Secretary, Douglas Alexander, etc, was palpable, indeed I overheard Alistair saying he hadn't expected the final few weeks to be so emotionally draining. Douglas came up and said the First Minister and Deputy weren't 'gracing us with their presence' (a Scotland Office official later told me they'd both pulled out at the last minute); instead John Swinney was the sole Scottish Government minister in attendance, along with his wife Liz. Lord Steel ('are you milking it?' he asked mischievously) and Judy were also in the congregation. As for the service itself, I slept through almost all of it.

Hung around for a bit outside and saw Ben Thomson from Reform Scotland, who seemed very chirpy, as well as some more journalists. Spontaneously I had lunch with an old friend from Whitehall at The Outsider on George IV Bridge. David Mundell (who later texted, saying 'Now we know your Scotland Office sources.') was also having lunch with Ruth Davidson upstairs. Later she came over to say hello and we agreed she'd had a 'good' referendum. I then finished writing my *Herald* column on Alex Salmond, a fairly pungent revisionist account of his political legacy, a necessary corrective to some of the sycophantic nonsense produced since Friday (including by me).

On Twitter, meanwhile, I was getting some of the blame for his resignation. Someone called Chris Darroch posted: 'I am so sad that this scum have induced his resignation. Torrance included,' and, later, 'Torrance the traitor. Pretentious ignorance of the worst kind.' He and others are pushing the '45' hashtag on Twitter. Also caught up with Salmond's Sunday interviews conducted, as usual, from Aberdeenshire. He told Andrew Neil that he was planning a book called *A Hundred Days* (funnily enough, also my preferred title for this diary) to be published before Christmas (sounds ambitious). The outgoing FM also told Sky and Channel 4 (later I heard from a friend that he refused to do BBC Scotland) that there were alternative routes to independence other than a referendum, which was a curious remark given he'd pushed for the referendum policy in the first place.

This came up when I did a Skype/telephone interview for Radio New Zealand just before collapsing in a heap in bed. They've just had elections there in which John Key's National Party 'broke' the Kiwi electoral system by winning an overall majority, something that isn't supposed to be possible (just like the SNP at Holyrood in 2011). Broadcasting to remote corners of the globe about events in a small northern European nation has been fun though I suspect the opportunities to do so will soon peter out. People keep saying 'now that' the Scottish Question has been settled, but it doesn't feel that way. Partly this is exhaustion – I haven't stopped since Thursday – and partly because the news cycle has already moved on to the SNP leadership race and the 'more powers' debate. In fact, I haven't stopped since May 2011 when all this began. The independence referendum has taken up more than three years of my life. But it's been fun: bloody exhausting, but fun.

Postscript

As I write this nearly seven weeks after 18 September 2014 – a date that will hereafter loom large in the history of not just Scotland but the UK – the ever-shifting political terrain serves as a reminder that 'nothing will ever be the same again' wasn't simply a hoary old journalistic cliché but, in this instance, a pretty accurate description of what came to pass following the historic Scottish independence referendum.

In my last diary entry a few days after a remarkable 85 per cent of Scots went to the polls, I reflected that it didn't feel as if the Scottish Question had actually been answered one way or the other. Sure, the outcome was relatively close, although in the context of a US presidential election more than 55 per cent of the vote and all but four local authority districts backing a 'No' vote would be described as a landslide.

Crucially, however, the Yes side maintained control of the political narrative. Within hours of the result and Prime Minister David Cameron's Downing Street declaration concerning 'more powers', English Votes for English Laws (inevitably shortened to 'Evel'), and all that constitutional jazz, Alex Salmond announced his resignation as SNP leader and, therefore, First Minister, but began developing a 'betrayal' narrative (rather shakily based on the fact Cameron had apparently linked the delivery of more powers to cross-party negotiations over English MPs' voting rights), something he and others sustained for the next few weeks.

Meanwhile the Smith Commission, charged with actually delivering upon the carefully-worded 'Vow', was set up to fail. Unless it went along with the SNP's definition of 'devo-max' then, ran an associated narrative, it would not be commensurate with the aspirations of the Scottish people. And while Unionist politicians were held to a certain interpretation of their promises, Nationalists quietly shed their own pre-referendum commitments. Both Salmond and Nicola Sturgeon, who soon emerged uncontested as his heir apparent, no longer believed the ballot was a 'once-in-a-generation' opportunity, while Section 30 of the Edinburgh Agreement (about respecting the outcome), quoted ad nauseam during the campaign, was also ditched. As ever, an impressively buoyant SNP was helped by many of its opponents. Labour Party politicians, who'd comprised the majority of Better Together activity, by and large allowed the referendum losers to write the first draft of history while turning, as was the Scottish party's habit, in on itself. Having initially declared her determination to fight on as leader and contest the 2016 Holyrood elections, within weeks Johann Lamont had resigned, and what a resignation it was. Ed Miliband, she charged, treated the Scottish

Labour Party like a 'branch office', while various 'dinosaurs' on the House of Commons benches didn't 'get' the post-referendum dynamic.

Lamont was, of course, correct in her analysis, although its public airing wasn't exactly helpful to a party that had never quite adjusted to its electoral defeat back in 2007. As the MP Jim Murphy led a trio of candidates attempting, to all intents and purposes, 'save' a once-dominant Scottish party machine, elements of 'the 45' agitated for another referendum. And although the wilder fringes (those who believed the referendum had, for example, been rigged) were kept in check by the SNP leadership, Sturgeon hinted at another ballot should Scotland be 'dragged' out of the European Union against its will following an in/out referendum due by the close of 2017.

Scottish and UK politics felt in greater constitutional flux than at any time since the turbulent 1970s and, looking ahead, there was scant comfort for those who dearly wished everything would 'get back to normal': a UK general election in May 2015, a Scottish Parliament contest in May 2016 and, within a year and a half of that, the aforementioned EU referendum. All three ensured the Scottish Question would be asked again, and again, and again. Only a foolish diarist would attempt to predict what might happen next.

David Torrance, London
November 2014

Great Scottish Speeches Vol. 1

Introduced and Edited by David Torrance
Foreword by Alex Salmond
ISBN 978 1 906817 27 4 PBK £9.99

Some great Scottish speeches were the result of years of contemplation. Some flourished in heat of the moment. Whatever the background of the ideas expressed, the speeches not only provide a snapshot of their time, but express views that still resonate in Scotland today, whether you agree with the sentiments or not.

Encompassing speeches made by Scots or in Scotland, this carefully selected collection reveals the character of a nation. Themes of religion, independence and socialism cross paths with sporting encouragement, Irish Home Rule and Miss Jean Brodie.

Ranging from the legendary speech of the Caledonian chief Calgagus in 83AD right up to Alex Salmond's election victory in 2007, these are the speeches that created modern Scotland.

...what has not faded is the power of the written and spoken word – as this first-rate collection of Scottish speeches demonstrates.
PRESS AND JOURNAL

Great Scottish Speeches Vol. 2

Introduced and Edited by David Torrance
Foreword by Alex Salmond
ISBN 978 1 908373 63 2 HBK £16.99

Following on the success of *Great Scottish Speeches*, Vol. 1 and ahead of the potentially radical changes to our political landscape after the referendum next year, David Torrance once again delves into the archives of Scottish public speaking to compile a second volume of memorable and inspirational speeches.

Featuring speeches from some of the most well-known and memorable speakers in Scottish history, *Great Scottish Speeches*, Vol. 2 is a worthy successor to his first collection. Not restricted to purely political oratories, Torrance shares with us a broad range of addresses from celebrated poets, musicians and writers with each speech being framed by an introduction, setting out its historical importance and contextualising what is to follow.

As Scotland embarks on a new process of discussion and debate about our constitutional future, it is timely to celebrate the different voices and strands of opinion which have taken the nation to our present place – and to encourage new voices for our future progress. Let the discourse begin!
ALEX SALMOND

Britain Rebooted: Scotland in a Federal Union
David Torrance
ISBN: 978 1 910021 11 8 PBK £7.99

Would federalism work in the UK?

Wouldn't England dominate a British federation?

How would powers be distributed between federal and Home Nation level?

What about the House of Lords?

In the run up to the historic referendum on Scottish independence, there was a plethora of tracts, articles and books arguing for and against, but there remains a gap in the literature: the case for Scotland becoming part of a 'rebooted' federal Union. It is an old, usually Liberal, dream, but one still worth fighting for.

It is often assumed that federalism is somehow 'alien' to the Scottish and British constitutional tradition but in this short book journalist David Torrance argues that not only has the UK already become a quasi-federal state but that formal federation is the best way of squaring the competing demands of Nationalists and Unionists.

He also uses Scotland's place within a federal UK to examine other potential reforms with a view to tackling ever-increasing inequality across the British Isles and create a more equal, successful and constitutionally coherent country.

A Constitution for the Common Good: Strengthening Scottish Democracy after 2014
W. Elliot Bulmer
ISBN: 978 1 910021 09 5 PBK £9.99

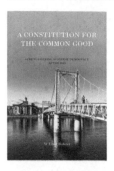

Nearly every democracy is built upon a written constitution; constitutions have been at the core of citizens' demands for better governance in places as disparate as Kenya, Tunisia and Ukraine. Constitutional change will remain central to the political agenda in Scotland for some time to come.

But what is a constitution for? Is it a defensive charter to protect the basic structures of democratic government, or is it a transformative covenant for a better society? How can the constitution sustain democracy and promote ethical politics while at the same time recognising and accommodating differences in society? What difference would a good constitution make to the poor? How can the constitution help ensure that the common good prevails over private vested interests?

A Constitution for the Common Good sets out a vision for how Scotland could reconstitute itself. It emphasises the connection between the constitution, democracy and the common good, arguing that democratic self-government is the true prize, regardless of the relationship of Scotland to rUK. A vital contribution to Scotland's ongoing constitutional debate, this book engages with fundamental questions of constitutionalism and democracy that are of enduring relevance to both citizens and scholars around the world.

Rethinking Our Politics: The Political and Constitutional Future of Scotland and the UK
Henry Mcleish
ISBN: 978 1 906817 83 1 £11.99 PBK

Our politics once again needs to inspire, enthuse, educate and be relevant to the needs and aspirations of the public and reconnect with the values that underpin our society. There are urgent issues that we need to deal with now – the most important of which being rampant inequality. We have to move away from the mindless tribalism and partisanship that too often dominates much of what passes as political debate.

Over the past year it has become clear that regardless of their stance on the referendum debate, the Scottish people are united on one front – the yearning for change for the betterment of their nation, their institutions and their politics. For McLeish, the referendum debate is merely the beginning. It is a symptom of the need for a more fundamental shift in the way we engage with politics in the UK and Scotland today.

Former First Minister of Scotland, Henry McLeish is well placed to diagnose the crisis at the heart of Scotland and UK politics. In *Rethinking Our Politics* he rails against the stagnation of the Union and makes a rousing and persuasive case for a complete overhaul of political thinking in Scotland, demanding that instead of making decisions on the basis of fear and insecurity, we rediscover the founding moral purpose of government. This is a 'must read' for those who care about the future of our nation.

Caledonian Dreaming: The Quest for a Different Scotland
Gerry Hassan
ISBN: 978 1 910021 32 3 PBK £11.99

Caledonian Dreaming: The Quest for a Different Scotland offers a penetrating and original way forward for Scotland. It identifies the myths of modern Scotland, describes what they say and why they need to be seen as myths. Hassan shows a Scotland in the grip of inexorable change as traditional institutions and power decline and new forces emerge, and outlines a prospectus for Scotland to become more democratic and to embrace radical new social policies.

Hassan drills down to deeper reasons why the many dysfunctions of British democracy could dog an independent Scotland too.
POLLY TOYNBEE
WRITER AND JOURNALIST, THE GUARDIAN

Caledonian Dreaming *is about grounded hope. This is a book that will inform, educate and illuminate. Alasdair Gray said: 'Work as if you live in the early days of a better nation'. While this is engraved in the Canongate Wall of the Scottish parliament building, Hassan has brought it to life in this wonderful book.*
JOE LAFFERTY

Luath Press Limited

committed to publishing well written books worth reading

LUATH PRESS takes its name from Robert Burns, whose little collie Luath (*Gael.*, swift or nimble) tripped up Jean Armour at a wedding and gave him the chance to speak to the woman who was to be his wife and the abiding love of his life. Burns called one of the 'Twa Dogs' Luath after Cuchullin's hunting dog in Ossian's *Fingal*. Luath Press was established in 1981 in the heart of Burns country, and is now based a few steps up the road from Burns' first lodgings on Edinburgh's Royal Mile. Luath offers you distinctive writing with a hint of unexpected pleasures.

Most bookshops in the UK, the US, Canada, Australia, New Zealand and parts of Europe, either carry our books in stock or can order them for you. To order direct from us, please send a £sterling cheque, postal order, international money order or your credit card details (number, address of cardholder and expiry date) to us at the address below. Please add post and packing as follows: UK – £1.00 per delivery address; overseas surface mail – £2.50 per delivery address; overseas airmail – £3.50 for the first book to each delivery address, plus £1.00 for each additional book by airmail to the same address. If your order is a gift, we will happily enclose your card or message at no extra charge.

Luath Press Limited
543/2 Castlehill
The Royal Mile
Edinburgh EH1 2ND
Scotland
Telephone: +44 (0)131 225 4326 (24 hours)
email: sales@luath. co.uk
Website: www. luath.co.uk